THE BRIEF REMARKER.

THE

BRIEF REMARKER

ON THE

WAYS OF MAN:

OR,

COMPENDIOUS DISSERTATIONS RESPECTING SOCIAL AND DOMESTIC RELATIONS AND CONCERNS,

AND THE

VARIOUS ECONOMY OF LIFE.

BY

EZRA SAMPSON.

——— ——— ——— "The spacious West,
"And all the teeming regions of the South,
"Hold not a quarry, to the curious flight
"Of knowledge, half so tempting or so fair
"As *Man* to *Man*." AKENSIDE.

NEW YORK:
D. APPLETON AND COMPANY,
346 & 348 BROADWAY
1855.

CONTENTS.

THE BRIEF REMARKER.

NUMBER I.

OF THE PECULIAR CAUSES OF SO PREVALENT A RESTLESSNESS OF DISPOSITION.

WHILE some ruin their circumstances by their indolence, others do it by their restlessness; always busy, but never pursuing any plan of regular industry. No sooner are they settled down in one business, than they change it for another. They are "every thing by turns and nothing long." Their attention thus dissipated turns to no account, and poverty overtakes them while they are flying so many different ways to escape it. Whereas a steady, straightforward course in almost any single business might have secured them a competence.

It is neither an imaginary nor a rare character, that I have now been describing: it is to be met with every where, in town and country. Thousands are undone by means of this single foible; every thing else in their habits and dispositions giving promise of success. This restlessness is owing sometimes to natural temper; but most commonly, perhaps, to the peculiar circumstances of the country in which we live. In China, a boy must follow the occupation of his father, and stick to that or starve. In India, no one can raise himself above the level of the caste in which he happens to be born. Nor is the mass of Europeans altogether free from shackles, that bind them down to occupations in which their own choice has had no concern. If a man there be bred a cobbler, he hardly may aspire to the honor of making shoes. But here, on the other hand, a man may put off his calling almost as easily as his clothes; or he may patch together several callings, and pursue them alternately or all at once, as best suits his own fancy. Here, the field of individual enterprise is alike open to all. Here, no one is of a family so humble as to be precluded from the possibility of raising himself, not only to opulence, but to office and rank. Here, wealth is shifting hands with such rapidity that, in one or two generations, the hills sink and the valleys rise.

Now, as this condition of things animates thousands with the spirit of enterprise, so it occasions in very many a restlessness and instability of feeling. Possessing freedom of choice, and having before them so many objects to choose betwixt, they never come to an election that fully satisfies them. Add to this, that the last twenty-five years have (by reason of the unexampled state of Europe) furnished instances, in almost every district of our country, of some rising suddenly to great opulence, by a single stroke in the experiments of speculation, and without any attention at all to the process of patient industry;—a circumstance that has operated powerfully on young minds, and on minds not young, in rendering them dissatisfied with slow gains or small profits, and impatient of the drudgery of any laborious calling. Not to mention that our country has, of itself, for a very long time past, furnished magnificent scenes, and numerous opportunities of speculation, altogether unexampled perhaps in the history of man.

Moreover, it is obvious to remark, that our enterprising youth are necessarily, as it were, tinctured with a romantic disposition. The books that they most read, are of the romantic kind; alike inflaming the imagination, and misleading the judgment, by descriptions "of a world where events are produced by causes widely and manifestly different from those which regulate the course of human affairs." Also, for almost the term of a whole generation, there has been constantly exhibited to view such a series of marvels in the civilized world, that the history of real life carries on it the appearance of romance.

Nothing very strange is it, therefore, that the minds of a great many are unsettled, notional, and fraught with extravagant expectations. And this is the less to be wondered at, as it is customary for our youth to step into manhood earlier than in former ages, or perhaps than in any country else. Commencing men at an immature period, and under such powerful impulses to wild extravagances of imagination, it would be marvellous indeed if they were not, many of them, averse to any sober, rational, and steady plan of life.

To contrast the past with the present in a short biographical notice of one of the first and wealthiest merchants of the last age, the writer remarks:—"It was an invariable rule with him to avoid every kind of dangerous experiment, and to confine himself to such branches of trade as admitted the surest principles of calculation."—This golden rule of business, which in former times of "steady habits" was sacredly regarded, not merely by that merchant, but generally;—this golden rule of business has, by a concurrence of unparalleled circumstances, been made to give place to rashness of speculation and a restless spirit of adventure—an evil, which nothing but length of time, and the smart-giving rod of stern experience will, in any likelihood, be able to cure.

NUMBER II.

OF TROUBLES OF OUR OWN MAKING.

There is in our nature such a restlessness of disposition, that we commonly make to ourselves more than half the evils we feel. Unsatisfied with what we are, or possess, we are still craving something past or to come, and by regrets, desires, and fears, are perpetually poisoning the streams of present enjoyment. The weather is too hot or too cold, too wet or too dry. If we have nothing to do, time hangs upon us an insupportable burden. If our circumstances compel us to daily labor, we fret to see others enjoying their leisure. Although we have food and raiment enough, and good enough, still we are dissatisfied that we are not rich. If, on the contrary, we chance to be rich, the weight of cares, the pains of getting, the difficulty of keeping, and the fears of losing, give us incessant disquiet and fatigue.

Mrs. Thrift has a decent competence, together with a kind husband, and fine children; but her heart is sick because she cannot live in the splendid style of her wealthy neighbor, Mrs. Modish. At the same time, Mrs. Modish, yoked to a surly, snappish, gouty husband, is secretly envying the condition of Mrs. Thrift.

Honest Abraham has a good farm, and is an excellent farmer, and free of debt; but his peace of mind is destroyed by being disappointed of an office ;—an office, too, without emolument. Farmer Thomas, his more artful neighbor who got the office, no sooner received his commission, than he began to dash away like a gentleman, and consequently neglected his farm, and impoverished his family; and by this time he sincerely regrets his having been so foolish as to barter solid pudding for empty honor.

Mercator, having acquired a snug estate by trade, grows uneasy, and sighs for a country life. Purling brooks, vocal groves, fragrant meadows, blooming orchards, and fields covered with a golden harvest, enchant his imagination. He sells his stock in trade, and purchases a farm, which he manages with about as much skill as a mere landsman would manage a ship at sea: it brings him in debt; and venting upon it no very gentle epithets, he longs to leave it, and go back to the situation he had abandoned.

Agricolus, weary of a dull, plodding way of living and of slow gains, leaves the plough and becomes a merchant. He sells his fast estate, and purchases with it goods, running in debt a few thousands, as he would needs have a handsome assortment. His goods are unskilfully chosen, and meet with a wretched market. Pay day comes, and his creditors, blest with excellent memories, are prompt in urging him to a settlement. But, alas! of money he has none. And now, "to break or not to break, that's the question." He struggles hard, makes new debts to pay old ones, sells at great loss; borrows money at 30 or 40 per cent., breaks at last; and whereas he merely imagined himself unhappy while holding the plough, he now feels that he is so indeed.

Thus mankind, from a restless disposition, render themselves wretched, when they might be much at their ease.

It would be worth to one, more than any, or even all of the arts and sciences, *to learn the art of living happily.* I don't mean *perfect* happiness, which is not to be enjoyed here; but such a degree of happiness as our Maker has put in our power. The art of living happily does not lie in stoical apathy; for as to the real and sharp afflictions of life, while one ought "to *bear* them like a man, he should also *feel* them like a man." Nor does he know the sweets of friendship, who feels little or no pain at being sundered from a near friend. Much less does it lie in the nauseating lap of gross sensuality; for the enjoyment of the mere sensualist is no higher than that of the pampered horse in the stable or stud, or the fattening pig in the sty. Indeed the brute has much the advantage, as it lives according to its nature and destination, while the man is haunted with a perpetual consciousness of the shameful degradation of his moral and intellectual faculties.

The following maxims, or rules of action might, if strictly observed, go far to increase the happiness, or, at least, to diminish the inquietudes and miseries of life.

Live constantly in the unshaken belief of the overruling providence of an infinitely wise and good, as well as Almighty Being; and prize his power above all things.

Observe inviolably truth in your words, and integrity in your actions.

Accustom yourself to temperance, and be master of your passions.

Be not too much out of humor with the world; but remember, it is a world of God's creating, and however sadly it is marred by wickedness and folly, yet you have found in it more comforts than calamities, more civilities than affronts, more instances of kindness towards you than of cruelty.

Try to spend your time usefully both to yourself and others. Never make an enemy, or lose a friend unnecessarily. Cultivate such an habitual cheerfulness of mind, and evenness of temper, as not to be ruffled by trivial inconveniences and crosses.

Be ready to heal breaches in friendship, and to make up differences; and shun litigation yourself as much as possible; for he is an ill calculator, who does not perceive that one amicable settlement is better than two lawsuits.

Be it rather your ambition to acquit yourself well in your proper station than to rise above it.

Despise not small honest gains, nor risk what you have on the delusive prospect of sudden riches. If you are in a comfortable thriving way, keep in it, and abide in your own calling rather than run the chance of another. In a word, mind to "use the world as not abusing it," and probably you will find as much comfort in it as is most fit for a frail being, who is merely journeying through it toward an immortal abode.

NUMBER III.

OF SELF-INFLICTED TORTURES.

NOTHING is more common than the discontent of those who have not even a shadow of cause for discontent. They are neither sick, nor pinched with poverty, nor called to sustain distressing hardships. They enjoy both food and appetite. They have raiment to put on, and friends to converse with; and if not rich, have fully enough for the moderate supply of all their real wants. Yet these enjoyments, these bounties of indulgent Heaven, are poisoned, as it were, by the discontent of their minds, so that they are wretched amidst health and competence.

What are the illusions that thus obstruct the sources of enjoyment, and, in this favored country, cheat so many out of the happiness of which Providence had put them in possession?—They are such as usually spring from one or other of the three following causes;—*perverseness of temper; false theories of worldly happiness; the influence of opinion.*

With respect to enjoying ourselves or not in life, more, a

great deal, depends upon temper than upon circumstances. Not that our enjoyments are not always considerably affected by our worldly circumstances, and sometimes in a very great degree; but if they are such, that we are able to supply ourselves with all the real necessaries and essential comforts of life, it is not our circumstances, but our tempers that are in fault, if we are not too happy to complain, and too grateful to repine. The root of our uneasiness is altogether in our own minds, and without a thorough change there, no change of place or of outward circumstances could quiet us. What though all our present ideal wants were satisfied? other ideal wants would presently start up, and we should still be weaving for ourselves the web of misery. A temper, that inclines to be satisfied with its present lot, is worth more than thousands a year; whereas restlessness of temper is one of the greatest of misfortunes. A full half of human troubles would vanish, and the rest be lightened, if there were a thorough cure of this one scrofulous disease of the heart.

Our false theories of worldly happiness constitute another huge class of troubles of our own making: and the effects of these false theories are the more deplorable, inasmuch as the disappointments, inevitably resulting from them, sour the disposition, and thereby enhance the numbers of the wretched victims of temper. Corporeal enjoyments are few and simple; neither wealth, nor any of the arts of refinement, can add considerably to their number, or any thing at all to their relish. The pleasures of sense are limited by narrow boundaries, which never can be passed without instantly turning pleasure into pain: and however much we may refine upon the pleasures of sense, our refinements can increase them but very little. The most refined epicure, for example, has scarcely any more enjoyment of the pleasures of the table, than one who confines himself to the plainest viands. Wherefore nothing is more plain and easy of comprehension than the true notion of mere worldly happiness:—the whole sum of it results from health, competence, the friendly society of neighbors and acquaintance, and the pure joys of domestic life. He that has these, though he have neither wealth nor rank, enjoys about all the world can bestow. But these real and unsophisticated enjoyments, which are bestowed in fully as large measure upon the peasant as upon the prince, are too vulgar for the fastidious taste of visionary speculatists; they must find a something that is quite above and beyond the common blessings of life, else they are determined not to enjoy themselves at all. Thus they lose the good, that lies fairly within their reach, by laying out their endeavors to grasp an abstract something, that is conceivable indeed, but not attainable;—an ignis fatuus, which the eye plainly sees, but which evades the touch, and baffles all pursuit.

The last brood of artificial troubles, which I proposed to notice, are those that are generated by the influence of opinion: I mean not one's own opinion, but the opinion of others. We are such strange and unaccountable creatures, that we are more solicitous to appear happy than really to be so; and hence we willingly abridge our real enjoyments for the sake of seeming to possess enjoyments superior to those that are altogether common to mankind. Now the general opinion of society (a very erroneous one indeed) makes the pomp of show a prerequisite for being deemed happy, or, at least, for obtaining the credit of refined enjoyment; and this general opinion, how much soever we may despise it in our judgments, has an astonishing influence upon our conduct and feelings; an influence that precipitates hundreds and tens of hundreds from a condition of competence to that of poverty.

That apt Remarker, Dr. Franklin, observes; "The eyes of other people are the eyes that ruin us. If all but myself were blind, I should want neither fine clothes, fine houses, nor fine furniture."—It is even so;—and it is this supreme regard to the eyes of others, that leads multitudes into extravagant and ruinous expenses. Without adequate funds, they build them fine houses, and purchase them fine furniture, and array themselves with costly apparel, that others may gaze upon them as persons possessed of taste and of refined enjoyments; and by these means they are presently stripped of the very necessaries of life.

NUMBER IV.

OF GREEDY AMBITIOUSNESS AFTER WEALTH—OMINOUSLY THE MASTER PASSION OF THE TIMES.

AMBITION'S thorny path is too narrow for two to go abreast. Each struggles hard to get forward of each; and the one that is foremost of all, must press onward with might and main, else some other will rush by him. He that stumbles is trampled over by the crowd behind him. It is all a scramble, in which the successful competitors are greeted with shouts of applause, and the unsuccessful assailed with the hisses of derision and scorn.

In a former age, it was the ambition of the celebrated Cardinal de Retz to be first in the hearts of his fellow-citizens, the Parisians. His munificence exceeded all former example; his liberalities were unbounded. The courtesy of his manners, and the fascinating charms of his address, won him universal friendship and admiration. At home he was crowded with visitors: when he rode through the streets, he was accompanied with a splendid retinue of nobility and gentry, all proud to do him honor; and whenever he entered the parliament, marked respect and homage were paid him there. But there happened an incident that put this friendship to the test, and proved it light as air.

Upon a time the Cardinal was thought to be on the eve of ruin. In that situation he went to the parliament, to clear him self of heavy charges, which his enemies had raised against him. The account of his reception there is thus given in his memoirs, written with his own hand.

"We went to the parliament. The princes had there near a thousand gentlemen with them; and I may say, hardly one from the court was missing there. I was in my church habit, and went through the great hall, with my cap in my hand, saluting every body; but I met with but few that returned me that civility, *so strongly was it believed that I was an undone man.*"

Neither is this a solitary example, nor one of rare occurrence. History abounds with examples that, in the falling fortunes of the great and noble of the earth, their friends fall off, like leaves from the trees in the first frosts of autumn. Sir Walter Raleigh, alike celebrated as a scholar, a gentleman, a statesman, a soldier, and a man of genius, in his last letter to his wife, after his most unjust condemnation to death, says: "To what friend to direct you I know not; for all mine have left me in the true time of need."

But not any longer to dwell on the scenes of high life, with which the generality of my readers have as little concern as myself, I will turn now to the walks of the more common sort.

In countries where distinction of orders is established by

law, ambition runs in two different channels. With not a few its main object is rank, titles, stars, garters, and ribbons; these baubles being by them preferred greatly to mere wealth, which is eagerly pursued by those, chiefly, who can have little or no expectation of attaining to the high distinctions of civil, ecclesiastical, or military rank. Whereas, in this free country of ours, where there is no distinction of orders, and no established rank of one family above another, the undivided current of ambition is towards wealth. Avarice is the general and the ruling passion The pursuit of gain is the only secular pursuit that is much valued or thought of; because, in the common estimation the grand point of honor is to be rich. Mammon is the idol, to which every thing else is made to bend. Offices are sought after for their emoluments chiefly. Nay, the august seats of legislation are unhesitatingly deserted for public employments, barren of honor, but of greater profit. Men are appraised, and rated high or low, according to the magnitude of their property. The common question, *What is he worth?* is answered only in one way. If his estate be small, he is worth little; if he have no estate left, he is worth nothing. It is but of small account, though he have an ample fund of moral and intellectual worth;—the worth that is most eagerly sought, most highly prized, and most generally esteemed, is pecuniary worth.

In the scramble of such multitudes after riches, very many must needs be unsuccessful; for in no country whatever, can more than a comparative few arrive at wealth. By far the greater part of the candidates, falling short of their expectations, endure the pangs of disappointment, and pine under the corrodings of envy. With some avarice defeats its own aim.

Their greediness of gain, if it impel them not to deeds of fraud or violence, which bring them to shame and ruin, yet spurs them on to engage in rash and ruinous adventures. The estates of others, as Franklin's Poor Richard said, are spent in the getting. Fondly anticipating a fortune, they dash away as if they really had it in hand. Others again counterfeit the splendor of riches, that they may put themselves and their families in the ranks of honor. But if they have fallen from these appearances, they had better, in the eye of fashion, have fallen from grace. Whatever of estimable and amiable qualities they may possess, they fare with their former visitors and familiars, as the Cardinal did with his, at the time he was thought "an undone man."

Industry, frugality, and thrift, are republican virtues. But a scrambling for money, as the chief good, is of bad omen. It produces meanness of sentiment and sordidness of disposition. A free people, whose passions are set altogether on the pursuit of gain, can hardly remain free very long; because the necessary consequence of such a spirit of avarice is fraud in private life, and venality and corruption in public life.

An able author, while treating incidentally of the fall of the Roman republic, remarks:—"The course that a free nation runs is from virtuous industry to wealth; from wealth to luxury; from luxury to an impatience of discipline and corruption of morals; till by a total degeneracy and loss of virtue, being grown ripe for destruction, it falls at last a prey to some hardy oppressor, and, with the loss of liberty, loses every thing else that is valuable."

NUMBER V.

OF THE TYRANNY OF FASHION IN LAYING ENORMOUS TAXES UPON COMMON-CONDITIONED FOLKS, AND GRINDING THE FACES OF THE POOR.

EVERY one, who reads English history, must know that Richard the Third had a humped back. And, as ancient story goes, humping became quite fashionable during his reign. The courtiers, the Lords, the Ladies, and the under gentry, patterning after royalty, wore, each, a fashionable crook in the back: so the English of that day were "a crooked generation," sure enough. Be this, however, as it may, in point of ridiculous absurdity it hardly exceeds what is very commonly seen among ourselves.

Though we would fain be called a Christian people, it is a fact, as notorious as sad, that an anti-christian deity is worshipped among us, in town and country, and by immense numbers of all classes, and of both sexes. Look where you will, you see all ranks bowing, cringing, bending the knee—to what? to Fashion. This is the goddess of their idolatry. They yield implicit obedience to her laws, however absurd and barbarous; and though she changes as often as the moon, they follow her in all her changes, and ape her in all her freaks,—humping whenever she humps. They are brought to endure cold and nakedness, when but for having followed her mandates, they might be comfortably clad. They reject and despise the diet which she forbids, though wholesome and palatable, and best suited, as well to their constitutions, as to their circumstances. They pay tithes to her of all they possess. Tithes did I say? It were well if only a tenth would satisfy her; she often claims even more than one half. Did she tax only the rich, who are able to pay, it would not be so bad; but she lays her rapacious hands on the middling classes, and even upon the poor. Nay, the knavish hussey seizes what ought to be laid up against old age and sickness, and also what ought to go to the creditor. By the decree of fashion, this republican, and otherwise free nation is thrown into castes, as really in some respects, as the East Indians have been by their Brahmins; and the only way to gain admission, or maintain a standing in the higher castes, is to dress gorgeously and fare sumptuously, no matter by what means. Hence the general struggle. The rich march foremost in the ranks of fashion, and the others keep as close to their heels as possible, following on in a long train, like files of geese. This is comic in appearance, but tragic in reality. It is amusing, at first thought, to see families, in narrow circumstances, struggling to make the appearance of high life; to see them vying, not only with one another, but with the rich, to exceed in finery and splendor; to see how much pains they take, and how many arts they use to dazzle the eyes of the beholder with the mockery of wealth. But on due reflection, one finds more reason to be sad than merry.—When we consider that these deluded people are following a phantom, that is leading them to ruin; that they are incurring expenses, which they are utterly unable to support; that they are bartering away solid comforts for an empty show; that by striving to live splendidly, they are losing the means of living decently and comfortably: when we consider that they are bringing wretchedness upon their children by leaving them to the buffetings of poverty, aggravated highly by their early acquaintance with fashionable life: when we consider, finally, that some of them are defrauding their creditors, by sacrificing on the altar of fashion what is needed for the payment of their just debts;—when we put these considerations together, we find them enough to excite deep regret and sorrow.

It is questionable whether great wealth conduces, on the whole, even to worldly happiness. It cannot cure an aching head, or soothe an aching heart; it is no shield from the shafts of misfortune, nor from the arrows of death; it brings to the possessor an addition of cares as well as of comforts, and is often the means of bringing moral ruin upon his children; and while it increases his power and influence, it increases, also, his responsibility.—The rich have, however, one exclusive privilege: they have a right to make a splendid appearance in the world, because their circumstances can well afford it. Fine houses, expensive furniture, stately equipage, and sumptuous fare, are within the bounds of their real means, and therefore not censurable in them. In one point of view, the profusion of their expenses is beneficial to the community, as it gives employment, and affords sustenance to industry. Yet there can be shown "a more excellent way."—Frugality is comely even in the rich. Not that frugality, which degenerates to parsimony, and causes the rich to wear the garb of poverty, from a sordid spirit of penuriousness; nor yet that frugality, which saves merely to increase a hoard of wealth, already too large; but it is a prudent saving from the grasp of profusion for the purpose of charity and beneficence.—Take the following example:—

Benevolus has both largeness of wealth and largeness of heart. Content with his present worldly store, he is resolved that his expenses shall about equal his income. He lives daily in the style of affluence, but never in the style of extravagance; and what he saves by frugality he bestows in charity. To the children of misfortune and want he is a friend and a father; of every useful and laudable undertaking he is a bountiful encourager. Does Benevolus aspire to be a leader of fashion? Yes. With all the weight of his influence he tries to make industry, prudent economy, and frugality fashionable; to make the moral and Christian virtues fashionable; to make it fashionable to behave well and to do good. Happy man! Happy the children of such a father, and the community that has such a pattern!

As the richest families may be beggared by extravagance, much sooner will it consume one's all when that all is but little—and what avails the ruffle without the shirt? Persons who are in small circumstances must prudently husband what they have, or it will quickly slip out of their hands. How unwise is it for them to make an ostentation of wealth which they do not possess, or to pursue fashion "when she runs faster than they can follow." Many thousands, by standing on tiptoe, and reaching after things too high for them, have fallen flat to the ground. If you follow fashion beyond your real means, depend upon it, the skittish jade will throw you into the mire at last.

NUMBER VI.

OF THE PAPAL RESCRIPT FROM THE COURT OF FASHION, INDIRECTLY FORBIDDING TO MARRY.

THE injunction of celibacy, or of the monastic life, by the Romish Church, being directly in opposition to the order and ordination of nature, has, more than any other single cause whatever, produced a huge mass of evils, both moral and physical, in those countries that have been under the papal dominion; evils too obvious to need pointing out, and too flagitious, some of them, to name. With prophetic reference, as we Protestants fully believe, to the doings of that corrupted church, St. Paul, in his second epistle to Timothy, expresses himself as follows:—"Now the spirit speaketh expressly, that in the latter times, some shall depart from the faith, giving heed to seducing spirits, and doctrines of demons."—And immediately after he particularizes the unnatural and monstrous rescript, "*Forbidding to marry*," as of the same infernal family, or nearly allied with "the doctrines of demons," aforementioned.

If, however, there were no "forbidding to marry" except in the Romish Church, we might hope that a full cure of the deadly evil is at hand. But this diabolical prohibition,—to wit, forbidding to marry,—has been enjoined and enforced even more extensively, in one other way, than it ever was by the canons of the Vatican.—Iwill explain my meaning by sketching a fragment of ancient history.

The ancient Romans were republicans after their kind, and continued such for a considerable number of centuries. Though they were pagan idolaters, and their worship was deplorably corrupt, yet, previous to their imbibing the atheism of Epicurus, they generally believed in a future retribution of rewards and punishments; which belief operated so powerfully upon them, that they were truly exemplary in some few of their social virtues. In particular perjury was scarcely known among them, and infidelity in the connubial state was no less uncommon. The Roman republicans were plain men and women, accustomed to daily labor, and quite unaccustomed to finery of apparel or luxury of living. A Roman, of even noble blood, tilled his little field with his own hands, and was proud of tilling it with superior industry and skill; whilst his wife made it her chief ambition to be an excellent housewife. While this state of things lasted, and a very long while it did last, the Romans were eager enough to get themselves wives. They married generally, and they married young; for they thought, and well they might, that whoso found a wife, found a good thing,—a real helpmeet, as well as a dear and faithful companion. And what is singularly remarkable, if true, it is recorded by a Roman historian, that there had not been known in the city of Rome, a single instance of divorcement during the whole space of five hundred years; though the law had put it in the power of the husband to repudiate his wife almost at pleasure.

Unfortunately for the Roman Republic, and more especially for the female part of it, a great and splendid event quite changed the morals, the taste, the habits, and the whole face of the country. One hundred and ninety years before the Christian era, the Romans, for the first time, entered Asia with an army, which, under Scipio, defeated and conquered Antiochus the Great, of Syria: and from hence they brought home such a taste for the luxuries of the East, as promoted and hastened the ruin of their commonwealth; and in no way more directly, than by a practical forbiddance of marriage. The Roman women, once so plain, frugal, and industrious, became enamored of the costly finery that was brought from the East. One of them, named Lollia Paulina, when dressed in all her jewels, is said to have worn the value of three hundred and thirty-two thousand pounds sterling. And though this was the most extraordinary instance of the time, yet it is reasonable to suppose that of the rest of the ladies, every one strove to get as near the top of the fashion as she could; and that with all the females, who thought any thing of themselves, the rage was to be fine and fashionable. This new order of things, while it precipitated the republic down the abyss of ruin, brought marriage almost into disuse: insomuch that Augustus, the first Roman Emperor, finding among the men a general disinclination to marry, was fain to pass severe penal laws, to force them, as it were, into the marriage bonds. But it was all to little purpose. Despot and tyrant as he was, he found it as impossible to compel the bachelors to marry, as

Peter the First long since did, to compel the Russians to shave off their beards. Was it owing to the licentiousnesss of the men? In part it was, no doubt; but not altogether. It was partly owing to their prudence. A Roman bachelor, naturally enough, would commune with himself thus:—"These extravagant flirts, of whose attire a single article costs more than one of them would earn in her whole lifetime, are fit only for show. I like mighty well to be in their company at courts and assemblies; but the gods save me from a union with them! If I marry, unless my wife bring me a fortune, she will quickly devour mine. Wherefore, I will look out only for number one, in spite of the edicts of the Emperor."

Consider, ye American Fair, that, in all times and countries, the like causes will produce the like effects.

NUMBER VII.

ON THE ELEVATION OF THE CONDITION AND CHARACTER OF WOMEN BY MEANS OF CHRISTIANITY.

In all ages of the world, the greatest portion of sorrow and hardship has fallen to the lot of the female part of our race. Amongst all the numerous tribes of savages and barbarians, in whatever quarter of the earth, or in the islands of the seas, females are despised and degraded, and a wife is but little better conditioned than a bond slave. "While the man passes his days in idleness and amusement, the woman is condemned to incessant toil. Tasks are imposed upon her without mercy, and services are received without complacence or gratitude." The laws and customs of Mohammedanism, as well as of Paganism, degrade and enslave the women; a degradation and slavery of vast extent, since by far the greater number of the human kind are either Mohammedans or Pagans.

It is only in Christian countries that women rise to their

proper rank, and are treated as companions and equals. For this happy improvement in their condition, they are indebted to Christianity, which, as well by humanizing and purifying the heart, as by the prohibition of polygamy, has loosed the bonds of their captivity, and, at the same time, adorned them with virtues, the most estimable and amiable.

The New Testament is the great charter of the rights of women; and not only the great charter of their rights, but the unerring directory of their duties, and the choice cabinet, as it were, of their most precious ornaments. As the benevolent system of Christianity frees them from vassalage, and exalts their rank in society, so it inspires them, at the same time, with a taste for what is morally excellent, and virtuous, and lovely. Nor is it a little remarkable, that of the religion, which so ennobles their sex, they are the first, the most general, and among the most effectual teachers. It is from women, that almost our whole sex, as well as theirs, receives its earliest instruction in religion and morality. Though they are neither missionaries abroad nor preachers at home, yet, as spreaders and promulgators of Christianity, they are hardly less useful than those venerable orders of men. Throughout all Christendom, as preceptresses, as mothers, and in their various domestic relations, they have the moulding of the minds of future men, as well as of future women, during those infantile years, in which the mind is comparable to soft wax, and when the impressions, which are made upon it, are the most indelible. So that it would not, perhaps, be extravagant to believe, that a full half of the whole Christian world has been christianized, or first imbued with Christian principles, by means of female teachers.

Scarcely any thing admits of clearer proof from history, that that the institutions for alleviating human misfortune and distress have grown out of the Christian religion; and nothing, surely, could confer greater dignity on the female sex, than its active and zealous co-operation in establishing such plans of general philanthropy.

All along, from the first age of Christianity, down to later times, there have been women, highly distinguished for their pious benevolence, and active beneficence; but, not having learned to form themselves into societies for joint acts of charity, their solitary or individual efforts could afford relief to but few. For the present illustrious epoch, in the christianized world, has been reserved the honor of multiplying and extending, far beyond all former examples, their humane plans and institutions. Multiplied as these have been, and multiplying as they are likely to be, no tongue can tell, no heart conceive, the benefits of the little streamlets, issuing in such innumerable directions from this single source;—benefits not only to the Receivers, but also to the Givers; for it is even "more blessed to give than to receive." The occupations of charity nourish and strengthen some of the best feelings of the heart, and, at the same time, are rewarded with the enjoyment of a higher pleasure, than the hoards of wealth or its pageantries can ever bestow. "What wonders and what pleasures has civilization procured to mankind!" So the philosopher exclaimed, and not without reason. The civilized man possesses manifold more enjoyments, and stands vastly higher in the scale of human beings, than the naked savage, or the rude barbarian. But it is not mere civilization, nor mere learning, that has imbued the heart with the genuine feeling of humanity.

See, on the page of history only fifteen centuries back, the ladies of Rome, that proud mistress of the world; see them seated in the amphitheatre, as delighted spectators of the mortal combats of gladiators; feasting their eyes with the bloody carnage, and their ears with the groans of the dying. And now see, on the other hand, tens and hundreds of thousands of females, of the present age, formed into societies for the alleviation of human distress; for the purpose of ministering to the widow, of sustaining the orphan, of clothing the naked, of feeding the hungry, or "healing the broken and weak." Behold these objects of striking contrast; and remember that the former had quite as much of polish, as much of elegance, and as much of learning as the latter. And what is it then, but the influence of Christian principles, that has made such an astonishing difference between them, in point of taste and sensibility?

NUMBER VIII.

OF SELF-IGNORANCE, AND SELF-ADULATION.

——"The nature of mankind is such,
To see and judge of the affairs of others
Much better than their own."

The above-cited sentiment has not abated of its force, nor is it the less applicable to human nature at the present instant, though two thousand years have passed away, since it came from the pen of Terence, the poet of Carthage. In one respect, very few, if any, are altogether free from the imputation of making use of deception. It is one of the strange properties of our fallen nature, that we deceive ourselves, even more easily than we are deceived by others; and, though we are mightily offended when others deceive us, we are pleased with the deception which we palm upon ourselves. We love flattery, because it enables us to flatter ourselves; and we dislike honest reproof or censure, because it impels us to fix our eyes upon our own fault or frailties.

We weigh our own actions, and the actions of others, not in the same balance, or else with different kinds of weights. We judge ourselves and our neighbors by different rules, which always gives the advantage to our own side. Imperfect we readily confess ourselves to be; but if one happen to impute to us any particular imperfection, we deem ourselves insulted, and instantly take fire. Mortal we know we are, and yet seem scarcely to expect either death or sickness; for these events, perhaps for the most part, come unawares. Probably there is not one *well* man in a hundred, who does not secretly think the fatal arrow more likely to hit almost any body else than himself. The young confidently expect they shall live to be old; and the old, who have already seen one generation pass away, are not without hope that they shall survive the greater part of another. The mass of mankind are, in short, perpetually deluding themselves one way or other; nor are the wisest and best quite free, in all respects, from self-delusion. Perhaps, if life were not, in any wise, gilded by the enchanting power of imagination, there would be little relish for most of those things, which God hath given us to enjoy under the sun.

A very ancient writer has told us of a poor laborer who, fancying himself a king, repaired daily to a hillock, where, as on his throne, he sat in state, and exercised regal authority over the imaginary subjects that surrounded him; who, being at length cured of that pleasant error of the imagination, complained hard of his doctors, that they had physicked him back again to poverty. Nor is he a solitary instance. The most of mankind, in some period or other of their lives, have, perhaps, indulged vagaries of the imagination, quite as groundless, if not quite so extravagant; and which, if they led them not astray from either duty or prudence, did them benefit, by sweetening their toils, and smoothing the path of life. The illusions of Hope (which no sooner is disappointed, than it springs anew in the human breast) constitute a large portion of the earthly happiness of mankind, and are the mainspring of their exertions in worldly affairs.

> "Dream after dream ensues—
> And still they dream that they shall still succeed,
> And still are disappointed."

However, speaking of worldly good only, their dreams afford them more satisfaction, than they ever find in realities.

But when the illusion relates to the moral qualities of our hearts, flattering us that our vices are virtues, or, at least, that they are less culpable for being *ours;* it is then that it is pregnant with infinite mischief.

Of all human knowledge, self-knowledge is accounted the most difficult of attainment; and why? Assuredly, it is not so very difficult in itself. We are conscious, not only of our own actions, but also of the views and motives by which we are actuated. The thoughts and affections of our hearts are all open to our own inspection. Why, then, is it hard for one so far to know himself, as to be able to pencil his own true picture with considerable exactness? The main difficulty arises from the blinding and deluding bias, that we have towards ourselves. It is by reason of this kind of sophistry, that, though we discern the mote in the eye of another, we perceive not the beam in our own;—that, though we are clear-sighted quite enough with respect to the faults of our neighbors, we are as purblind as moles in regard to as great, or even greater faults in ourselves; that, at best, we weigh our own faults with more than some grains of allowance, but those of every one else, excepting our particular friends, without any allowance at all. Finally, to the same cause it is owing, that we magnify into shining virtues, such deeds of our own doing, as we should think but lightly of if done by persons in whom we had no particular interest.

The sophistry, with which we cheat ourselves, runs into our social intercourse and our dealings. In estimating the characters of those about us, we are apt to judge of them according to the particular bearings they have to our own dear selves. If they are near of kin, or close friends, our favoritism blinds us to their frailties, and magnifies in them every thing that has the appearance of excellence; but if they are aliens from our hearts, we are apt enough to judge them with all that severity, which appearances can in any way justify. So, too, in matters of dealing, it is a hard thing, indeed, for one to determine right in one's own cause; the opposite positions of *mine* and *thine* not unfrequently swaying men of honest intentions. For which reason it is, that in all the intercourse and business of life, the frequent use or application of the golden rule is, in point of morals, of such immeasurable importance; since, in innumerable cases, it is only by changing places ideally with those we have concerns with, that we can know exactly how to do them justice.

And not only is the daily application of that divine rule so necessary in all our business, but it is alike necessary in the management of conflicting opinions. The free exercise of private judgment is, what every man claims for himself, and yet almost every man grudges it to others. And hence it is, that disputes upon matters of opinion are, so commonly, acrimonious. Whereas, if we were no less willing that others should enjoy the free exercise of private judgment, than to enjoy it ourselves, our disputes would be conducted with fairness, and good temper.

NUMBER IX.

OF THE WIDE DIFFERENCE BETWEEN WISDOM AND CUNNING.

In one of the tragedies of Sophocles, there is an admirable moral, couched under the veil of heathen fable.

Philoctetes, to whom Hercules had bequeathed his bow and arrows, went, with the other princes and chiefs of Greece, to the siege of Troy. He was son of the renowned Achilles, and no less distinguished for his valor than his birth. But, having been bit by a serpent, an incurable and most painful ulcer ensued; and his perpetual groans and lamentations disturbed and disheartened the whole Grecian camp. For this reason, the chief of that military confederacy had him conveyed to Lemnos, a desolate island, where he remained ten years, alone, and in intolerable anguish. At the expiration of that time, it being declared by an oracle, that Troy could never be conquered without the arrows of Hercules, then in the possession of Philoctetes, Ulysses and Neoptolemus were jointly sent to Lemnos to obtain them of him.

Ulysses, notorious above all men for craft and intrigue, and well knowing that Philoctetes bore the Greeks an implacable hatred for their barbarous usage of him, laid a cunning plan to get the arrows from him by fraud, which he communicated to Neoptolemus, at the same time insisting that he should become the instrument of its execution. Neoptolemus, who was a generous-hearted young prince, is at first struck with horror at the base proposal, and says:

"I was not born to flatter or betray,
——— What open arms can do
Behold me prompt to act, but ne'er to fraud
Will I descend. ———————
——— O King! believe me,
Rather, much rather, would I fall by virtue,
Than rise by guilt to certain victory."

Ulysses, however, (so easy is it for an arch deceiver to corrupt the integrity of an inexperienced youth,) gained his point at last, by his cunning sophistry, and honeyed persuasions; and Neoptolemus submitted to an act of treachery which his soul abhorred. He first insinuated himself into the confidence of Philoctetes, by a train of falsehoods, and then robbed him of his arrows, which he bore off to the ship, that lay ready to sail back to the coast of Troy. But, reflecting afterward upon the baseness of the deed, and stung with remorse and pity, he, notwithstanding the invectives and threats of Ulysses, went back and restored the arrows to Philoctetes.

After all the arts of persuasion to induce Philoctetes to go to the siege of Troy, or at least to send his arrows thither, had been used in vain, and there seemed no possibility left that the point could be gained by any human means, Hercules descended from Leaven and effected what mere man could not do, a change of will in Philoctetes, who then voluntarily went with Neoptolemus to the Grecian camp, carrying with him his bow and arrows, and, by means of them, Troy was conquered.

This, in short, is the moral of the fable:—Open and honest policy, aided by the powers above, was crowned, finally, with more complete success than could have been obtained by the deep-laid, fraudulent plan of the crafty Ulysses.

The arts of falsehood and trick, whether on a large scale or a small one, are but foolishness, however subtilely managed.

> "The secret snare when Falsehood spreads,
> *Herself* she fetters in the subtile threads."

Craft, partaking, as it does, of moral turpitude, which it perpetually strives to conceal, exposes itself by its very attempts at concealment, as the serpent tells us where to strike him by covering his head. Whether in the private or public walks of life—whether in the common intercourse between neighbors and fellow-citizens, or in the great concerns of princes and statesmen —an honest policy will be found to wear best. Our great and beloved Washington, whom Heaven crowned with such marvellous success, had nothing of the craft of Ulysses. With a mind good as it was great, he sought noble ends by honest means—by means that he could never blush to own. He was admirable for his real, unsophisticated wisdom; for the wisdom that soared above the base arts of intrigue, and which was without guile, without hypocrisy.

"Cunning," says Mr. Locke, in his excellent treatise on Education—"cunning, which is the ape of wisdom, is the most distant from it that can be; and as an ape, for the likeness it has to a man, wanting what really should make him so, is by so much the uglier; cunning is only the want of understanding; which, because it cannot compass its ends by direct ways, would do it by trick and circumvention. No cover was ever made either so big or so fine as to hide itself. None were ever so cunning as to conceal their being so."

There are few particulars in which mankind more often misjudge than in this. They are apt to think that the artful and unprincipled, because they display considerable cunning, are of course men of superior parts; whereas, generally speaking, their minds are narrow. You will seldom find one of them possessed of true clearness and largeness of understanding.

So again, many a doting father is secretly gratified with the slyness and the fox-like tricks of his boy; when, in reality, he has all reason to apprehend that the boy is getting to be a confirmed villain in grain, and will have a genius for nothing else.

The fox is the most noted of any of the inferior animals for craft and roguery; yet the fox is one of the most miserable of all the brute creation. He has not a friend upon earth. The honester dog hunts and attacks him with peculiar malice. Every four-footed animal seems to bear him a grudge; the weaker shun him, and the stronger pursue him. The very birds, knowing his knavish craft, hover in the air over him, and seem to express their apprehensions and their hatred. They alight upon the trees and hedges, as he is slyly creeping along the ground beneath, and with loud cries and chatterings, give warning of his approach, as who should say, "yonder goes a cunning, beguiling, greedy rogue—take special care of yourselves." And thus, also, it fares with those of Adam's children who have much cunning, but no principle of honesty.

NUMBER X.

OF THE TEMPORAL ADVANTAGES OF UPRIGHTNESS OF CHARACTER.

"My son, sow not upon the furrows of unrighteousness."
Advice of the son of Sirach.

Dr. Franklin, founding his theory upon the principle that the human body is specifically lighter than water, tells us, in substance, that one fallen into that element might escape drowning, for some considerable time at least, were he to abstain from struggling and plunging, and to let his body down with the feet foremost, remaining thus in a perpendicular position, except throwing his head as far back as possible; because in that position, the face would be quite above the surface of the water.

This prescription, or direction from the venerable Doctor, who knew, as well as any man, how to keep his own head above water, is, of itself, or in its plain literal import, well worth the being held in remembrance. But craving indulgence for the license, I mean, withal, to make an analogical use of it.

Young men, as soon as they are entitled to the rights of personal independence, launch out in what is figuratively called the ocean of life. Indeed we are, all of us, on that ocean; some in deeper, and others in shoaler water; some going forward smoothly with the tide, and others having the tide against them; sometimes we have fair wind and weather, and at other times we are under a dark sky, and assailed with tempestuous winds, that raise aloft the foaming billows.

What then is the safest way, at all times, and for persons of all ranks and conditions? It is told in only three words;—*Mind the perpendicular.* Many a young man, and many a man not young, have I seen ingulfed and lost, not by reason of his wanting skill and alertness, but because he failed to keep himself in a perpendicular attitude; whereas, on the other hand, never did I see a single one totally submerged, who had always been duly careful in that particular.

If, even, there were nothing to hope or fear beyond the grave, honesty would be the best policy; inasmuch as it carries one through this world with most safety, in the long run, as well as with honor. "He that walketh uprightly, walketh surely." He travels in a plain and safe path; a fair character is his passport, and the laws of society are his protection. As long as a man holds fast his integrity, he cannot be quite undone; for though, by adverse gusts he be sadly plunged, his *face* will still be above water. Though he should suffer the loss of all things else, yet the consciousness of strict integrity will buoy him up, and the knowledge that others have of his integrity, will give him a chance to repair his broken fortunes, or, at the least, will secure him that good name, which is "better than precious ointment."

On the contrary, "he that perverteth his way shall be known."

Though deceit and knavishness may sometimes procure momentary advantages, they are but momentary, and are much more than countervailed by the lasting ill consequences, which they never fail to bring after them. For not only does dishonesty draw after it many inward disquietudes, but it lays one under very heavy disadvantages, with respect to his intercourse with the world. Notwithstanding all his arts of cunning, it will be known; and when a man's character is of that sort, as to fill with suspicions every one that knows him, even his honest acts will be thought to spring from base motives, or to have some dark design. It will be suspected that the plague of leprosy still remains, either "in the warp or in the woof."

It greatly behooves young men to form fixed resolutions, at the outset of life, never to swerve from the perpendicular, in a single instance,—no, not even in the most trivial one; for one trespass against the laws of honesty leads to another, as it were by a sort of natural and necessary connection. So that, though there be many who, in their intercourse with the world, have never been guilty of one dishonest act, yet there are few who have been guilty of one, and but one. Because the first, by compromising the moral principle, weakens the power of resisting the next temptation; because one knavish deed often requires another, and sometimes several others, to cover it; and lastly, because rooted knavishness of heart is harder of cure than any other moral malady, inasmuch as the corruption of the principle of integrity is the corruption of the very source of all moral virtue.

He that has seen a rogue in grain, a thoroughly practised rogue, turn to a downright honest man, has at least seen one marvellous thing.

NUMBER XI.

AN EXEMPLIFICATION OF TRUE CHRISTIAN HONESTY.

The following line of Pope,

"An honest man's the noblest work of God"—

has been pronounced unworthy of that celebrated poet, forasmuch as honesty is but a vulgar virtue, as common to the meanest, as to the greatest abilities. Honesty, though commendable, is so far from being one of the noblest of human qualities, that the honest man may, nevertheless, be but a plain simple man, of contracted intellect, of very little education, and of a low condition. *This* the noblest work of God! Fy upon such nonsense!

Now, to adjust this matter between the poet and the critic, it will be necessary to take a cursory view of the different standards of honesty, according to one or other of which reputedly honest men square their conduct, and of the different principles, by which they are governed.

Men, sometimes, act honestly from policy, rather than from

a principle of probity. They believe, and believe aright, that "honesty is the best policy." According to this sound maxim they mean to act, and they greatly find their account in it. In short, none are wiser in their generation than those who are honest altogether from policy. While carefully minding to keep themselves within the hedge of the law, they, without mercy or pity, take every advantage that the law will let them. They escape the infamy and punishment, which commonly befall the impolitic wights, who are versed in the black art of downright roguery. Thus they walk in a plain and safe path. An honest reputation is their passport, and the laws of society are their protection. These are your *hard* honest men, who are honest merely for their own safety and profit, and are just as selfish in their honesty as in every thing else. True enough, the poet is worthy of reprehension, if he meant them. But, though the fear of disgrace or punishment, and the desire of a fair character may give birth to a creditable, but contracted and spurious kind of honesty, which has in it nothing of the dignity of virtue; yet the truly honest man, however low in circumstances, or mean in parts, is one of Virtue's nobility.

The truly honest man would be just as honest without law, as with it. Guided by the paramount authority of conscience, he neither withholds aught, nor exacts aught on the mere plea, that civil law is on his side.

The truly honest is he, who makes it a cardinal point to do to others, as he would be done unto; and who decides with justice, when self-interest and justice are in opposite scales.

The truly honest man is never ostentatious of his honesty. Ostentation of it is always an ill sign; it looks like putting on a patch to hide a blemish.

But enough of definition. One good example is worth a score of definitions: and the following example, all will allow to be a good one. The anecdote is given in St Pierre's Studies of Nature.

"In the last war in Germany, a captain of the cavalry was ordered out on a foraging party. He put himself at the head of his troop, and marched to the quarter assigned him. It was a solitary valley, in which hardly any thing but woods could be seen. In the midst of it stood a little cottage; on perceiving it, he went up and knocked at the door; out comes an ancient Hernouten, with a beard silvered by age. 'Father,' says the officer, 'show me a field where I can set my troops a foraging.' 'Presently,' replied the Hernouten. The good old man walked before, and conducted them out of the valley. After a quarter of an hour's march, they found a fine field of barley. 'There is the very thing we want,' says the captain. 'Have patience for a few minutes,' replied his guide, 'and you shall be satisfied.' They went on, and at the distance of about a quarter of a league farther, they arrived at another field of barley. The troop immediately dismounted, cut down the grain, trussed it up, and remounted. The officer, upon this, says to his conductor, 'Father, you have given yourself and us unnecessary trouble; the first field was much better than this.' 'Very true, sir,' replied the good old man, 'but it is not mine.'"

Such an example of honesty, I repeat, is worth a score of definitions. Here we have not an abstract notion of honesty, but we see it, as it were, embodied. Here we behold the express form and visage of genuine, *Christian* honesty, acting on the principle of loving one's neighbor as one's self. And what though the exemplar was an obscure and a lowly man, distinguished neither for parts nor learning? In the moral frame of his mind there was a nobleness of heavenly origin; a nobleness far superior to eminent natural parts, which belong alike to the best, and the worst of human beings.

Compare this humble Hernouten, or Moravian, with the illustrious chieftains who figured in that German war, and whose bloody deeds are emblazoned on the page of history. Compare his disinterestedness with their selfishness; his philanthropy with their greedy avarice, and fell ambition; his tender and scrupulous regard to the rights of his neighbor, with their unfeeling spirit of plunder and rapine;—and judge which party is entitled to stand higher on the scale of genuine honor.

One of the best religious confessions extant is that of Zaccheus, a rich publican, who, probably, had been not a little dishonest and extortionous:—" Lord, one half of my goods I give to the poor, and if I have taken any thing from any man by false accusation, I restore him fourfold." This is practical orthodoxy.

NUMBER XII.

OF THE PREVAILING HABIT OF PROMISE-BREAKING IN COMMON DEALING.

In the polite world, forms of speech are used, which are not meant to be understood according to their obvious meaning. For instance, when one man says or writes to another, Your humble servant, or, Your most obedient, he intends not to bind himself to clean the boots of the one he thus addresses, or to do him any sort of menial service; and much less does he mean that he is ready and willing to yield him obedience, in all cases whatsoever. It is hardly worth while, however, to enlarge on this topic, as the aforesaid forms of speech have almost become obsolete, at least in these United States. Pledges of humble service, and passive obedience, mutually given in the interchange of civilities, are now as rare in this country, as they were once common. This is no matter of regret; for it is not a flower that has been plucked up, but a weed.

But there is one other form of words, which seems to have

come into general abuse, over this whole country; and the more is the pity, as these last are words of grave import, as well as of obvious sense: I mean the phrase, so abundantly used,—*I promise to pay.* In other times, these words were passed with timid caution, and when passed they were held sacred; but they are now coming to be words of mere form, meaning nothing; very like the old complimentary phrases,—Your humble servant—Your most obedient. Not but that the promisee always interprets the text as of old, according to its literal or expressed meaning. But the promiser perverts the text, that he may accommodate it to his own heterodox notions; or, rather, after the Romish doctrine of mental reservation, he mentally interpolates the word—*never*—making it run thus;—I promise (*never*) to pay.

It would be endless to recount all the mischiefs that are flowing in upon society from this prevailing heresy; nor is it needful, since most of them are too obvious to escape notice. Wherefore, not to mention the sore disappointments, the indignant heart-burnings, daily arising, in ten thousand instances, from this single source; nor yet to mention its destructive influence upon all confidence between man and man:—passing over these topics, and others akin to them, I shall consider the matter merely as it affects the interests of the delinquent party.

Be it supposed that he is a man, possessed of several estimable qualities; that he has a large stock of what is called good nature; that he is obliging and compassionate; that, in the main, he is a moral man; and, finally, that there is no apparent blemish in his character, save this alone.—Give the delinquent all these good qualities, and yet "the dead fly, in the precious ointment," spoils the whole compound.

There is a smack of immorality in every instance of voluntary word breaking; and in this, as in every other vice, one step naturally leads to another. The good-natured man, who has neglected to fulfil his promise, is fain to cast about him for an excuse, and if he cannot find one he makes one.

This can hardly be done for the first, or second time, without a considerable struggle with moral principle. But it soon becomes feasible, and as natural, almost, as to breathe. In the process of this ill habit, he quite loses his moral feelings as respects strict veracity; and almost every day he lives, he deals in fiction without any sort of compunction.

Neither is this all; he is the occasion of falsehood to others. He steps over to one of his neighbors, to borrow. His neighbor respects him for his sundry good qualities, but knows well the particular infirmity of his character. He is loth to lose his friend, and quite as loth to hazard his money. What does he do? He, also, proceeds to frame fictitious excuses. "I am very sorry, sir, that it is not in my power to oblige you. There is no man living, that I should be more ready to serve; but—but—," and then out comes the excuse, lie and all.

The man who makes it his general practice to shuffle off, as much as possible, the payment of his honest debts, not only forfeits all claims upon the confidence of society, but loses a main portion of self-respect. He often meets with fellow-beings, with whom he cannot so much as interchange the customary salutation, without enduring the feelings of self-abasement, and in conversing with whom he is compelled, as it were, to have recourse to prevarication and quibble.

And what does he gain by it, in his secular affairs? Nothing at all. He is a loser even there. If he frequently suffers the compulsory process of law, he is a ruined man. Or if he procrastinate, till he has quite exhausted the patience of his creditors, and then pays, seemingly rather to avoid the expense of law than from an honest principle, still he loses that credit, which, to his secular affairs, might be an incalculable benefit; and in seasons of pressing emergency, if he have not sufficient resources in himself, he can find them nowhere.

A strict regard to one's word or promise, is one of the first of social virtues. Wherefore, young men, who are entering, or have just entered the threshold of business, would do well to keep in memory the following maxims. Be as careful of *taking*, as of *giving* credit. Never run in debt beyond what, you have a moral certainty, or, at least, a reasonable prospect of being able to pay in season. Never defer payment when it is needed, and you have the power to make it.

NUMBER XIII.

OF THE HEAVY TAX LAID UPON ALL WORLDLY EMINENCE.

The following advisory monition of an inspired prophet, to his dear and familiar friend, contains a volume of instruction:—"*And seekest thou great things for thyself? Seek them not.*"—Nothing is more certain than the vanity of human greatness, not only by reason of its being transitory and perishable, but, also, because it is often accompanied with much more than an ordinary share of trouble and vexation.

If we first consider the first and greatest of all worldly distinctions—I mean extraordinary gifts of nature—even these, for the most part, are heavily taxed by the impartial hand of the Giver. The few geniuses (few, indeed, in comparison to the number of those who lay claim to that high distinction), so far from being the happiest, are often the most wretched of mortals. The irritableness and spleen of distinguished authors, and especially of poets, are proverbial. The same texture, and tone of the system, which qualify them for soaring into the regions of fancy, and for paintng nature in all her hues, do utterly disqualify them, at least in many instances, for enjoying, in an equal measure with the rest of mankind, the common comforts and blessings of life; not to mention the bitterness of rivalry, and the torments of jealousy, which they are fated to feel and endure. So that, as regards ease and comfort, plain common sense, with controlled passions, is better, by far, than genius, when taxed, as it so often is, with morbid sensibility, and with passions, violent and ungovernable.

The greatest *Beauties* are seldom the most amiable, the most discreet and respectable, or the most happy of women; while, not rarely, their very beauty has been their ruin.

And, indeed, if we were to make a general survey of the extraordinary gifts of nature, and to weigh together, in an even balance, their advantages and disadvantages, as respects the comfort of the possessors, we should find that, in many instances, if not in most, the latter are fully equal to the former.

Neither are the gifts of fortune exempt from heavy and grievous taxation. Vast wealth brings upon its possessor a load of incessant care; generates dispositions and feelings incompatible with quiet enjoyment; and often makes profligates of her children. Nay, even Power, that idol of human ambition, —even Power,—for which riches, themselves, are chiefly coveted,—is often accompanied with more of vexation than of substantial enjoyment. Royalty, itself, has its disquietudes, and dire vexations. Mary, Queen of England, and joint partner in the throne, in a letter to her husband, William the Third, then in Ireland, thus pathetically describes the troubles of her exalted station.—"I must see company on set days. I must laugh and talk, though never so much against my will. I must grin when my heart is ready to break; and talk, when my heart is so oppressed, that I can scarce breathe. All my motions are watched, and all I do so observed, that, if I eat less, or speak less, or look more grave, all is lost in the opinion of the world." —How unenviable is such a lot as this, and, yet, how envied!

While on a time I was reading, in General Lee's memoirs, that Washington, when speaking on the subject of death, used often to declare, that *he would not repass his life, were it in his option*—while reading this extraordinary passage, I was touched with a momentary surprise. What! methought, can it be so? The man whose life was covered with glory, beyond that of almost any other mortal,—could *he* be unwilling to travel over again the same brilliant path, and to enjoy anew the same high honors? Could *he* find such a life tedious and irksome? A few moments' reflection was sufficient, however, to convince me, that the thing was neither incredible nor wonderful. In the seven years' war, and the eight years of his administration, his solicitude and anxiety, lest haply, by some improper step, he should commit the interests of his country, far outweighed, in all probability, every thing of real enjoyment, that mere human power and greatness can bestow. Nor is it unreasonable to think, that, during those fifteen anxious years, many a day-laborer,—nay, many a menial servant enjoyed a greater portion of unalloyed worldly comfort, than did the illustrious man, whom the world held in such admiration.

The object of the foregoing train of reflections is not, at all, to decry Genius, or Beauty, or Riches, or Power; but, rather, to show that man or woman, in moderate circumstances, and ungifted with any uncommon endowments, may be quite as happy without these splendid distinctions, as those are who possess them. For the enjoyment of every essential comfort that this world can afford, there is need only of health and competence, together with a contented mind, a pure conscience, and a thankful heart.

Between the periods of birth and burial how short a space! How very soon will come the time, when, with all the vast congregation now treading this stage of mortality, no distinctions but of the *moral* kind will remain!

NUMBER XIV.

OF THE INESTIMABLE VALUE OF A PIOUS, DISCREET, AND FAITHFUL MOTHER.

It has been often observed, that some of the most illustrious of human characters were early moulded to the model of excellence by the maternal hand. Of this I might adduce, from the records of history, a goodly number of instances; but, for the present, I shall mention only one.

Sir Philip Sidney—born about the middle of the sixteenth century—was the wonder of the age in which he lived; for though he died when a little more than thirty years old, his fame, as a wise and profound statesman, was spread over Europe.

Nor was he less distinguished for religious and moral virtues, and particularly for generosity and tenderness of nature. It has been remarked of him, that "the most beautiful event of his life was his death."

Receiving a mortal wound in a battle in Flanders, the moment after he was wounded, when thirsty with the excess of bleeding, he turned away the water from his own lips, to give it to a dying soldier, with these words; "Thy necessity is still greater than mine."

This extraordinary man was indebted, for the rudiments of his education, to his illustrious and excellent mother, the eldest daughter of the Duke of Northumberland, who, in a preceding reign, had been beheaded. "Her tender melancholy, occasioned by the tragical events in her family, together with the mischance of sickness that had impaired her beauty, inclined her to hide herself from the gay world, and to bestow her attentions almost exclusively upon the education of her children." "It was her delight," says a biographer of Sir Philip, "to form their early habits; to instil into their tender minds the principles of religion and virtue; to direct their passions to proper objects; to superintend not only their serious occupations, but even their amusements."

Had not the loftiness of the house of Northumberland been fallen; had Lady Mary, the eldest daughter of that house, been a leader of fashion at the royal court—a distinction to which her rank would fully have entitled her; her Philip would, in no probability, have been the exalted character that he was.

To see a mother, herself accomplished, and capable of shining in the first circles of fashionable life;—to see her forego the pleasure of amusement, and the ambition of show, for the sake of bestowing personal attentions upon her children; to see her spend the best of her days in fashioning their minds and manners upon the purest models, guiding them with discretion, and alluring them to the love of excellence alike by precept and example; to see this is to behold one of the most charming spectacles, any where furnished in this fallen world.

And what though it be not in the power of such a mother to make a Philip Sidney of her son? What though nature has gifted her children with no uncommon strength, or brightness of intellect? Yet with the divine blessing, she may have such influence upon the moral frame of their young and tender minds, that they shall be disposed to improve their natnral talents, whatever they may be, and to employ them honorably. The benefits, in this respect, which highly capable mothers might confer on their children, during a few of the first years of their earthly existence, are far beyond the power of calculation, since these benefits would, probably, descend from one generation to another, down to distant posterity. "Delightful task!" In comparison with the pure and sublime enjoyment, which the faithful performance of it gives, poor and wretched, indeed, is the whole sum of pleasure, that can possibly be extracted from the amusements of fashion.

Lamentable, however, would be the condition of things in this respect, if either wealth, or rank, or superior talents, or any great degree of literary acquirements were indispensably necessary in a mother, to fit her for the noble and all-important task, which that relation devolves upon her. So far from it, a woman of mere plain sense, whose reading extends but little beyond the divine volume that contains our holy religion, and whose worldly circumstances are narrow, and even indigent, is capable, nevertheless, of conferring unspeakable benefits upon her little ones. As she is the first in their hearts, so, in their esteem, she is the first of women. Her example is their model; they copy her ways; they hang upon her lips. The moral and religious love, inculcated with maternal tenderness by her, they never quite forget; and very often, it is the means of forming their characters for life.

Precious is the mother, whether of high, or low degree, who, in this respect, acts the real mother, to the best of her abilities. Hardly can she fail of stamping upon the minds of her children some salutary impressions, which will never be quite effaced. Except in the rare instances of most unnatural perverseness, their hearts will ever cleave to her. They will not forsake her when she is old. Their filial kindnesses will soothe and solace the infirmities and decay of her age. And when she is called "to put off the mortal, and to put on the immortal clothing," the genuine expression of their hearts will be,—"We loved, but not enough, the gentle hand that reared us.—Gladly would we now recall that softest friend, a mother, whose mild converse, and faithful counsel we in vain regret."

NUMBER XV.

TRUTHS SAID OF BOYS, WHICH BOYS WILL NE'ER BELIEVE.

Our life is beset with perils at every step, but no period of it is, perhaps, quite so perilous as that, in which the boy is stepping into manhood. Then it is that his feeling is fervid, his hope vivid, and his self-confidence at the highest. Then it is, that he listens with most rapture to the voice of the siren, that his heart is most susceptible to the allurements of pleasure; and it is then, that he spurns alike the trammels of restraint, and the counsels of friendship.

Untaught by experience, he despises the experience of others; wise in his own conceit, he scorns the monitions of age and riper judgment; full of himself, he perceives no need of direction or advice, and regards it as an insult to his understanding. He feels a sentiment of indignation and disdain toward those, who should presume to teach *him* how to behave. His sense is deceived, "his soul is in a dream, he is fully confident that he sees things clearly, and yet he sees them in a false mirror, exactly such as they are not."

Nor is it, always, the youth of the least promise, that are in the most danger. So far otherwise, those of forward parts, of lively imaginations, and of strong passions withal, are in peculiar hazard during those green years, in which is the critical period of transition from the condition of boys to that of men. The very qualities, that distinguish them and set them above their fellows, diminish the likelihood of their establishing a sober staidness of character, and, ofttimes, are the means of launching them into the whirlpool of dissipation, where all is lost; where reputation, morals, and whatever is estimable in human beings, are all ingulfed together.

How many instances do the perilous times, we live in, furnish—how many deplorable instances of hopeful boys, abandoned and lost ere they were out of their *teens!* And by how much the more their parents had doted upon them, by so much the more are their hearts wrung with anguish.

Far less is the danger, for the most part, while the immature youth remains under the parental roof, or in "the well-ordered home." There he finds it not so easy to shake off salutary restraints; there he needs must feel some respect for the opinion of the society, in whose bosom he was born and educated, some reverence of parental authority, and some regard to the feelings of near kindred. But when he leaves the haven of home, and is pushed off into the stream of life, it is more than an even chance that he will founder in the stream, if he have not previously been under the governance of moral and religious principle. In his new situation it often happens, that he finds new enticements to lead him astray, and, at the same time, feels himself loosened from the authority and influences which had, heretofore, repressed his wayward propensities; and if vicious, but genteel and artful companions get the first hold of him, his ruin is, in all probability, sealed.

It was in clear view of these affecting circumstances, that the celestial poet, Cowper, penned the following lines:

——"My boy, the unwelcome hour has come,
When thou, transplanted from thy genial home,
Must find a colder soil and bleaker air,
And trust for safety to a stranger's care."

It is hard to mourn over the *death*, but it is, sometimes, still harder to mourn over the *life* of a beloved child. When parents see the one who, they had expected, would be found the solace of their age, the honor of their family, and an ornament to society—when they see him, at the instant of their highest hopes, turn to the ways of folly; no heart but a heart thus exercised, can conceive the sharpness of the pang. This is sorrow indeed; and that the best they can do to prevent it, or, rather, all they can do, is to lay themselves out, in good earnest, to train up their children in the way they should go.

Good education is the thing in the world, the most important and desirable, but it is of wider scope than most people imagine. What is called learning, is only a part of it, and so far from being the most essential part, it is but the husk. In vain will you employ your endeavors to educate your children, unless you give seed to the heart, as well as culture to the understanding; unless you make their moral frame, the subject of your assiduous and well-directed care; unless you take, at least, as much pains to make them well-principled and of virtuous manners, as to make them shine in learning and accomplishments: for intellectual improvement, if their morals be neglected, will tend to render them wise only to do evil. If you train up your boy to a strict regard to truth, honesty, and integrity, and to a deep reverence for all that is sacred; if you train him up in habits of industry, temperance, and love of order;—it is then, and only then, you can reasonably expect, that he will pass through the perilous crisis before him uncontaminated, and that his manhood will be crowned with honor.

NUMBER XVI.

OF THE CONTEMPT OF WOMANKIND.

"When pain and sickness wring the brow,
A ministering angel thou."
SCOTT.

THE man, who expresses or feels a general contempt of womankind, evinces thereby, either that his acquaintance has been mostly with the baser sort, or that his heart is devoid of the common sensibilities of our nature. A satire upon *Woman!* It is revolting; it is dastardly and brutish. Individuals are deserving of the lash of satire, but not the species. Of women, as well as of men, there are the artful and treacherous, the unfeeling and cruel, the mischievous, the disgusting, the abominable.—The sex, nevertheless, is entitled to a high degree of respect, esteem and love.

Of one, in the dark ages, who was the gloomiest of bigots, and the most ruthless of persecutors, it is recorded that "he never looked in the face of a woman, or spoke to one."

In like manner,

———"aside the devil turned,"

when the first of female forms presented itself before him. Woman was, "the last, best gift," to man; moulded out of that part of his flesh and bone, which lay nearest the heart. And what though she was first in the transgression? Was she not principal, also, in the restoration? And when the Divine Restorer, *born of a woman*, was in poverty and need, who were they that ministered to him? *Women.* When the disciples had fled through fear, who stood by, and so deeply sympathized in his last agonies, undismayed by the ferocious countenances of the murderous throng? *Women.* Who so affectionately prepared the embalming spicery, and were the first to visit the sacred tomb? *Women.* To whom have all the after generations been most indebted for the pious culture of infancy and childhood? *To women.* The Eternal Wisdom has, if I may use the expression, cast the minds of the two sexes in different moulds, each being destined to act in a sphere peculiarly its own.

"For contemplation he, and valor form'd,
For softness she, and sweet attractive grace."

The one is destined and fitted for the more active and perilous scenes; the other for the duties and trials of domestic life; the one to protect, the other to lean on the arm of her protector; the one to exhibit the sterner virtues, the other the milder; the one possessing more of active courage; and the other, more of fortitude, of resignation, of unweariable patience, and more of the benevolent affections. This is nature's distinctive line, which, on the part of female character, can never be overleaped, without producing disgust or ridicule. Hence it is, that, of all affectation, none is more displeasing than a woman's affecting the spirit and manners of the other sex. We have a sort of admiration of the heroic intrepidity of the Spartan women; of their contempt of danger; of the stoical apathy, or rather the exultation, with which they received the news of their sons and husbands dying bravely in battle. We admire them as prodigies, but neither love, nor esteem them as women. And why is it that the atheistical *woman* is regarded with such singular horror? Why is the foul oath, the heaven-daring blasphemy, doubly horrible in the ear of decency, when proceeding from the lips of woman? It is because we contrast the outrage with the attributes of timidity, gentleness, delicacy and sensibility, belonging more peculiarly to her sex.

One of the most deplorable wants in woman, is the want of *heart*; the want of genuine sensibility, of the radical affection of sympathy and benevolence. It is a want, which neither beauty, nor wit, nor the rarest accomplishments of person or mind can, by any means, compensate. On the other hand, the most attractive graces of the female character are not the artificial and showy ones; but those of a meek and quiet spirit, and of beneficent dispositions, guided by moral principle and the discretion of sound sense:—in a word, graces, the same that our holy religion inculcates and inspires.

In the fair daughters of Eve, domestic excellence is the predominating excellence; in comparison with which all the ornaments, that literature or manners can bestow, are as tinsel compared with fine gold.

How much soever woman contributes to refine and amplify the innocent pleasures of health and prosperity, yet still more doth she contribute, when she acts the woman, to alleviate the pains of adversity. In our sickness and sorrows, she is indeed as "a ministering angel." What heart else is so sympathetic? What hand else is so soothing? Who watches by the sick bed with most care, with most assiduity, with the most inexhaustible patience? Who, in spite of feebleness of frame, foregoes sleep, and patiently endures a course of remitless watchings of incredible length? Who, so often, devotes life, and the pleasures of life to the needs of a helpless parent? to the solitary chamber of decrepit age? It is *woman*;—the well-educated, the enlightened, the Christian woman.

NUMBER XVII.

OF THE INCREASE OF CONSEQUENCE ORDINARILY GIVEN A MAN BY MARRYING.

Families are clusters of little commonwealths, which can hardly subsist without government, and whose well-being depends greatly upon the manner, in which they are governed.

The ruler of a family, with respect to the children, belonging to his household and under his care, stands in the relation of a magistrate. A sort of magistrate he is, of very ample powers; for he is clothed at once, in a certain measure, with legislative, judicial, and executive authority.

In this character, it concerns him to act with the utmost impartiality. To be partial is to be unjust; and the injustice being perceived and deeply felt, (as it scarcely ever fails to be,) discontent, heart-burnings, and bitter murmurings will ensue. Favoritism is the bane of government, in the smallest communities, as well as in the largest. And look! often it is the favorite child, that wrings the hearts of the doting parents; and no less often the child, that shared least in their regards, comes, at last, to be the solace and the prop of their declining years.

It behooves, that the ruler of a family establish no domestic rules and laws, but such as are reasonable in themselves, and conducive to the real good and welfare of the little community he governs. Else he acts the part of a tyrant; and one, who is a tyrant in his own house, would be a tyrant over millions, if he had it in his power.

As the laws for his household should be enacted with all the prudence and forethought he is master of, so, also, they should be executed with discretion and cool judgment. What would be thought of a judge, who should proceed to pass a penal sentence without conviction, or without giving a patient hearing and a fair trial, or who should fly into a violent passion upon the judgment-seat, and foam with rage while in the act of passing sentence? Every one would think him utterly unfit for his place, and would cry out,—shame upon him! Now the ruler of a family acts as a judge; while the party, arraigned before him, has neither the benefit of counsel, nor the privilege of trial by jury. In these circumstances, it is peculiarly fit and necessary, that the judge should not act passionately, but with cool deliberation.

Paternal magistracy must be supported by general decency of behavior, or, inevitably, it will fall into contempt. It is an old Latin maxim, "*Maxima debetur pueris reverentia*,—in English," *Very great respect is due to children.* Parents must respect themselves, in the presence of their children. A governor, or a justice of a court, who respects not himself by a steady observance of the laws of decency, brings his office and authority into contempt: and it is so in domestic government. Nor does the requisite decorum of parental authority, at all, imply moroseness and habitual sternness. So far otherwise, the father who is courteous and affable, and, in a proper manner, even intimate with his children, increases, by it, their esteem and respect, as well as their love.

A unit standing alone, however great a unit it be, is still the least of numbers ; but place it in close alliance with another unit and, instantly, there is produced the respectable number 11.

Ordinarily, a man multiplies his importance in society by marrying. Instantly, he multiplies the number of his kindred ; the relations of his wife being to him, as his own. The circle of friendly acquaintance is enlarged, by the addition of those, with whom she had been in the habits of friendship. It is now, that society begins to have fast hold of him ; and it is now, that he, himself, begins to cling to society in earnest. He is no longer a citizen at large, whose home is everywhere, or rather nowhere. He now feels that he has, indeed, a particular home, and is attached to the spot. And what though he have neither rank, nor wealth, nor talents, to distinguish him abroad ? He, nevertheless, is a man of consequence in his own family. Of that little community he is the legitimate head, by a right more divine, than any regal authority can boast of. There is at least one individual who participates, deeply and feelingly, in all his interests and fortunes. His prosperity and his adversity, his joys and his sorrows, are hers. However obscure, he comes now to be a man of some authority. His children are the subjects of his rule, as well as the objects of his paternal care and love. He says to one, Go, and he goeth ; to another, Come, and he cometh ; and to a third, Do this and he doeth it. Nor is any ruler else obeyed with so much alacrity and good-will, as that father, who acts the father with a proper mixture of discretion and tenderness. The eyes of his little subjects glisten with joy, while they are fulfilling his wishes, and obeying his behests.

Moreover, ordinarily, a man is more likely to be a virtuous member of society for marrying. He feels doubly bound to good behavior, by placing himself in this relationship. It is not only his own interest that is at stake, but the interests of the partner, whose earthly destinies are so closely connected with his ;—the interests, too, of the beloved offspring of their union. If he bring a blot upon himself, she, together with their children, shares in the infamy. Full well he knows that, if he take to bad courses, he plunges those who are most near and dear to him, as well as himself, into an abyss of wretchedness. This circumstance cannot fail of bearing, with considerable weight, upon minds not entirely lost to the common sensibilities of human nature.

NUMBER XVIII.

OF THE USE AND NECESSITY OF SMALL CHANGE IN SOCIAL AND DOMESTIC COMMERCE.

THE commerce of neighborly social life is carried on, chiefly, by small change. Vast favors are seldom bestowed, and heavy obligations are seldom incurred. It is the constant interchange of little obliging attentions, that constitutes connubial happiness. It springs from an uninterrupted series of little acts of mutual kindness, light as air of themselves, and costing little or nothing, but of immeasurable importance in their consequences; as they furnish the only kind of food, that will long sustain that delicate kind of friendship, and as the absence of these small attentions occasions, first coldness, then distrust, and finally alienation. Setting aside the brutish and the dissolute part of the community, wives and husbands disagree oftener, by much, about trifles, than about things of real weight. Perhaps nine in ten of their disputes and squabbles grow out of little things, such as trivial neglects, petty faults, or a word unkindly spoken. Nay, merely a hard look, sometimes, lays the foundation of a hard quarrel. A husband never can please his wife any longer, than his general conduct evinces that he is, in most respects, well pleased with her; and still less, perhaps, may a wife expect to please or gain her husband otherwise than by treating him with conjugal affection. If, for even his real and gross trespasses, she administers acids rather than sanatives, the oil of vitriol instead of the healing balsam, she will but increase the moral malady, that she wishes to cure.

If we extend our view to the larger circle of social intercourse which comprehends relations, friends, and acquaintance of every kind and degree, we shall find, that the frequent interchange of courteous attentions and little kindnesses is the thing, that keeps them united together, and pleased with each other; and that, in default of this, they presently lose all relish for one another's company. The truth is, as our tempers are oftener ruffled by trifles than by things of moment, so, on the other hand, our affections are won more by a long series of trivial obligations, than by one single obligation, however great.

Man, put him where you will, is a proud-hearted little animal. And hence, we become attached to those, who are in the habit of treating us, as if they thought us worthy of their particular notice and regard, and, at the same time, cold and secretly resentful toward such, as habitually neglect us in these little points: even though the former never have done us a single important favor, and the latter, in some one instance or other, have essentially befriended us.

With regard to neglect and trespasses in those little things, which constitute the main substance of social life, the worst of it is, that they are incapable of free discussion; and of course, the wounds from them admit of no healing. We are deeply touched with omissions or slights, for which it would be ridiculous to expostulate or complain. They leave a sting, which secretly rankles in our memories, and festers in our imaginations, and inwardly we feel sore, while we are ashamed to fret outwardly; the cause of our provocation being an undefinable, nameless something, upon which we never can ask for an explanation, and, consequently, can never obtain any satisfaction.

True enough, all this is often ill-grounded, or the offspring of mere jealousy. But that makes the case more remediless; for ill-grounded enmities are the most obstinate, because, as their causes exist altogether, or chiefly, in the imagination, the imagination is ever busy in coloring and magnifying them; whereas, when the offence, though real, is of a definite form and shape, it may be got over.

I have seen two friends dispute and quarrel violently about an affair of moment, and then settle it, and, presently, become as kind and loving together as ever. And I have seen other two friends, who never quarrelled together at all, become first cold, and at last utterly estranged, by reason of a neglect or slight, on the one side or the other, which, of itself, was too trivial to be so much as mentioned to the offending party.

There are those, who are willing to oblige, but are unwilling to receive obligations, though never so small, in any way or in any thing; and they boast of it as a noble quality. But whatever they may think, themselves, they violate, in this respect, the general law of social commerce, which requires some degree of reciprocity, or a mutual exchange of commodities. One, who is in the way of often receiving from another little kindnesses, which he is never permitted to requite, sinks into a dependent; and his nominal friend is not, indeed, a friend, but a patron. The show of utter averseness to being obliged, in any case whatever, is, commonly, understood aright; it is taken for pride, or contempt, or coldness, and naturally gives displeasure; while, on the contrary, to accept little obligations with frankness, and to be alike willing to oblige and to be obliged, is the proper line of social intercourse.

I will only remark further, that the little daily attentions, upon which social feeling and happiness so much depend, ought to be natural and spontaneous, and not loaded and stiffened with ceremony: and that the only way to make them quite natural and spontaneous, is to have written on the heart that first of social laws, "*Thou shalt love thy neighbor as thyself.*"

NUMBER XIX.

OF THE GREAT SOCIAL LAW, ENJOINING IT UPON EACH TO YIELD PLACE TO EACH.

In the crowded streets of a great city, where multitudes are passing in opposite directions, while some are crossing obliquely, and others at right angles, it is necessary for every one to give way a little to those he meets; by which means they will have a free passage. Were the whole multitude to pass directly onward, without any one's yielding an inch of ground to any body else, all would be obstructed more or less, and confusion must ensue.—Or, if a churlish individual should take it into his head, to march forward in a straight line, and, in no case, make way for man, woman, or child, nor even for a procession, he would be sure to jostle against some one or other, at almost every step, and would receive many an insult, and, perhaps, hard blows, for his obstinacy and impudence.

And very much so it is in our journey through life, and with respect to our general intercourse with mankind. "In the march of life, no one's path lies so clear, as not in some degree to cross another's; and if each is determined, with unyielding sturdiness, to keep his own line, it is impossible but he must both give and receive many a rude shock." In society, in neighborhoods, and even among close friends, there will spring up rivalries, and be, sometimes, a clashing of opinion, and if all were mutually obstinate, there could be no bounds nor end to contention. Whereas, by the exercise of mutual condescension, social harmony is preserved, and the pleasures of society enjoyed.

The exercise of condescension is ranked among the precepts of the gospel, and is enjoined as a duty upon Christians, who are expressly told, from divine authority, *to be patient towards all men,—to be courteous.* Hence it follows, that the extremely obstinate man, who will not yield an ace in matters of interest or opinion, but runs foul of every one that chances to cross his path, does really transgress the rules of the gospel, as well as those of decorum.

Here let me not be misunderstood. Condescension has its bounds, and those bounds are strongly marked. One should never yield opinions, much less principles, that are of great and serious importance. One should never sacrifice conscience to please friends, or for fear of foes. One should never "follow a multitude to do evil." One should never suffer himself to be conformed to the world in vicious practices and customs, or in fashions, which, though innocent in themselves, are too expensive for him to follow. One should never yield any thing to importunity, which self-justice forbids him to yield at all. In these points, the person, who would go through the journey of life *well*, must be firm and inflexible. But in matters of indifference, or of no serious consequence, whether respecting opinion or interest, a yielding, accommodating spirit is not only desirable, but a moral and Christian duty. And even in points which are not to be yielded, one should maintain firmness in such a manner, if possible, as to make it evident that he acts from principle rather than from obstinacy.

It would be easy to apply these observations, to the various relations of social life, in all which the custom of well-ordered society, imposes upon us a regard for the opinions and feelings of others; but more particularly are they applicable to those in the married state, for it is here that mutual obstinacy of temper, meets with daily and hourly opportunities and occasions of collision. " Trifles light as air," are perpetually disputed between them, and with as much warmth and pertinacity, as if they were articles of faith.

Courtesy of manners is the congruous drapery of a benevolent mind, and is both seemly and pleasing, at all times, and in every relation of life. Nor does it need any laborious study to attain it. A great part of the essence of courtesy, or of genuine politeness, is expressed in these three words, "*Never prefer yourself.*" This rule of social intercourse, which is of excellent use, is the more highly to be regarded, as it is drawn, not from the school of pagan philosophy, but from the pure fountain of the gospel. One of the parables of our blessed Saviour begins thus,—" When thou art bidden of any man to a wedding, *sit not down in the highest room.*" That is, in modern phrase, *prefer not thyself.*

They, who carefully abstain from giving to themselves any undue or even questionable preferences, will seldom meet with incivilities from others.

NUMBER XX.

OF THE NECESSITY OF LEARNING HOW TO USE MONEY.

——" To know
That which before us lies in daily life
Is the prime of wisdom; what is more, is fume,
Or emptiness, or fond impertinence."

MILTON.

THERE is one inferior, or subordinate branch of knowledge, which great learning overlooks, and great genius contemns; though, in all ages of the world, learning and genius have suffered sore hardships and perplexities for the lack of it: I mean the knowledge of the use of money.

This is, it must be owned, a vulgar kind of knowledge; amply possessed, not unfrequently, by minds of the baser sort. So far is it from entering into the scope of scholastic education, that few are more destitute of it than some of the deepest scholars. The studies they pursue are altogether foreign from this, and the classical authors which they most admire speak of it with contempt. It is the ambition of the studious boy to be a fine scholar. This object, along with virtuous dispositions, embraces, in his estimation, every thing desirable in character. After a painful, and laudable course of exertions, he attains it. He steps forth, into the busy world, in the majesty of learning. By all men, that are scholars themselves, his parts and his progress are admired. He has great talents, rare talents, shining talents, and all sense but common sense. He knows the reputed number of the visible stars in the firmament, and not a few of them he can call by their names. He has explored the depths of natural philosophy. In metaphysical acumen he is keen, and can split hairs as with an edge, finer and sharper than a razor's. In the most celebrated languages of antiquity, and, perhaps, in several modern languages, he is marvellously skilled. But in respect to that ordinary traffic, which all, who have bodies to feed and clothe, must be concerned in, he knows less than a market boy of the age of twelve. And how will he ever get this kind of knowledge? His books teach it not, and, besides, to make it an object of practical attention, is repugnant, alike, to his habits and feelings. Thus richly endowed, and, meanwhile, deplorably lacking, he steps into the busy world:—and experience tells the rest.

It is no uncommon thing, to find men of excellent parts, and profound erudition, who, nevertheless, of the little affairs of practical life are as ignorant as children. In their dealing, they are exposed to daily impositions; the sharks of society prey upon them, and they perceive it not. If they employ laborers, they know neither how to direct them, nor how to estimate their services; and are quite as likely to find fault with the honest and faithful, as with those who defraud them, and artfully cover the cheat. If they have an income which, rightly managed, would be sufficient, it melts away in their improvident hands, and they suffer want. In whatever pertains to abstract science, they are entitled to rank with the great; but in every thing that relates to the supply of their daily necessities, or those of their families, they are the least among the little. Though they have an accurate knowledge of the map of the heavens and of the earth, as they know nothing, or next to nothing of the things about them, they are more pitiable for their ignorance, than enviable for their learning.

This sort of helplessness does not, however, befall the learned only: it is, alike, common to the inheritors of opulence. As they who, from childhood, have been altogether engaged in scientific pursuits, know less of the economy of a family, than of the economy of the visible heavens; so they, that are born to the inheritance of wealth, are naturally inclined to despise the very name and appearance of economy, as little and mean. Possessing a superfluity of money, which they never knew the getting of, they squander rather than spend it; and in a very little while, the fruits of a whole age of painful industry are utterly wasted and gone: not always from any uncommon depravity of heart, but sometimes, nay often, from merely the lack of ordinary prudence; of that worldly prudence, the study or observance of which they deemed beneath their condition.

"The *love* of money" (not money itself) "is the root of all evil." There is almost no evil, to which the inordinate love of money has not given birth or aid. But if things were to be estimated, merely by the abuse of them, Literature, Science, the lights of Reason and even Reason itself, must fall under reproach. What though money be the idol of griping avarice, and the pillar of devouring ambition? What though it minister, in a thousand ways, to the lusts of men? What though to many it opens the floodgates of vice? What though the sordid seek it as the chief good, and the knavish snatch it by whatever means?—Is money itself in fault? Is it not a blessing after all? If it be not a blessing, then it follows that the naked, famishing savage is as well off as the well-fed and well-clothed European or American; that vile, smoky cabins are as comfortable as choice houses; and that civilization itself is no better than the forlorn state of nature.

Money is, indeed, a great blessing, and the knowledge of using money as not abusing it,—charitably, whenever charity calls, but, always, discreetly—is an interesting branch of knowledge, and well deserves a place in our systems of education. For it is far more important to learn to guide our affairs with discretion than to "speak with tongues." Neither is any other science so often and so urgently needed, as homely household science—or practical skill in managing those little domestic and personal concerns, which every day of life brings along with it.

NUMBER XXI.

OF THE WONDERFUL BOY.

There is a remarkable variety in the growth of mind, from the first visible dawnings of reason, to the full maturity of its powers. Of minds, that finally attain to an uncommon degree of intelligence, some have a slow growth; an ample harvest of fruit succeeds to no extraordinary blossom. Neither their childhood nor their youth gave promise of the parts, which the process of time gradually and slowly developed. It has been remarked of the late Patrick Henry, so celebrated in the annals of Virginia, "that he did not appear at the bar until he was about thirty years old, and that he had attained nearly to forty, before the extent of his talents was discovered by the public, and, probably, before it was known to himself." Other minds have a rapid growth, and shortly become stationary, or even go to decay; and the maturity of age disappoints the high expectations that had been built upon the singular forwardness of childhood and youth. Their premature brightness passes away, and is presently gone, like the passing blaze of a meteor.

"The wonderful boy, being no longer a boy, is no longer a wonder." Not that this is the fact in all instances: there have been men of gigantic minds, who discovered marks of superiority in mental stature, almost from the cradle. One remarkable instance of it, was Dr. Samuel Johnson, and another, the late Chief Justice Parsons. Of the latter the Hon. Judge Parker in an address to a Grand Jury observes:—"From the companions of his early years I have learned, that he was comparatively great before he arrived at manhood; that his infancy was marked by mental labor and study, rather than by puerile amusements; that his youth was a season of persevering acquisition instead of pleasure; and that when he became a man, he seemed to possess the wisdom and experience of those, who had been men long before him."

But notwithstanding these, and sundry other similar instances, experience teaches that the wonderful boy not seldom makes but an ordinary, and, sometimes, an inferior man: and this is owing, perhaps, for the most part to the two following causes.

In the view that is taken of childhood and immature youth, the partial or superficial observer is very apt to mistake loquacious vivacity for brightness of intellect, and a forward pertness for genius; and the fond hopes that are founded upon this common mistake, are at length blasted of course. In the progress of age there is discovered the want of solidity and depth. The mind has no bottom. It retains its sprightliness through life; but it is still the sprightliness of childish years.

But the most common cause of the deplorable failure of youths of great promise, is the indiscretion, not to say vanity of their friends. It is quite common for parents to mistake their own goslings for swans; to think their children very bright, if they have merely common sense. But if any one of them happen to be more forward for his age than is usual, he makes a prodigious figure in their partial and doting eyes; nor can they be content to smother or conceal the delicious sensations of their hearts. They exhibit the prodigy of intellect to their acquaintances and visitors; and these, out of courtesy, praise the wonderful boy to his face, and express quite as much admiration of his parts as they feel—and, peradventure, a little more.

Young master listens—"nothing loth"—to these notes of adulation. Ere he is out of his teens, he thinks himself too wise for instruction, and too important for advice. He looks down with scorn upon the beaten tracks of life, and must needs strike out some eccentric path for himself. Or, depending on the mere force of genius, he despises plodding industry even of the intellectual kind, as fit only for vulgar souls. The deplorable consequences are inevitable.

A boy flattered much for his genius, or a girl, for her beauty, is, of all human wights, the most likely to become tumid with vanity, which alike deforms the mind and hinders its growth.

The natural gifts of the mind are dealt out with a frugal hand; to none so abundantly as to supersede the necessity of mental labor; and to few so sparingly, that they may not, under the enjoyment of suitable means, and with well-directed industry, attain to a respectable standing for knowledge; and whatever difference there may be between men in regard to the original powers of their minds, the most common and the greatest difference between them, arises from a diligent cultivation of these powers on the one hand, and a slothful neglect of them on the other. With respect to intellectual, as well as to worldly treasure, it is the hand of the diligent that maketh rich; while the sluggard, who neglects to cultivate and improve his mind, will find that mind a wretched waste at the age of fifty, of however great promise it had been at the age of twenty. Like rare-ripe fruit, its maturity and its decay will be simultaneous.

NUMBER XXII.

OF BRIDLING THE TONGUE.

"The tongue can no man tame."

If this were not the language of inspiration, experience has proved it to be the language of truth. The tongue is the most untamable thing in nature. "Every kind of beasts and birds, and of serpents, is tamed and has been tamed by mankind." But not so with the tongue. Who, amongst the sons of men, ever yet tamed his own tongue? Not one.—A person can *bridle* his tongue, or *hold* it; but no sooner does he take off the bridle, or let go his hold, than this little member runs wild, and out slips something from it, in the moment of passion or of levity, which the speaker, presently, wishes back.

Mark Anthony, it has been said, tamed lions, and drove them, harnessed to his chariot, through the streets of Rome. Had he tamed his own tongue, it had been a greater wonder still.—The rattlesnake has been tamed, and so has the crocodile: but the tongue, never. Pythagoras imposed on his pupils constant silence, for months, and years together. But what did it all signify? No sooner were they permitted to talk, than they gabbled a deal of impertinence.—Besides, to withhold the tongue from speaking at all, is destroying its end and use, rather than taming it. The gift of speech is too precious to be thrown away. Let the tongue be accustomed to speak, and to speak as it ought to. "A word spoken in season, how good is it!" Unruly tongues, on the contrary, produce "a world of iniquity."—Some are "full of deadly poison." Such are they, that curse men and blaspheme God, and which utter lies for mischief, or for sport. Such too is the deceitful tongue, "whose words are smoother than oil; yet are they drawn swords." There is the sly, whispering tongue, and babbling, tattling tongue: each of which "separateth very friends." "The words of a tale-bearer are as wounds." He wounds others thereby, and himself too. For the mouth of such a fool is his destruction.

An impertinent, meddling tongue makes bad worse, even when employed in offices of friendship. When Job was smit from head to foot, the busy tongues of his wife and his friends were a sorer plague to him than all his pains. And thus it often happens, that a person under misfortune suffers as well from the meddling tongues of friends, as from the malicious tongues of enemies.

There are *fiery* tongues. "The tongue is a fire." Such is the tongue of the passionate man, or woman, whose mouth, foaming with rage, casteth abroad words, which are as "firebrands, arrows, and death." Such also is the tongue of the slanderer and back-biter, which, being itself "set on fire of hell," puts whole neighborhoods and communities in a flame, and setteth on fire the course of nature." How many a sweetly fashioned mouth has been disfigured, and made hideous, by the fiery tongue in it.

What, then, is to be done with this unruly little member, which "boasteth great things," and occasioneth infinite mischief in the world? Since no man, or woman even, can quite tame it, what is the best way to manage it?

First, correct the heart, and keep that with all diligence. The foolishness of the lips is first uttered in the heart. "For out of the abundance of the heart the mouth speaketh."

Next, carefully bridle the tongue. Keep the bit upon it at all times; especially in the moment of sudden anger, and in the hour of joy and conviviality.

Self-command, as respects the tongue, is as necessary as it is difficult. For we are told from divine authority, "If any man offend not in word, the same is a perfect man, and able also to bridle the whole body."

As it is of the utmost importance that we rule our own tongues, so, on the other hand, it is of no small importance, that we be guarded against the unruly tongues of others. And here I will lay down one caution, and commend it to the particular remembrance of the young and inexperienced. Beware of close intimacy with those, whose tongues are calumnious towards almost every one except the present company, to which they are ever smooth and fair. For, he who commonly indulges himself in calumniating or ridiculing the absent, plainly shows his company, what it has to expect from him, after he leaves it.

NUMBER XXIII.

OF SAYING TOO MUCH.

THE art of holding the tongue, is quite as necessary as the art of speaking, and, in some instances, it is even more difficult to learn.

In a biographical notice of a celebrated speaker in the British House of Commons, it is remarked that "*he never said too much.*" This is, in truth, a rare commendation of a public speaker. One who, without circumlocution or parade, comes to the matter in hand at once, and pertinaciously sticks to it throughout—who seizes on the strong points in the argument, and sets them to view in the clearest light—who says all that is proper and nothing more—whose every sentence, and almost every word, strikes home, and who "minds to leave off when he has done"—such a public speaker, whether in the Forum, in the Pulpit, or at the Bar, will never tire his hearers.

But my present business is not with *Speakers*, but with *Talkers;* the last being much the most numerous tribe, and entitled, of course, to the first notice.

Man, or even *woman*, when enjoying freedom of the tongue, and gifted with the faculty of using it fluently, is a great deal more apt to say too much than too little.

When a room full of ladies are all speaking at the same instant, only with this difference, that some tune their voices higher and some lower, it is pretty clear that they say too much. But this is tender ground, on which I would tread lightly.

They who expect to be listened to by every body, but are unwilling, themselves, to listen to any body; who will hold you by the sleeve or button, if you attempt to escape them, and din you the harder, the more you show signs of weariness;—this tribe of talkers (as all but themselves will readily admit) say too much.

Persons, who have wit, or (what is as bad) who think they have it, are in particular hazard of saying too much. It is one of the hardest things in the world, to make a temperate use of real or of self-supposed wit, and more particularly, of the talent for raillery. And hence many a one, not wanting in good nature, and meaning nothing more than to show off his wit, multiplies enemies, and sometimes wounds his best friends. To make use of a line in one of Crabbe's poems,

"He kindles anger by untimely jokes."

They who talk merely with the intent to shine in company, or for the sake of showing off to advantage their own parts and learning,—always say too much.

The fond pair, who entertain their visitors, by the hour, with setting forth the excellent qualities, or clever sayings of their own children, or with mawkish details of the rare conjugal affection that subsists between themselves,—say too much.

Those who are inordinately fond of speaking in the first person—*I myself*,—it is more than an even chance that they will say too much. When a young man, whose stock of wisdom is small, is more eager to expend it in talking, than to increase it by patient listening—he is very apt to say too much.

Old men are prone to say too much, when, getting into the *preter-pluperfect* tense, they represent the former days as every way better than these. As if the human family, notwithstanding the perpetual accumulation of experience, were constantly retrograding instead of advancing; and as if men and women, nowadays, were like grasshoppers in comparison of their progenitors.

It is seldom that men do not say too much, in their convivial moments. It is then, that they are peculiarly apt to let off with the tongue something which they are sorry for on the morrow; for "when wine is in, discretion is out."

As to those persons, whose staple of conversation is telling stories in long metre, though it is hardly to be expected that they can be prevailed with either to refrain or to abridge, yet the following direction from *Chesterfield travestie*, may be of use to them, as a general regulator.—"When you mean to introduce an interesting story, make out a kind of preface about an hour's length, by way of impressing upon your hearers the pleasure they are about to receive. If they should be disappointed, that is not your fault. You did your best; and so much time has been passed away, at least to your own satisfaction."

I will conclude with a caution.—Let not him that talketh not, despise him that talketh. There have been some wights of the human family, both male and female, who have obtained the reputation of abilities and wisdom by their grave taciturnity,—

every body thinking that they could say a great deal if they would--when in sober truth, their habitual silence was owing rather to dearth of ideas or to dulness.

To be humdrum in company, is as wide from the true mark as to be garrulous.

NUMBER XXIV.

OF THE SALUTARY EFFECTS OF THE NECESSITY, LAID UPON MAN, TO LABOR.

NECESSITY is the mainspring of industry, and the mother of useful arts. The earth was given to the children of men, in a rude and forlorn condition. And why? Assuredly, not because it was out of the power, or beyond the benevolence of the Creator, to have rendered the whole face of it "like blooming Eden, fair," and so fertile every where, as to yield a plentiful abundance for human sustenance, without any human labor, care, or forethought. This did not, however, consist with the plan of Divine Wisdom.

Man is a being compounded of mind and matter; and a great part of his necessary employment is such, as tends to evince the superiority of the former over the latter. The stubborn glebe he meliorates, softens, and fructifies. Regions of forest he subdues, and turns them into fruitful fields, and blooming gardens. The droughty soil he irrigates, and the fenny he drains. Earth, Air, Fire, and Water, are all laid by him under contribution, and he compels them, as it were, to minister, not only to the necessities and comforts, but to the embellishments of life. In ten thousand ways, by skilful contrivance, and the dint of industry, he overcomes the resistance of stubborn matter, and forces it to yield to his use—to his comfort—to his adornment. And by all this busy round of contrivance and of labor, the faculties of his mind are developed, his body is made more strong and healthy, his morals more virtuous or less corrupt, and his life unspeakably more contented and happy. For he rejoices in the work of his hands, nor feels he the burden of time, which hangs so heavily on the sons and daughters of sloth.

Man is nowhere found more degraded, than in climes the most delicious, and upon a soil that produces, spontaneously, an abundant supply of his wants. It is *there* that his faculties are torpid, his mind and his heart most deeply corrupted, and his existence superlatively wretched. If we may credit the accounts of voyagers, some of the South Sea islands are earthly paradises in regard to climate and soil, but border upon the infernal regions as to customs, morals, and manners; both the men and the women being so deeply corrupted, that their abominable vices alone, not only prevent any increase of population, but threaten even to extirpate them entirely from the face of the earth. Nor would it, perhaps, be much better with the human race over the world, if the whole world were in a condition that superseded all necessity for labor.

If it seemed meet to the all-wise Creator, that man, in his primeval state, should be subject to labor—that he should be made *to dress the garden, and to keep it*—much greater is the urgency for industrious habits in his lapsed state, in which idleness is sure to be prolific of vice. And, accordingly, upon the moral change of human nature, the earth, too, underwent a change. The thorn and the thistle grew up, in place of the fragrant flower and the nourishing plant. The heat consumed by day, and the frost by night. The inert matter, that he had to deal with, became doubly intractable. Obstacles to sloth, and imperious calls to industry, multiplied. So that man was compelled to eat his bread in the sweat of his face.

Happy necessity! the necessity that prevents a frightful mass of moral evil, and produces an immensity of good. Without it, the wickedness of man would be doubly great upon the earth; and so far from enjoyment—feeling the fulness of satiety, and the intolerable burden of time—like Milton's fiend in paradise, he would " see undelighted all delight."

Among the vain sons and daughters of men, there are those who despise labor, even though their circumstances urgently need it. As if the point of honor lay in being useless, improvident, and helpless. This is *Folly's* pride. Whoso despiseth labor, despiseth an ordinance of heaven. Not only is labor made necessary by the law of our general nature, but it is enjoined by a positive law from above.—" *Six days shalt thou labor, and do all thy work.*" The truly wise, so far from despising it, ever hold it in honor. To honor useful labor—to encourage the industrious—to bring up children to early habits of industry and frugality—and, on the other hand, to discountenance and hold in reproach a life of sloth, of improvidence, and of dissipation,—

are indispensable, and ought to be engrained in the public mind. They are truly republican sentiments and habits; and as far as they prevail, so far will there be order and thrift in any free republic, and especially in this free country, in which there is such an unbounded scope for industry.

NUMBER XXV.

OF THE DESIGN AND USE OF THE THUMB.

THE whole frame of the human body so clearly evinces design, and, of course, an all-wise Designer, that atheism would appear the extreme of folly, if even there were no other arguments to confute it, than those which are, in a manner, forced upon us, whenever we take a careful survey of ourselves.

The mechanism of the eye is marvellously complex, and yet nothing in it is superfluous; every part bearing a necessary and obvious relation to the purpose for which it was formed. Nor is the mechanism of the ear less adapted, in every part, to the design of its formation. These wonderful organs of sense are given us, however, in common with the lower animals, of which there are some, that far excel us in clearness of sight, and quickness of hearing. But the human body has one appendage, which belongs not to any of the brute creation, and which evidences design or contrivance, as clearly as the eye or the ear. I mean *the Thumb.* This puny member, which scarcely ever is noticed by poet or philosopher, has been the main stay of the human family, in all ages and countries.

Had the human body lacked this little limb of labor, man would have been the most forlornly helpless of all animals, and, indeed, the whole race must nearly have perished thousands of years ere the present time. He neither could have tilled the ground, nor drawn a fish from the water. He neither could have felled the forests, nor furnished himself with weapons of defence against the ferocious beasts, with which they were inhabited. He would have been alike incapable of making, and of using any of the instruments necessary for his sustenance, or clothing, or defence. Suppose that the thumb, and that only, had been overlooked in the general contrivance of the human body, suppose that all the organs and members of the body, and particularly the *hands*, were exactly as they are now, save that, instead of four fingers and a thumb, there were five fingers standing parallel to each other:—the body, in that case, would have been a machine wonderfully curious, but utterly inadequate to the purposes of human life. Suppose further, that, as a recompense for the want of a thumb, man had been gifted with a double or treble portion of intellect; he, notwithstanding, must have been helpless and wretched; for it would be out of the power of finite intellect to suply that deficiency, or even so much as to provide for the mere necessary wants of the body.

Man, upon his expulsion from paradise, was cast into a wilderness world, and a wilderness it must have remained to this day, but for the thumb upon his hand. He was commanded to subdue the earth, and was authorized to exercise dominion over the beasts of the field;—things as much out of his power had he been thumbless, as arresting the stars in their courses. But this feeble being, through the constant aid of the thumb, what wonders has he wrought! See the forests felled; see blooming gardens and fields waving with golden wheat; see villages, towns, cities, the spacious and well-furnished tenements of man; see his convenient and comely attire, the fulness of his cup, and the comforts of his table; see thousands of ships proudly traversing the ocean, freighted with the superfluities of some countries for the supply of the wants of others; see the finer works of art, pictures, statuary, engravings, embroidery;—see all these, and a thousand other things, and you will recognize in every one of them the agency of the thumb. Nay, all our books of Divinity, Law, Physic, Surgery, History, Biography, Philosophy, Poetry, or of whatever name or description, were first *thumbed* out by the laborious penmen of them. So true is it, that, as the hand is the instrument to all other instruments, it is the thumb, chiefly, that ministers ability to the hand.

The thumb points to duty. Its admirable contrivance manifests both the wisdom and the goodness of the Contriver. It plainly shows, at the same time, that man is destined by his Maker, to employments of manual labor; and, consequently, that manual labor, so far from being a reproach to him, is one of the essential duties of his nature and condition, and ought rather to be held in honor than in disgrace. And if there be some exceptions, they include but a very small proportion of the human family: for, of the whole world there *are* not more, perhaps, than a hundredth part, who are fairly exempted by rank, or fortune, or mental occupations, from the necessity of laboring with their hands.

"*Sucking the thumbs*," is a proverbial phrase, denoting a total neglect of employing them in any useful way, answerable to the design they were made for. A great many of this "untoward generation" have the vile trick of "sucking their thumbs;" —a great many, too, whose circumstances imperiously demand a better use of them. It is a pitiful practice, whether in man or woman, directly leading to poverty and want, and, not unfrequently, to the worst of vices. It behooves that parents keep a sharp look out, lest their boys and girls get into this way, so dangerous to their morals, so deadening to all their faculties, and so destructive of their future prospects in life.

But there is one use of the thumb, that is infinitely worse than not using it at all; it is employing it in spreading abroad falsehood and moral poison, with the pen, and with the type. It were far better to be born without thumbs, than to use them so abominably.

NUMBER XXVI.

OF IDLERS.

There are multitudes who pass along the stream of life without laboring at the oar, or paying any thing for their passage; so that the charge of their fare falls, most unreasonably, upon their fellow-passengers. This is an evil of a very serious and dangerous nature; for such idlers not only burden the community, but corrupt it. To say that it were as well for their country that they had never been born, and that they are unworthy to be numbered in the census of its population;—to say this, is saying too little. They not only do no good, but they do much harm; they not only prey upon the fruits of other men's industry, but they deprave public morals. It is in the nature of this kind of gentry to multiply very fast if they are not checked; for besides that they commonly bring up their children, if children they have, in their own way of living, they are perpetually making proselytes from the families of their neighbors; leading astray, by their examples and enticements, a great many youth, who, but for them, might have been industrious, and useful to society.

In some countries, the wisdom of legislators has been much employed on this subject, and the arm of executive power has enforced industry, as a political duty which every person owed to the State. The Hollanders in particular, in the early age of their Republic, considered idle persons as politically criminal, and punished idleness as a crime against the commonwealth. Those, who had no visible means for a livelihood, were called before the magistracy, to give an account how they got their living; and if they were unable to render a satisfactory explanation on this point, they were put to labor. Those thrifty Hollanders are said to have employed, also, the following singular expedient. They constructed a kind of box, sufficiently large for a man to stand therein upright, and exercise his bodily faculties. In the interior of it there was a pump. The vagrant or idler was put into this box, which was so placed in the liquid element, that the water would gush into it constantly, through apertures in its bottom and sides; so that the lazy culprit had to work at the pump with all his might, and for several hours together, to keep himself from drowning. The medicine, it is said, was found to be an infallible cure for the disease; insomuch, that no one was ever known to work at the pump for the second time.

I do, by no means, recommend those old Dutch laws and customs for domestic use here. Sacred Liberty! I would not hurt a hair of thy head. Yet every thing ought to be done in this case, which can be done consistently with that personal liberty, which our free constitutions of government guarantee to every citizen of the United States. How far our laws, in consistency with the rights of citizens, might go towards restraining notorious idleness and dissipation with respect to adults, it is not for me to say. I leave it to men, gifted with superior wisdom. Thus far, however, I will venture to affirm—that as children, in some sense or other, do actually belong to the community, so it ought to be in the power, and to be made the duty of the political guardians of the public welfare, to see to it that they be brought up in such a manner, that they may be likely to strengthen and adorn, rather than to weaken and deprave society. For which reason, when idle profligate parents are manifestly leading their children in their own footsteps, they ought to be taken from the dominion of such unworthy parents, and placed under the care of those, who would accustom them to habits of virtuous industry. It would be an act of charity to the children themselves; and would give to the general community a vast number of sound and useful members, who, else would grow up to prey upon its earnings, and poison its morals. If all suitable pains were taken with the rising generation to induce them to form sober and industrious habits, by example, by the incitements of persuasion, and even by reasonable force whenever force is necessary, the effects would be happy beyond measure. An infinite mass of mischief and crime would be prevented; the officers of justice would have little to do; our jails would, comparatively, be empty.

I will only add, *Public Sentiment*, as it now stands in some, if not in most parts of our country, must needs be rectified; else idleness and dissipation will continue to gather numbers and strength. So long as an idle, worthless fellow, perchance a gambler and sharper, by means of a fine coat, a lily hand, and graceful bows, is able to take rank of an industrious, worthy young farmer, or mechanic, who gets an honest living by the sweat of his face,—it will be vain to denounce idleness, or recommend industry. Under such circumstances, young men, whose ambition is more than a match for their moral principle, very naturally turn idlers, or set out to live by their wits, well knowing that if they can only keep up a gentlemanly appearance, by almost whatever means, they will be much better received, and rank much higher than if they were plain, industrious, laboring men.

Lo, a ball! a splendid ball,—And who enters now? Who is he, that all the gentlemen greet so heartily, and all the ladies notice so readily? It is Mr. *Flash*, an itinerant, who, without funds, without industry, without any visible means, always dresses in high taste, and has at his fingers' ends every punctilio of fashionable manners—He is quite the *gentleman*, every inch of him.

NUMBER XXVII.

OF PRODUCTIVE LABOR, OTHER THAN THAT OF THE HANDS.

" KNOWLEDGE is power." This was a favorite maxim of Bacon, so eminent in the ranks of philosophy.

The weakness of man is marvellously strengthened by his knowledge. It is by his superior knowledge, that he gains dominion over the various races of animals, of which many are much stronger, and swifter than he; over the stubborn earth, and over the powerful elements, Fire, Air, and Water. Naked came he into the world, and naked must he ever have remained, had not the inspiration of the Almighty given him understanding, and furnished him with motives to employ this noble faculty in an infinite variety of useful ways.

Man is feeble of body; his main strength lies in his mind. Apart from his superior intellectual faculties, he would be one of the most helpless, forlorn, and wretched animals, upon the face of the earth.

The invaluable worth of knowledge, and of education by

which it is acquired, has been ever, in all civilized countries, the standing theme of profound discussion, or, more often, of splendid but empty declamation; so that only scanty gleanings are left to the modern pen. There is, however, one respect in which the subject has been neither exhausted, nor frequently touched; it is the intimate connection between knowledge and *Productive Labor.*

Productive Labor, so essential to the sustenance and support of the general community of man, is twofold—*direct*, and *indirect.*

Direct productive labor consists of that bodily exercise, that "sweat of the face," by means of which we are furnished with food and raiment, and with all the various necessaries and elegancies of life.

By this it is that life is sustained and decorated, and it is in this way that the great bulk of mankind is necessarily employed. Those who labor with their hands in husbandry, and in the various useful arts, are, as it were, the strong pillars that support the living world. But then they are, in no wise, entitled to arrogate the honor to themselves exclusively :—" The hand cannot say to the eye, I have no need of thee."

Indirectly, there are in the common vineyard productive and efficient laborers, other than those who work with the hands. They are the ones who invent, conceive, plan, guard and regulate. So that, after all, *mind* is an essential and a most eminent operator throughout the whole process.

I will barely suggest a few particulars; leaving it to the reader to enlarge upon them, and to combine them with others which are alike obvious.

Very little would it signify, though we had hands to labor, if we knew not how to use them; nor should we know how to use them skilfully, but for the inventions of those who have gone before us. Without the aid of the arts our hands must be idle, or work to no purpose. In all the multitudinous occupations that are now going on, whether upon land or water, whether for the sustenance or the adornment of life, there is a never-ceasing dependence upon the arts. And how were the arts explored, and how brought to the state of wonderful perfection, in which they now are? By intense labor of the *Mind*. From one generation to another, very many who labored not at all with their hands, have labored abundantly, and most efficiently and usefully, with their intellects. Their inventions and improvements have directed and guided manual labor, and have facilitated and abridged it in a marvellous manner and degree. And assuredly, theirs is to be regarded as belonging to the highest class of productive labor; assuredly, he that contributes to the general stock of knowledge in the arts, is a benefactor of the public, and is entitled to the gratitude of all; assuredly the laboring man is bound to encourage the arts, which so mightily aid the work of his hands. Nor ought he to think lightly of mere science; it is the mother of the arts, and in sundry instances it has, undesignedly and unconsciously, led to the discovery of them. The star-gazers of ancient Chaldea never once dreamed of the vastly important practical purposes, to which the world, in succeeding ages, would apply the knowledge of astronomy.

Again, it is to be considered and distinctly remembered, that the laboring classes spend their strength for nought, unless the fruits of their industry be securely guarded from plunder and robbery, and against the hand of rapaciousness, in whatever manner, or under whatever guise it may assail them. Hence, of necessity, there must be government, laws, and courts of justice; and of necessity, also, there must be lawgivers, executive and judicial officers, advocates, &c. Now, all these must be paid out of the common stock. But provided they discharge their duties ably and faithfully, and are content with reasonable recompense, no laborer is more worthy of his hire. By no means are they to be regarded as drones in the hive. As they are the necessary guardians over the general treasure which manual labor accumulates, so they have a right to a share of it;—at the same time, on the part of the general community, special care must be taken lest the guardians of its rights and its property, like the ravenous sons of old Eli, should make such free use of the *flesh-hook*, as to leave little else to the commonalty but the broth.

Moreover, since laws can afford us no effectual protection, unless the morals of the community be preserved from general corruption, it clearly follows that the professional men, who faithfully devote their time and attention to the interests of pure morality, are really, though indirectly, productive laborers, in even the secular sense of the term. I will particularly instance the venerable Ministers of our holy religion, who—laying out of the question all considerations of the future life—do, I presume to affirm, greatly increase the amount of productive labor, by the weight of their exhortations and influence against idleness and profligacy, at the same time that they no less contribute to the security of the fruits of labor, by the generally moralizing effects of their ministrations. So, also, the well-qualified and faithful instructors of our children and youth are to be regarded in nearly the same point of view—as among the most productive and useful of laborers.

Neither is it true that no labor is hard, except that of the hands. So far otherwise, many an excellent man, by intense labor of mind in his profession, has worn himself out much sooner than he would have done, had he employed an equal measure of industry in the labors of the field.

NUMBER XXVIII.

A SORROW-SOOTHING SCOTTISH LEGEND.

Old age is justly considered as situated on the confines of the grave; and, of course, the ravages that death makes in that uttermost province of human life, excite no surprise. It is an adage nearly as ancient, perhaps, as time, that the old must die. Indeed, the aged may be said to die while they live. By little and little, they are losing, almost every day, somewhat of the very stamina of life; and, even if no mortal disease supervenes, their earthly tabernacles must, ere long, be dissolved of mere decay. This natural process of dissolution is often so gradual as to be little perceived, and least of all by the subjects of it; but the process is constantly advancing, whether perceived or not. So far, therefore, from its being a marvel that the aged die at last, the marvel is that they live so long, considering the extreme brittleness of the thread of life, and the many hairbreadth escapes from death, which they must have had during such a great length of time.

On the contrary, *premature* deaths occasion not merely the bitterness of transient sorrow, but that rooted anguish which rises from disappointed hopes. And it is particularly so with regard to children, cut off in the flower of youth, or in the bud of infancy. Parental affection "hopeth all things;" and when the object of its fond hope is snatched away, it faints under the stroke, and is ready to say repiningly,—"It were better not to have had the gift at all." But when this object is an *only* child, the cup of anguish is not merely full, but it overflows. Bereavement of this last description is frequently noticed, in the Holy Scriptures, as most deeply affecting; and, accordingly, pious writers, in all ages and countries, have been assiduously anxious to pour the balm of consolation into hearts, thus torn with anguish.

With such benevolent views, no doubt, was fabricated the ancient legend, or fable, with which I shall conclude these reflections. It originated in the Scottish highlands, whose inhabitants have, in great part, borne a resemblance to the people of the patriarchal ages; having, from time immemorial, led a pastoral life, and been remarkable for frugal plainness of living, for sobriety, and for zealous attachment to the holy religion they profess. And a singular circumstance, which to *them* has given peculiar efficacy to the legend hereafter related, is, that they have been, and are, generally speaking, so tinctured with superstition, as firmly to believe in the frequency of supernatural visions and apparitions. I will only remark further, for explanation, that every highland householder, agreeably to an ancient custom, makes a festival for his friends and neighbors, on the death of any one of his family; which funeral is called, *The late Wake.*

A married couple of the Scottish highlands, had lost thrice their only child, each dying at an early age. Upon the death of the last, the grief of the father became boisterous, and he uttered his plaints in the loudest terms.

" The death of the child happened late in the spring, when, in the more inhabited straths, sheep were abroad; but, from the blasts in that high and stormy region, they were still confined in the cot. In a dismal, snowy evening, the man, unable to stifle his anguish, went out, lamenting aloud, for a lamb to treat his friends with, at the late wake. At the door of the cot, however, he found a stranger, standing before the entrance. He was astonished, in such a night, to meet a person so far from any frequented place. The stranger was plainly attired; but had a countenance expressive of singular mildness and benevolence, and addressing him in a sweet, impressive voice, asked him, what he did there, amidst the tempest. He was filled with awe, which he could not account for, and said, he came for a lamb.—'What kind of lamb do you mean to take?' said the stranger. 'The very best I can find,' he replied, 'as it is to entertain my friends; and I hope you will share of it.' 'Do your sheep make any resistance when you take away the lambs, or any disturbance afterwards?' 'Never,' was the answer. 'How differently am I treated,' said the traveller. 'When I come to visit my sheepfold, I take, as I am well entitled to do, the best lamb to myself; and my ears are filled with the clamor of discontent by these ungrateful sheep, whom I have fed, watched, and protected.' He looked up in amaze; but the vision was fled."

If it be proper to add any thing at all here, I can think of nothing better than the Epitaph of Mr. Wesley's, upon an infant child :—

> "When the Archangel's trump shall blow,
> And souls to bodies join,
> What crowds shall wish their lives below,
> Had been as short as thine!"

NUMBER XXIX.

OF MATERNAL TENDERNESS—OR THE SORROWS OF THE DAUGHTER OF AIAH.

Amongst the short but admirable sketches of nature, which the historical part of the Sacred Volume furnishes, there is one that has been very little noticed; though had it been found in any other book of so early date, it would have been quoted, again and again, with peals of applause. It is recorded in the 21st chapter of the 2d book of Samuel, and consists of a simple, unvarnished tale of maternal tenderness, taken from real life.

In the beginning of barley-harvest, seven sons of Saul were hanged up, all together, and it was ordered that their dead bodies should remain upon the gallows or tree, exposed to the birds and beasts of prey. Two of those young men were the sons of Rizpah, Saul's concubine, whose conduct on that distressing occasion is described as follows:—"Rizpah, the daughter of Aiah, took sackcloth, and spread it for her upon the rock, from the beginning of harvest until water dropped upon them out of heaven, and suffered neither the birds of the air to rest on them by day, nor the beasts of the field by night."

The sacred historian records this story as worthy of notice and remembrance, and, according to the usual manner of the penmen of the Holy Bible, he merely records it; adding not a word of comment, or a single reflection of his own. Indeed, it is, of itself, a picture which needs no coloring, and which no art could improve.

What was the moral or religious character of Rizpah, we are not told. Her being called Saul's concubine is no evidence that she was an abandoned character; for concubine, probably, means here nothing more or worse than a wife of the secondary or subordinate rank, agreeably to the custom tolerated, though not sanctioned, under the Mosaical dispensation. Nor do we know if the two unhappy sons had treated their mother, at all, with filial kindness. Considering that they were branches of Saul's ungracious house, the greater likelihood is that the mother had suffered many a pang from the churlishness of their behavior. And be it even so, she but acted the genuine character of *Mother*, when she forgot the undutifulness of her sons in the yearnings of her compassion.

If we except the few, in whose hearts natural affection has given place to the ambition of making a figure in the eyes of the public,—maternal tenderness is of universal extent, unless in those benighted regions where it has been blighted by a horrible superstition. This species of affection is one of the primary qualities of human nature, and no talents nor accomplishments can supply its place. It is one of the main pillars of our race, which, without it, would quickly tumble to ruin.

The child that has the mother with it, though born in the

most abject condition of life, has one friend at least;—a friend, who loves it as naturally as she loves herself, and guards and fosters it from the same powerful feelings of nature, from which she guards and fosters her own life. And what though, as to the greater part of mothers, the maternal tenderness partakes more of animal instinct than of any rational exercise of the mind? What though it is apt to run into a blind, excessive, and pernicious indulgence? What though their misguided fondness for their infant progeny is aptly represented in the fable of the ape, that stifled her youngling with the violence of her embrace?—All this only shows that the gifts of nature are pervertible, and that ill may be educed from good. The affection itself, peculiar to the maternal bosom, is implanted by the hand of God: it is a precious part of female nature, and of immeasurable importance in its consequences.

As a celebrated writer remarks, "The authority of a father, so useful to our well-being, and so justly venerable on all accounts, hinders us from having that entire love for him that we have for our mothers, where the parental authority is melted down into the mother's fondness and indulgence."

Experience fully testifies to the truth of the above remark, and, at the same time, evinces the wisdom of the divine economy in this important particular. Filial affection, which is one of the most useful affections of our general nature, obtains its root and earliest growth from maternal tenderness. The fond and doting mother has our first love, which by degrees extends itself to the other parent. Whereas, but for the indulgent softness of female nature, which so irresistibly attracts the affections of our infancy and early childhood, there would be much less of pure, unsophisticated filial love than there now is in the world.

Alas for the conduct of those children, who neglect their mother when she is old! It manifests an unfeelingness of heart, and a brutality of disposition, exceeding the ordinary bounds of human depravity.

While I am upon the subject of maternal tenderness, I will notice one of the bitterest of the bitter drops in the cup of early widowhood; it is the loss of the only human being, who can so naturally participate in her yearnings to her infant offspring. This is exquisitely expressed in one of the poems of Mrs. Opie, a young widowed mother.

> "When to my heart my child I fold,
> She only deepens every sigh:
> I think, while I her charms behold,
> How she'd have pleas'd her father's eye.
> And while I from her lisping tongue,
> Soft childhood's artless accents hear,
> I think, with vain remembrance wrung,
> How she'd have charm'd her father's ear."

NUMBER XXX.

OF PRUDENCE IN THE ORDINARY CONCERNS OF LIFE.

"I, Wisdom, dwell with Prudence."

AND what is this close intimate of wisdom ?—Not that niggardly, craving propensity, which occasions one to toil and moil like an emmet, without cessation, and without enjoyment—not that sordid disposition, which, appropriating every thing to *self*, withholds bread from the hungry—not the worldly spirit, that makes all its calculations with the sole view to present loss and gain—not the jealous temper that keeps, by day and night, a catlike watch, and dares trust nobody—not the slyness that habitually prefers stratagem to openness of conduct—not the cowardice that shrinks from the responsibility, or the danger, to which duty calls.—Though by a *moral* abuse of words, these, severally, have been dignified with the name of Prudence, they are very unlike that genuine prudence, with which wisdom deigns to dwell.

Prudence of the right stamp, is the *practical* exposition both of a correct judgment and a correct heart. It regards the future as well as the present ; immortality as well as time ; and each according to their respective importance. It seeks the attainment of worthy objects by worthy and suitable means. It keeps the end in view, and the means it properly adapts to the end. It shuns the evil that is avoidable, and what is unavoidable it meets with resignation and firmness.

An ounce of genuine prudence is worth a pound of unbridled genius. What signifies fine sense, exalted sense, even the best *theoretical* sense in the world, if it produces worse than nonsense in *practice?* What signifies it that one has great parts and great learning united, if, notwithstanding, he acts the part of a fool?

> "How empty learning, and how vain is art,
> Save where it guides the life, or mends the heart."

Look at Bibulus, the most exalted, yet the most self-degraded of men! Seemingly, he never *thinks* foolishly, nor ever *acts* wisely. Endowed with uncommon talents, and possessing the advantages of superior learning, his whole life, nevertheless, is a series of inconsistencies, errors and follies; and all from the want of prudence, without which no man is truly great, nor can be useful to others, or even to himself.

Prudence consists of soundness of judgment, together with firmness of resolution to follow the dictates of judgment. For want of such firm resolution many act absurdly, though they speculate wisely; being drawn astray, contrary to their better knowledge, by indolence, by timidity, by ungoverned passion, or by their propensities to particular ruinous vices.

Prudence, as particularly respects the concerns of this life, is a gift of Nature, distributed like intellect, in different degrees among mankind. Some discover the rudiments of it even from childhood. Others are naturally rash, headstrong, and disposed to follow the impulse of the moment, without either foresight or reflection, till taught to their cost, and, sometimes, happily cured in the school of experience. While others again, notwithstanding excellent advantages for learning discretion, continue, as to this particular, radically defective to the end of their lives. They have quickness of apprehension, readiness of wit, volubility of tongue, and, besides, Dame Experience has severely disciplined them in her school. But, all this notwithstanding, they still have the weakness of infancy in this particular; in middle age, and even to old age, their minds are yet in the cradle.

But though the prudence, of which I am now speaking, is a natural gift, it is an improvable gift. Where there are any rudiments of it at all in the young mind, it may, by proper means, be strengthened and increased; and it is one of the essential parts of education to lead the pupil into the habit of forethought and reflection, and to cultivate in him a sturdy growth of well-directed *Resoluteness*; which, in fact, is a main pillar of the human heart. As many persons are imprudent for want of education, so, unquestionably, the ruinous imprudences of many others are owing to a perverted or an unsound education; an education that leads them to contemn the condition allotted to them by Providence, and to restless aspirations after one that is unattainable.

Some certain circumstances have been the means of imbuing a whole population with remarkable prudence, continuing for ages. In Holcroft's Travels in Holland it is remarked: "The Dutchman living in continual danger of inundation, and of losing not only the fruits of his industry, but his life, becomes habitually prudent. His foresight is admirable, his perseverance not to be conquered, and his labors, unless seen, not to be believed." The Scotch, also, have, time out of mind, been, as it were, inoculated with prudence, as it relates to the various branches of economy; and it is clearly accounted for from the peculiar circumstances of their history. In some other countries (unfortunately, in our own, for one instance), a concurrence of several extraordinary circumstances has occasioned very many thousands to be imprudent, rash, and desperately adventurous. And as on the large scale, so on the small, a sound education, correct habits, and a just way of thinking, in early life, generally lead to prudence of conduct in its following stages; and so contrariwise.

One of the many important branches of prudence, is carefully to avoid incurring enmities, as far as it can be done consistently with uprightness of character, and a good conscience. For seldom does one *unnecessarily* make an enemy of his fellow-creature that he does not find cause to regret it afterwards; and as seldom has one had reason to be sorry that he has used the *soft answer which turneth away wrath.* But instead of arguing this point, I will merely adduce a very curious and very instructive specimen from the Memoirs of Franklin.

"In 1736," observe the Reviewers, in the *Analectic Magazine*, "Franklin was chosen clerk of the General Assembly of Pennsylvania; his first promotion, as he calls it in his narrative. The choice was annual, and the year following, a new member made a long speech in opposition to his re-election. We copy what he relates on this occasion, because it is every way characteristic."

" 'As the place was highly desirable for me on many accounts, I did not like the opposition of this new member, who was a gentleman of fortune and education, with talents that were likely to give him in time great influence in the House, which indeed afterwards happened. I did not, however, aim at gaining his favor by paying any servile respect to him, but after some time took this other method. Having heard that he had in his library a certain very scarce and curious book, I wrote a note to him, expressing my desire of perusing that book, and requesting that he would do me the favor of lending it to me for a few days. He sent it immediately; and I returned it in about a week with another note, expressing strongly my sense of the favor. When we next met in the House, he spoke to me (which he had never done before), and with great civility; and he ever after manifested a readiness to serve me on all occasions, so that we became great friends, and our friendship continued to his death. This is another instance of the truth of an old maxim that I had learned, which says, "he that has once done you a kindness, will be more ready to do you another, than he whom you yourself have obliged." And it shows how much more profitable it is prudently to remove, than to resent, return and continue inimical proceedings.' "

NUMBER XXXI.

OF THE VAST IMPORTANCE OF MANNER IN GIVING COUNSEL AND REPROOF.

To exasperate is not the way to convince; nor does asperity of language or of manner necessarily belong to the duty of plain dealing. So far otherwise, a scolding preacher, or a snarling reprover, betrays alike a gross ignorance of the philosophy of the human mind, and the absence of Christian meekness; and however zealous be his aim to do good, the provokingness of his manner will defeat the benevolence of his intentions.

The following remarks are from the pen of a man, as distinguished for Christian piety, as for superior genius—the immortal Cowper. "No man" (says that evangelical poet) "was ever scolded out of his sins. The heart, corrupt as it is, and because it is so, grows angry if it be not treated with some management and good manners, and scolds again. A surly mastiff will bear perhaps to be stroked, though he will growl under that operation, but if you touch him roughly he will bite. There is no grace that the spirit of self can counterfeit with more success than that of zeal. A man thinks he is fighting for Christ, when he is fighting for his own notions. He thinks that he is skilfully searching the hearts of others, when he is only gratifying the malignity of his own, and charitably supposes his hearers destitute of all grace, that he may shine the more in his own eyes by comparison."

Nor is either scolding or ridicule the proper way to cure men of their religious prejudices: for by inflaming their anger, it renders their prejudices the more stubborn and inveterate. It is no matter how absurd, or even how monstrous their errors and prejudices may be; if you offend them by the grossness of your manner, there is little hope of your convincing them afterward by the cogency of your reasoning.

The Baptist missionaries in India, at the first insulted, as we are told, the superstition which they attacked; and ridiculed and reviled the Bramins, in the streets and at their festivals, when the passions of the blinded and besotted populace were most likely to be inflamed. But experience taught those pious and apostolical men, that this was not the right way to make converts: for which reason, in 1805, they made a declaration of the great principles upon which they thought it their duty to act. "It is necessary," say they, "in our intercourse with the Hindoos, that, as far as we are able, we abstain from those things which would increase their prejudices against the gospel. Those parts of English manners, which are most offensive to them, should be kept out of sight; nor is it advisable at once to attack their prejudices, by exhibiting with acrimony the sins of their gods; neither should we do violence to their images, nor interrupt their worship."

Now if this forbearance from every thing provoking, whether in language or in manner, was expedient in dealing with the errors of the grossly idolatrous pagans, it is, assuredly, not less expedient for fellow-christians, in their treatment of the real or supposed religious errors of one another. Bitter revilings and contumelious denouncements always provoke, but never convince. If they are used instead of argument, they betray a conscious weakness, for it is much easier to revile and denounce than to argue. And furthermore, we are quite as apt to be furiously in the wrong as to be furiously in the right; or, if even we know ourselves to be right as to matter, we put ourselves in the wrong as to manner, if we make use of foul weapons rather than of those which the armory of reason supplies.

Manner is to be carefully studied by every one, whether in a public or a private station, who undertakes to reclaim the vicious or convince the erring; for what would be beneficial if done in one manner, would be worse than labor lost if done in another. A haughty, supercilious manner never wins, seldom convinces, and always disgusts; whereas that which indicates meekness, and unmingled benevolence and compassion, rarely fails of some salutary impression; especially, if suavity of manner be accompanied with force of reasoning, and a due regard be had to time, place, and circumstances.

No very long while ago, Mr. ——, an American clergyman, as distinguished for pious zeal as for eminent parts, was passing a river in a ferry-boat, along with company of some distinction, among which was a military officer, who repeatedly made use of profane language. Mr. —— continued silent till they had landed, when asking him aside, he expostulated with him in such a moving manner, that the officer expressed his thanks, and his deep sorrow for the offence; but added withal, "*Sir, if you had reproved me before the company, I should have drawn my sword upon you.*"

There are some who glory in it, that by their plain-dealing they wound the pride of those they deal with. Peradventure with greater pride they do it. Often we are so little aware of the obliquities of our own hearts, that we may be feeding and nourishing pride within ourselves, whilst we are zealously aiming our blows at the pride of others. Our love of chiding, our coarse bluntness, which we fondly term an honest plain-heartedness, or a warmth of zeal, may, possibly, spring from other motives than those of pure Christian benevolence.

In the governance of children, very much indeed depends on *Manner*. If you *provoke your children to anger*, little will they regard, at the time, the wholesome counsel that is mingled with the provocation you give them. Reproof is ever a bitter pill to the receiver, and when administered, even to *children*, it must be done with visible marks of tender affection to sweeten it; else it will be more likely to do harm than good.

NUMBER XXXII.

OF TRUTH-SPEAKING AS DENOTING COURAGE.

"Dare to be true; nothing can need a lie;
The fault that needs it most, grows two thereby."

It requires no inconsiderable degree of courage always to speak the truth. And hence, in the fourteenth and fifteenth centuries, commonly termed the age of chivalry, the two points of honor in the male sex, were Valor and Veracity; particularly a steadfast adherence to plighted faith, or one's word and promise; lying or falsehood being considered as indicative of cowardice, and abhorred rather for its meanness than for its moral turpitude. Accordingly, the chivalrous knights, whilst little regarding any part else of the second table of the holy decalogue, and least of all the *sixth*, *seventh*, and *tenth* commandments, would, nevertheless, suffer any pains and penalties in preference to the imputation of word-breaking, lying, or prevarication. In the old Romance, *Amadis de Gaul*, King Lisuarte being reduced to the dire alternative of breaking his word, or delivering up his daughter into the hands of an utter stranger, he is represented as exclaiming,

"My daughter must fare as God has appointed; but my word shall never be wilfully broken."

The age of chivalry has long since past; but some of its relics have floated down the stream of time, and are visible even at the present instant. In some of the high circles of fashion, as well among descendants of Europeans in other countries as in Europe itself, Valor and Veracity are considered not merely as indispensable requisites of a gentleman, but as almost the only points of honor that are necessary to his character. A man may be a blasphemer of God and religion, a notorious profligate, an inmate of the brothel, a seducer of female virtue; he may be all this, and yet be received into what fashion calls *good company*, with as cordial welcome as if his character were pure as the driven snow. But if he lie under the imputation of either direct cowardice or of the indirect cowardice of uttering a wilful falsehood, he is despised, banished, and proscribed, as unfit for the company of ladies and gentlemen. For which reason, a man of this sort of high fashion, when charged directly or by implication, with being a coward or a liar, finds his chivalrous spirit roused, and lifted to the highest pitch. Call him a foe to God, a debauchee, a violator of the connubial ties,—and he is able to laugh it off; for it does in nowise touch his honor: but call him a coward, or a liar, and he thinks nothing but your blood can wash away the stain.

Apart, however, from the notions of chivalry, the vice of lying ranks among the meanest of vices. It is the vice of slaves. It is the vice that chiefly abounds among nations in political slavery and with that low and wretched class of our fellow-beings who are in personal bondage. Slavish fear prompts them to prevaricate and lie, as it were in self-defence. Nor is it the less mean for its becoming an attribute of freemen. Its meanness, as well as its guilt, is increased by this circumstance; since in the last case there is far less urgency of temptation, and a far clearer knowledge of duty. Assuredly, with people possessing freedom and enjoying the light of Christianity, a strict regard to truth should be considered as a cardinal point in character, and every species of wilful falsehood should be held in utmost disgrace; not merely in disgrace for its meanness, but in abhorrence for its moral turpitude.

Though, as I observed before, it requires courage to speak the truth at all times, and under all circumstances, yet this sort of courage is of no difficult attainment in the school of Christian morals. And as to the rest, speaking the truth is one of the easiest things in the world; for it is merely the expresssion of one's own perceptions, or of what lies clearly in his own memory. The veriest child, that has attained the use of the organs of speech, is capable of this. Whereas, to speak falsehood requires effort and art. Falsehood is *fiction*, and needs invention and contrivance so to frame and fashion it as to make it bear the semblance of truth. As he that dances upon the rope, is not a moment at his ease, but must constantly employ effort to keep his balance, even so it fares with a liar. His mind is ever on the alert to escape detection. And after all, the very expedients he uses for this end, often produce the consequences which he wishes to avoid. He proceeds, with cunning art, to cover one lie with another, till at last, the covering being too thin or too narrow, the whole series is clearly seen through.

I will only remark further, that lying, even in its simplest and must inoffensive forms, is by no means free of all mischief. Confidence is the cement, or rather the main pillar of society. Without it friendship is but a name, and social intercourse a sort of war in disguise. And as falseness of speech, in any shape or degree whatever, has a tendency to destroy or weaken social confidence, so it tends, of course, to unhinge society. From this, as well as from the more solemn and more awful view of the subject, it clearly follows that nothing is of greater necessity in the moral education of children, than to teach them betimes to pay a strict regard to truth

NUMBER XXXIII

OF VULGARITY.

There are but few words in our language, that have a more grating sound in the ears of those who lay claim to good breeding, than the word vulgarity, insomuch that many a one had rather be thought vicious than vulgar. And what is vulgarity? This is rather a puzzling question, for the word is nowhere clearly defined, nor is it capable of being exactly marked out by a definition. Profaneness, filthiness of speech, and a clownish awkwardness of manners, are only the grosser parts of vulgarity, which extends itself to almost innumerable particulars of human conduct, and not unfrequently into the fashionable ranks of society. But though it is in a manner undefinable, it admits of being explained, as it were, by piecemeal; and this may be the better done by contrasting it with a quality, which every body of any decency of mind and character, professes to hold in respect.

Vulgarity, then, is the direct opposite of courteousness. But here, again, arises a question — *What is courteousness?* Your dictionary will tell you, it implies something elegant—something beyond the reach of plain men and women of the common sort. But so it is not. When St. Paul, addressing himself to Christians of all worldly grades and classes, even down to menials or slaves;—when addressing himself to the lowest as well as to the highest, he bade them "*be courteous*," assuredly he did not mean that they must needs all be of elegant manners. No: it is full likely that Paul himself did not excel greatly in that particular: it was not, surely, the *elegance* of his manner, that made Felix tremble. Courteousness must mean, therefore, a something which is within the reach of all sorts of people; and in its primary and best sense, it may be understood to mean exactly such a behavior as spontaneously springs from a heart, warm with benevolence: —whilst, on the contrary, vulgarity, as respects people of some rank in life, is the growth of cold selfishness always, and often of selfishness and narrowness of intellect combined. Vulgarity, in some shape or other, betrays itself as clearly at the very top as at the very bottom of the scale of life.

Cardinal de Retz remarks of Cardinal Richelieu, a most puissant prime minister of France, "that he loved to rally others but could not bear to be rallied himself." So, also, it is said of the Great Frederick of Prussia, that his manner was to harrow up the feelings of his courtiers and attendants, by breaking his cutting jokes upon them without measure or mercy; well knowing that they durst not offer any retort. These two instances clearly show that vulgarity may be found in the palace as well as in the cottage. The like may be frequently seen among the *little* great; many of whom take a delight in wounding the feelings of those below them, merely because they *are* below them;- -a detestable fault, which *sudden* wealth, or *sudden* consequence of any kind, is peculiarly apt to draw after it. I say a *detestable* fault, because scarcely any thing betrays a more reprobate heart, than an unfeeling, brutal conduct toward inferiors; as it usually springs from the odious compound of arrogance, vanity, and cowardice.

We have no more right, wantonly or causelessly, to wound the mind than to wound the body of a fellow-being; and in many instances the former is the more cruel of the two.

Some persons, even in the blessed deed of giving alms to the needy, poison the gift by an ungracious manner of bestowment, accompanying it with a sour look, or, peradventure, with a bitter taunt. One of the wisest of the ancients noticed this species of vulgarity, and reproved it with the sound words following: "My son, blemish not thy good deeds, neither use uncomfortable words when thou givest any thing."

There are some again, both men and women, who value themselves highly upon a coarse bluntness, which they themselves call downright honesty and plain-heartedness. "We can't flatter, not *we*—*we* must speak truth—if they will take it—so—if not—*we're* plain."

But hark! not so fast. Pause a moment, and examine your own hearts, and, perchance, you may find that your manner partakes more of pride or sourness, than of benevolence. If you wish to amend the faulty, assuredly this is not the way. Again, have you no faults at all of your own? Hardly will you pretend to absolute immunity in that respect. Well, then, ask your own hearts if you are willing to receive the same measure, which you mete out to others. If you can bear, in all cases, to be told roundly of your own faults, even the minutest of them, then, and not otherwise, you may seem fairly entitled to the privilege of giving it off so roundly to others. Then, and not otherwise, may you be at liberty, to deal out your bitter pills, without any regard at all to gilding or sweetening them.

In short (for many things must I leave unsaid), any body, that knows the world, might easily show that the family of the *Vulgars* has branched out into a great many divisions and subdivisions; one or other of which embraces not a few, who would be very loath to own themselves members of that unhonored household.

NUMBER XXXIV.

OF THE VERY GREAT INFLUENCE OF USE OR CUSTOM, AS RESPECTS CHILDREN, UPON THEIR DISPOSITIONS AND CHARACTERS IN AFTER-LIFE.

> "Just as the twig is bent the tree's inclin'd."
>
> POPE.

IT can hardly be imagined how much we are under the power of custom: it binds and fixes our inclination in almost any direction. That which we are accustomed to, almost whatever it may be, acquires our attachment, and we are uneasy without it. If our customary food have been plain, simple, or never so coarse, it is sweet to our relish; on the other hand, if we have been accustomed altogether to dainties, we shall feel a kind of loathing for the ordinary provisions of the human kind. The *Black Broth* of the Spartans (they being always used to it) was to them delicious, though loathsome to every body else.

I once dined at an inn, in company with a lady who had "fared sumptuously every day." It was a plain dinner, and substantially good, but not such as she had been accustomed to, and the very sight of it threw her into tragical distress.

She was not hectical, nor in any manner sickly. Her form was the index of nothing less than of habits of abstemiousness. But, alas! her stomach turned against every thing. She barely tasted of this, of that, and of the other morsel, and laying down her knife and fork, her visage could scarcely have been more rueful, had she been under the hands of the executioner.

Man is said to be "a bundle of habits." And what is habit? Habit is the aptitude we acquire for what we are accustomed to, whether it relates to the body, or the mind, or both. As by frequency of repetition, we come to be more ready and expert in whatever we have to do; so, also, by frequency of repetition, the appetite, the taste, the inclination, acquire a settled direction that way. Nay, if the thing we are accustomed to gives us little or no pleasure, its absence gives us pain.

"I remember," says the far-famed Burke, "to have frequented a certain place every day, for a long time together; and I may truly say, that so far from finding pleasure in it, I was affected with a sort of weariness and disgust; I came, I went, I returned, without pleasure; yet if by any means I passed by my usual time of going thither, I was remarkably uneasy, and was not quiet till I got into my old track."—And he proceeds to say, "They who use snuff, take it almost without being sensible that they take it, and the acute sense of smell is deadened so as to feel hardly any thing from so sharp a stimulus; yet, deprive the snuff-taker of his box, and he is the most uneasy mortal in the world."

It might indeed be shown, in a great variety of instances, some of an indifferent, and others of a moral nature, that being accustomed to a thing induces, for the most part, such a settled habit as is aptly denominated a second nature. But my object is to apply the general principle to the all-important concern of education.

Training up a child in the way he should go, consists not altogether in pointing out the way, but also, and chiefly, in accustoming him to walk therein. As the tree grows up straight or crooked, according to the direction given it when a plant, so, in a great measure, it is with animal nature. Of this truth we are deeply sensible in its application to the inferior animals, and our practice accords with our way of thinking. In training up young animals for use—a colt, for instance, or one of the canine breed—much care is taken to break them betimes of their faults, and to render them docile, and such as we wish them to be at mature age. Because experience teaches us, that if their faults are permitted to grow up with them, they will become inveterately fixed, and exceeding hard to cure. We know that if the one be suffered to kick, and the other to snarl and bite, at every body that comes near them, or if any other vicious trick be permitted to "grow with their growth," it would be unreasonable to expect to fashion them aright in after-time, when age shall have matured and confirmed their ill habits, and redoubled their obstinacy. Rightly judging on this point, we are *practical*, because, forsooth, it would be a pity the young animal should be spoiled for want of attention to his training.

How much less care, in this respect, is ordinarily paid to the training of the human offspring! Not that we are sparing of pains and expense for the purpose of imbuing the young mind with the rudiments of learning. But having done this, we unscrupulously leave undone a still more important part, namely, the care to settle those habits, without which the possession of learning can turn to no good account.

It is foolish to expect that children, accustomed to do evil, will in after-life learn to do well; no less foolish than to look for the growth of a fragrant flower in the spot, where you had dropped only the seed of a thistle. For the generality of human beings are, throughout life, such, or nearly such, as early custom has fashioned them; no animal being more wilful, more obstinate in the wrong, or harder to be cured of the ill habits which early custom has riveted.

Consider it, ye who are parents of young children. If it be your choice that they should be idle men and women, rear them up in idleness. If you would render them helpless all their days, never compel nor permit them to help themselves. If you wish them to be fastidious and squeamish about their food, feed them daily with dainties. If you would have them gourmands, cram their little bodies well, from morn till eve. If you would entail upon their mature age various ill humor,—as sullenness and obstinacy, discontent and peevishness,—indulge and foster betimes these wayward propensities. If you admire a quarrelsome, a violent, a revengeful spirit, permit their little hands to strike, and their little tongues to lisp out rage. Again, if you would train them up for cheats and liars, laugh at their cunning tricks, their artful falsehoods and equivocations; or, if you rebuke them, let them see withal that you are more pleased with their wit, than displeased at the inceptive marks of their depravity.

But if your desires and wishes be quite the reverse of all this; why then, take care against teaching your children, what it will be necessary for them to unlearn at a riper age. Take care to make such impressions on their tender infancy, as you would wish should be permanent and lasting. Never let it be out of your memories, that "habits woven into the very principles of their nature are unspeakably better than mere rules and lessons, which they so easily forget."

NUMBER XXXV.

ON THE ADVANTAGES OF THE LONG-PROTRACTED WEAKNESS AND DEPENDENCE OF CHILDHOOD.

There are none of the inferior animals that come into the world so helpless, and continue helpless for so great a length of time, as the human progeny. The young of the lower part of the animal creation are endowed with strength and activity, and, in many instances, with a sagacity that astonishes the beholder, and sets his philosophy at defiance. Very shortly they quit the dam, and become their own providers. But the infant is puling in the mother's arms for many months, and dependent on parental care for as many years.

Is this remarkable circumstance in the economy of our nature meant to be a burden, or a blessing? A blessing doubtless. Because in the helpless condition of the infant, which continues so long dependent on others, is laid the groundwork of the social ties. We learn first to show kindness at home. It is there that the social principles of our nature, ordinarily, are first put in exercise, and drawn forth into practice.

The keystone of the fabric of society is laid in marriage, and the strong pillars of the superstructure are established in infancy. The helpless progeny—for a long while helpless—incessantly occupy the kind attentions of the parents, who are the more attached to their offspring from the very circumstance of their utter weakness and dependence. The mother in particular, how cheerfully she foregoes her accustomed amusements and pastimes, and how constantly she confines herself to the charge of her infantile brood! With what unspeakable tenderness does she nourish and cherish them, and watch over them day and night! With what heartfelt joy does she perceive in them the dawning of reason and listen to their lisping prattle. And if too discreet to blaze abroad their little feats of activity, their pertinent questions, and their witty remarks—so much beyond the ordinary condition of their age—yet all these she treasures up in her heart:—and in that fond heart are continually blooming new prospects, new hopes, and new joys.

The affection of parents for their offspring is a species of affection that belongs to our universal nature. Whether in the civilized or in the savage state, in every clime, and among all the tribes of man, parents love their children. This primary human affection was exercised as soon as men began to multiply upon the earth. Ever since that period it has been a ruling passion, every where, and under all the different modifications of society; and though, strictly speaking, it is not of itself a moral virtue, yet to be without it, is to be a monster.

On the other hand, the long term of the infantile, dependent condition of children, is what chiefly generates filial affection, accompanied with respect, reverence, and obedient dispositions.

What if the human offspring, like the young partridge or quail, could shift for themselves almost as soon as born? What if they could presently become their own protectors, and their own providers? Small, if any, would be their regard for their parents: feeble, if any, would be the ties of filial love. But, by means of their long condition of dependence and tutelage, there are superinduced in their minds sentiments and habits of love, respect and submissiveness:—sentiments and habits, which seldom wear off in the succeeding periods of life, but are carried into society with unspeakable benefit.

On the same ground rests the whole fabric of education. The child, conscious of weakness and utmost dependence, finds none on earth to look to for protection, food and raiment, but the tender and ever attentive parents, who, of course, in *his* estimation are of pre-eminent wisdom and worth. Hence he receives their instructions into willing ears, hearkens to their advice, and treasures up their precepts in his memory. In their hands he is capable, in some important respects, of being moulded like soft wax.

Thus every family is of itself a little government. Every family is also a little academy, in which education, good or ill, has its beginning. Clusters of families form a particular society; and clusters of societies form a commonwealth or nation, which is exalted by righteousness, or debased by vice, in proportion as the discipline of the general mass of the families, that compose it, is good or bad.

NUMBER XXXVI.

OF THE MORAL BENEFITS ACCRUING TO PARENTS BY MEANS OF THE GOOD INSTRUCTION THEY GIVE THEIR CHILDREN.

The benefits resulting to children, from a due attention to their early instruction in the rudiments of learning and virtue, have frequently been the subject of able pens. Both in prose and in verse they have been described so clearly, and with so much fulness, that it would be difficult to add to what is written already. But it has been too little considered, of what unspeakable benefit good family instruction is to parents themselves.

He that is teaching another, is teaching himself: and more especially is it so in a moral point of view. Those attentions, which parents give to the moral and religious instruction of their offspring, have a powerful tendency toward guarding and strengthening their own moral and religious feelings and habits. Hardly can they in serious earnest dehort their children from vice, without experiencing an increase of resolution to guard against it in their own lives; or earnestly inculcate upon them the necessity of virtuous conduct, without acquiring an increase of desire and of carefulness to act virtuously themselves. They must needs be sensible that example has more influence on the young mind than precept, and that their good precepts will be thrown away unless they be careful to exemplify them in their domestic life and habits. They cannot but be conscious that their own example has a most powerful and decided influence in training up their children to honor or disgrace, to happiness or misery: and, consequently, they have in their children a constant stimulus to a virtuous, respectable course of behavior.

While your attention is daily employed in training up your child in the way he should go, you are at the same time nurturing in yourself the things that are virtuous and lovely; you are ameliorating your own temper and disposition; and are attaining a double security against aught of word or act, that has the appearance of vice, or even of indecorum. So true is it, that your daily efforts to render your example worthy of the imitation of your child are daily remunerated—richly remunerated, by the benefits resulting from it to the frame of your moral nature, independently of the benefits accruing to the child. Nor would it be hazarding too much to say, that the parents who have discharged the parental duties faithfully and discreetly, never yet failed of reaping, for themselves, an amount of profit far exceeding all the pains, even though the welfare of their children were altogether out of the question.

The scene of marriage was originally laid, not amongst "the thorns and thistles" of the curse, but in the blissful abodes of paradise. The first divine benediction was pronounced upon the conjugal union of man and woman: and in no wise is it evincive of the narrowness of superstition to indulge a religious belief, that virtuous marriage has generally, in some respects or other, been crowned with the blessing of God, from the time it was first consummated in the garden, up to the present day.

> "Domestic happiness, thou only bliss
> Of Paradise, that has surviv'd the fall!
> Thou art the nurse of virtue."———

A well chosen conjugal relation tends to smooth the natural asperities of man, to soften his manners, to sweeeten his temper, and to expand his heart. The bachelor thinks of *himself;* the married man of his *family.* The former becomes the more selfish by reason that he has none but self to look after and provide for: the latter the more benevolent, for his having a wife and children dependent upon the daily kindness of his attentions. Having learnt first to show kindness at home, he is the better disposed and qualified to extend the charities of life to those about him in the circle of society. Other things being equal, the single circumstance of his having a family of his own, as it connects him more closely with society, so it renders him a more feeling, a more beneficent, and a more estimable member of it.

It is agreeable to the order of nature, that we learn first to show kindness at home, and to those near about us; that we regard, in the first place, the little parcels of human beings with whom we are the most intimately connected—our families, our near kindred, our neighbors and familiar accquaintances. The daily exercise of practical benevolence toward these, has a tendency to expand our hearts, and to replenish them with humane sentiments towards the rest of our fellow-beings. The braggart philosophers of modern time inverted this order of nature, and by means of that inversion they made philanthropy to be a mere ideal phantom, instead of a practical principle. Under the pretence of embracing the whole human species, alike, in the bonds of affection, they left no room in their hearts for any individuals of that species—not even for those who were nearest them in blood. Rousseau, the apostle, if not the father, of this counterfeit philanthropy, turned his own infant children (all of spurious birth however) into a foundling hospital, and never afterward, as it has been said, took the least notice of them, or so much as inquired about their welfare. Rousseau loved every body *collectively*, but nobody *particularly*; he was an enthusiastic friend of the human race considered as a whole; but there was not, perhaps, one individual of that race, that he would have put himself out of the way to serve.

NUMBER XXXVII.

ON THE CONDITION OF OLD AGE—WITH DIRECTIONS FOR LIGHTENING ITS BURDEN.

We are naturally desirous of long life, and yet are unwilling to be old; agedness being regarded by us as the most dreary period of our earthly existence, not only as it borders upon the grave, but, also, by reason of the grievous infirmities with which it is so commonly visited. It is affecting to contemplate the ruins of art, —the once superb palaces and cities of antiquity lying in unsightly rubbish; it is more affecting still to contemplate the ruins of that curious workmanship of nature, the human body; and most affecting of all is it to contemplate the ruins of *Mind*.

In the life of the Dean of St Patrick's, Dr. Swift, the following anecdote is peculiarly affecting. That celebrated genius, for a considerable time, had anticipated with anguish the calamity that befell him in the loss of his mental faculties. Not long before the calamity came upon him, he was riding out in the company of a number of ladies and gentlemen. On a sudden he put spurs to his horse, and rode forward till he was out of sight of his companions; who, when they came up, found him upon his knees, under an aged oak, whose upper branches were dry and sapless while the stock was yet green. Upon being questioned about the singularity of his conduct in that instance, he replied, he had been making his fervent supplications to God, that he himself might not, like the tree he was under, be withered at the *top*.

There is often a *premature* decay in mind. Ere the corruptible body stoops with age, the immortal part shows evident signs of impairment. It not only grows forgetful, but feebler in intellect; and this not unfrequently happens to persons, well informed and of excellent intellectual faculties. In so far as it comes by the immediate act of God, or from contingencies which cannot be prevented or foreseen, it is a calamity that we can only deplore with humble reverence of the righteous hand that inflicts it. But in most cases it is owing to preventable causes: such as intemperate drinking, gluttony, debauchery, and the general train of kindred vices, which war against the whole man, and bring both the body and the mind into premature decay and ruin. But not to speak of the causes which are so well known, and so generally acknowledged, I will mention one that has been little noticed—*it is the habitual dereliction, or inaction of our rational faculties.*

Intellect often degenerates for want of exercise. Mental exercise is no less necessary for sustaining the faculties of the mind, than is corporal exercise to the vigor and alertness of the body. Nothing so much strengthens the memory as the frequent employment of it, by which it gains strength, as it were, mechanically; whereas, on the other hand, habitual disuse never fails to abate its power. Also, our reason is a faculty, to which exercise gives development, growth, and strength. We learn to reason by reasoning, as we learn to walk by walking. As one whose limbs have for a long time been confined and motionless, loses, in some degree, the power of walking, so one who suffers this faculty of reason to remain inactive, loses in some degree, the power of reasoning. Moreover, even speech is lost by long disuse. Some who had, for several years, been in a condition of solitude and utter seclusion from the company of fellow beings, were, when first restored to society, unable to articulate their mother tongue. Such, in particular, was the case of Alexander Selkirk, whose real history is veiled under the fictitious but pleasing tale of Robinson Crusoe. Now it is obvious that age naturally delights in repose; in a conditon of quiet, both of body and mind; of quiet bordering on inaction. It is visited with the feeling of lassitude not easily overcome; for which reason, the most of those whose prime has been spent in vigorous labor of thought, do in the evening of life remit this labor, considerably or altogether, and their minds fail for lack of exercise.

It is, further, obvious to remark, that age seldom enjoys an equal participation in social intercourse. "Iron sharpeneth iron; so a man sharpeneth the countenance of his friend." The mind can doze over a book, but engaging conversation arouses its dormant powers, and tends more, perhaps, than any thing else to give it tone and tension. But a great many of the aged are solitary and desolate. The companions of their youth, and even of their riper years, are mostly gone, and they have found none to supply their places. Living, as it were, alone in the world, their minds are no longer expanded and quickened by a living intercourse with society.

If the topics, which have now been merely suggested, were

considered in all their bearings and consequences, it would, I conceive, appear at least as a probable fact, that the imbecility of minds once strong, is more frequently the effect of their own torpid inaction, than of the impairing hand of time.

To those who wish for the prolongation of their rational faculties (and who would not wish it?) I will venture to suggest the following short hints.

1st. "Be temperate in all things"—in your desires, as well as in your enjoyments.

2d. Cultivate contentment and cheerfulness of temper. "A cheerful heart doeth good like a medicine." Like a medicine, it harmonizes and invigorates the body and the mind; while morbid melancholy and peevishness powerfully tend to impair both.

3d. So educate and so train up your children, if children you have, that they will, likely, be not only the props, but the delightful companions of your old age.

4th. When the years draw nigh, or are actually come, in which the hand of time begins to bear hard upon you, beware of sinking into mental torpitude or inaction; by reading and contemplation, exercise daily the faculties of memory, of reason, and of judgment.

5th. Neither withdraw from society, nor give society occasion to withdraw from you. As fast as the friends of your youth drop away by death, make to yourselves other friends from among the succeeding generations. It is not good that the old should consort with none but the old; it tends to deepen the shade of the gloomy valley which they are passing through, and to accelerate the impairment of their minds. The company and conversation of the young,—nay, even the prattle of little children is animating to well-tempered age: and, on the other hand, age, that carries with it experience and good information, and possesses a due mixture of pleasant humor with becoming gravity, has it in its power to please, as well as to profit, the decent and ingenuous part of younger society.

In conclusion: Lay hold of wisdom, as the only sure anchor of age. "In her right hand is length of days." The firm belief and steadfast practice of our holy religion,—as it yields the consolation of hope, which as to the aged can no longer spring from the prospect of earthly enjoyments,—so it tends much, in every way, to invigorate the understanding and to preserve it from decay.

NUMBER XXXVIII.

OF THE SILLY QUARREL BETWEEN A VENERABLE OLD COUPLE ABOUT A LITTLE GOAT.

Tobit of old and his wife Anna, unluckily fell into a quarrel upon the question, how she came by the kid that he heard bleating in his house. He very uncourteously accused her of stealing it; while she, in return, broadly hinted that, notwithstanding his pretensions, he was no better than he should be. "*Behold, thou and all thy works are known.*"

"The tongue can no man tame." And besides, it is agreeable to the laws of pneumatics that the lightest bodies should rise the highest, especially in a tempest. Wherefore, in spite of the degrading subjection in which the wife was held under the husband in that age and country, Anna had the last word; and a cutting word it was. Poor Tobit, it seems, had more than his match; for the retort that his wife made upon him was so keenly sarcastic, and touched him so deeply, that he fell a weeping. Indeed he was not much to be pitied, as he was manifestly the aggressor. Had he patiently inquired into the matter instead of blurting out his provoking suspicions, the bitter fray between them had never been.

This apocryphal text, which, peradventure, was never treated of so formally and methodically before, embraces several points of sound and wholesome doctrine. 1st. The serenity of connubial life is very apt to be disturbed by sudden and unexpected gusts, unless special care be taken in this particular. If both husband and wife be of a mild and even temper, there is no danger; or if one be so, and the other hasty, the danger is not so great; but if both be inflammable, there is need of the utmost watchfulness. A couple so tempered may, notwithstanding, be faithful, generous, noble-spirited, and kind-hearted, and may live together very lovingly in the main; but if they fail to keep a sharp look-out, now and then a gust arises, all of a sudden, and quite unexpectedly to themselves, and the house is made to ring from side to side. Some one, in his speculations on this subject, has recommended it, that a hasty couple should accustom themselves, ere they fly into a passion with one another, to utter in their hearts thrice the three following cooling words—Bear and forbear.

2d. The most part of domestic feuds, perhaps nine in ten, spring from trifles.. "Behold how great a matter a little fire kindleth." A word unfitly spoken, a sour look, a neglect, touches and stings the mind, and sometimes fires the tongue, and occasions a boisterous dispute; even though neither party can accuse or blame the other, in any matters of considerable moment.. For the prevention of this kind of domestic evil, permit me to offer the following recipe: "The Jesuits," according to an Italian author—"The Jesuits, with whom none could vie in the pleasures of civil life, were exceedingly attentive to appear to each other in the most amiable light. The polite behavior of the first day was uniformly preserved by them, during the many years they continued together; so that the honeymoon of their consociation, if this expression may be allowed, lasted for their lives. This reciprocal complaisance, at first merely adopted, was improved by habit into a solid, uninterrupted, and happy friendship."

The application is obvious.—Go, and do likewise.

3d. As amongst neighbors, so in domestic or conjugal life, sharp contentions arise from judging of matters prematurely, or before they have been duly investigated and weighed. In this respect, Tobit was sadly out of the way. He should have questioned Anna mildly about the bleating kid; asking her in a pleasant tone, how and whence it came; and, if not satisfied with her answers, he should have searched elsewhere for the truth. But no. Such was the flurry of his spirits, that he acted with as much assurance and decision upon a mere impression, as if he had had proof positive. Neither is this a solitary instance: the like has often happened to the great discomfort of social and domestic life. It ought to be deeply engraven on the mind and memory of man and woman, that "he that answereth a matter before he heareth it, it is folly and shame unto him."

4th. In the state of matrimony, hardly any thing is more discomforting, or more deadening to the delicate affection of love, than overmuch suspiciousness of temper. Groundless suspicions, repeatedly manifested, never fail to cool the love and excite the ire of the suspected party. And here again, Tobit deserves the lash of severe censure. He acted the part of a suspicious husband. And no wonder that Anna, an honest as well as industrious housewife—no wonder that she was stung to the quick at being suspected of so heinous an offence It was no wonder that her spirits were aroused, and being well gifted in that particular, that she used her tongue in the able manner she did.

One thing more, and I shall have done. Let no man take occasion from this subject to ridicule or despise marriage. It has passed into a proverbial saying, that there are but few happy matches: and, in one sense, it is true. There are few in comparison of the whole, who are *very* happy in marriage. But permit me to ask,—are there a great many that are *very* happy in the single condition? Is the bachelor entitled to glory in his choice, or to boast of a superior degree of felicity? He, who has no one that naturally cares for his person—no one that takes a lively interest in his concerns—no one that participates of his feelings of joy or deeply sympathizes in his adversities, sicknesses and sorrows—no tenderly-throbbing bosom, on which to rest his weary head.

On the reverse of this picture, behold the married man. Perhaps his wife is not, in some respects, quite as he would wish. Perhaps she has turns of unpleasant humor, and sometimes gives him pain by her peevishness or obstinacy. Yet she is faithful to him, and to his interests. Though, at times, she herself assaults him, with her tongue, *on no account will she suffer any body else to do it.* His joys and his sorrows are hers. In his outgoings, her heart blesses him; and after days or weeks of absence, she affectionately greets him on his return. His food, his apparel, the decencies of his appearance, are objects of her daily attention. His every ailment of body meets her sympathy, and quickens her care. In his heavy sicknesses, scarcely does she give sleep to her eyes, or slumber to her eyelids.

> "With a soft and silent tread,
> Nimble she moves about the bed."

Anxiously she watches the symptoms; carefully she administers the medicines; she responds to every groan, and with eagerness catches at every glimmer of hope.

Judge now, which of the two is the happier man.

NUMBER XXXIX.

OF FRIENDSHIP, AND THE CHOICE OF FRIENDS.

" Give me the man, whose liberal mind
Means general good to all mankind;
Who, when his friend, by fortune's wound,
Falls, tumbling headlong to the ground,
Can meet him with a warm embrace,
And wipe the tears from off his face."

In the choice of friends, much regard is to be had to the qualities of the *head*, but much greater still to those of the *heart;* for if *that* be radically wanting in integrity and honor, the more alluring is every thing else in personal character, the more dangerous. Catiline, with the worst of hearts, was possessed of personal accomplishments in a transcendent degree. He had the art of accommodating his manners and conversation to people of all tempers and ages. Cicero said of him; *He lived with the sad severely, with the cheerful agreeably, with the old gravely, with the young pleasantly.* All accomplished as he was, the viciousness of his moral character was manifoldly the more seductive, contagious, and pernicious to the community at large, and to the young especially. He easily insinuated himself into the friendship of the Roman youth, whom he corrupted and ruined.

Close intimacies, suddenly formed, often end in disappointment and disgust, and to the injury of one or other of the parties. It is a dangerous imprudence to trust any one as a friend, without good evidence of his being trustworthy ; without good evidence that he has neither a treacheous heart, a fickle temper, nor a babbling tongue. Often, very often, have the young of both sexes smarted under the consequences of such imprudence.

Equality in point of external circumstances, is not always a necessary preliminary to intimate and permanent friendship. The friendship between David and Jonathan, for unshaken fidelity and sublime ardor, has scarcely a parallel in history; yet the one was a shepherd of mean rank, whilst the other was of blood royal, and heir apparent to the throne. But though it is not always necessary that two close friends should be equal in their worldly conditions, it is necessary that their deeds and offices of kindness be reciprocal, else one becomes a *patron* and the other a *dependent*. If one be greatly outdone by his friends in acts of kindness, or receive benefits at their hands which he can never in any wise repay, they will regard him as their debtor on the score of friendship, and he himself must be wounded by the mortifying consciousness of bankruptcy in that respect. Hence there have been instances of proud-hearted men becoming the enemies, and even the destroyers, of their greatest benefactors, in order to rid themselves of a burdensome debt of gratitude.

One should be careful to show as much fidelity, as much attention, as much kindness to his friend, as he would require of him in similar circumstances.

Between frail imperfect creatures, there cannot be perfect friendship; and when one discards a friend for some trifling negligence, for an ungracious expression, or for his not having added the hundredth to his ninety-nine obliging acts, he is not worthy of having a friend, nor can he have one long.

It has been said that warm friends make warm enemies; but it is seldom so, except in cases of flagrant infidelity on the one side or the other. The truth is, very warm friendships (unless in the domestic state) are rarely lasting, by reason that they are above the ordinary tone of human nature, and therefore require much attention, and a constant exchange of obliging offices to keep them good. Whenever attention abates on the one side or the other, such friendship experiences a chill, and gradually cools down at length to indifference; but no positive enmity necessarily follows.

The friendship between persons notoriously wicked (if friendship it may be called) naturally turns to fear. As they know they cannot trust one another, so they constantly harbor a mutual jealousy, bordering upon, and often ending in downright hatred.

There is too much truth, generally speaking, in the following lines of Goldsmith:

> "And what is friendship but a name,
> A charm that lulls to sleep;
> A shade that follows wealth or fame,
> But leaves the wretch to weep."

When a man falls into misfortune, it often happens that some of those he had most befriended while in prosperity, are the first to forsake, and even to censure and reproach him. The reason is plain: they forsake him because they think him a pigeon no longer worth the plucking; and they reproach him to balance old scores.

The book in the world that best unfolds the human heart, is the Bible. There we find a man of vast substance; as liberal as he was rich, and as pious as liberal. A man who was "eyes to the blind, and feet to the lame," who "was a father to the poor;" and whose charitable hand and consoling voice "made the widow's heart sing for joy." While "the candle of the Lord shined upon his head," unbounded respect was paid him. The old as well as the young, princes and nobles as well as peasants, did him obeisance. He had friends without number: *close* friends—friends fixedly determined never to forsake him in his *prosperity*.

With unerring aim, and to answer the mysterious purposes of infinite wisdom, heaven's arrow was pointed at the bosom of this very man. In a single hour he fell from the height of prosperity to the lowest depths of human wretchedness. Bereft of all his child renat a stroke, reduced to poverty and need, covered from head to foot with disease, he sat upon the ground,—left there to weep his woes by himself. His friends as well as his fortune had left him. They stood aloof, and, with scorn rather than commiseration, eyed him afar off. He called after them —"*Have pity upon me! have pity upon me!*"—but called in vain. Even the very few that drew near, *ostensibly* to comfort him did but add grief to his sorrow. With rugged hands and unfeeling hearts, they tore yet wider his bleeding wounds, but poured in no balsam.

Suddenly, "the Lord turned the captivity" of this self-same man, and even doubled the prosperity of his best days. And no sooner was *that* known, than his old friends, who had forsaken him, came back of their own accord, and were ready enough to fasten themselves upon him. *Then*, and not till then, "came all his brethren, and all his sisters, and all that had been of his acquaintance before, and did eat bread with him in his house." His good *cheer* restores him to their good *liking*.

Yet, unfeeling as the world is, there are some in it, and I hope not a few, who are the same in the black night of adversity as in the sunshine of prosperity. These are of the right stamp. —Reader, hast thou a friend of this sort; one who was thy father's or thy mother's friend in distress; one who has readily befriended thyself in time of utmost need?—Then hast thou a pearl of inestimable worth—lock it close to thy bosom.

NUMBER XL.

OF THE IMPORTANCE OF LEARNING TO SAY, NO.

A VERY wise and excellent mother gave the following advice, with her dying breath—"My son, learn to say, No." Not that she did mean to counsel her son to be a churl in speech, or to be stiff-hearted in things that were indifferent or trivial—and much less did she counsel him to put his negative upon the calls of charity and the impulses of humanity; but her meaning was that, along with gentleness of manners, and benevolence of disposition, he should possess an inflexible firmness of purpose—a quality beyond all price, whether it regards the sons or the daughters of our fallen race.

Persons so infirm of purpose, so wanting in resolution, as to be incapable, in almost any case, of saying No, are among the most hapless of human beings; and that, notwithstanding their sweetness of temper, their courteousness of demeanor, and whatever else of amiable and estimable qualities they possess. Though they see the right, they pursue the wrong; not so much out of inclination, as from a frame of mind disposed to yield to every solicitation.

An historian of a former and distant age, says of a Frenchman who ranked as the first prince of the blood, that he had a bright and knowing mind, graceful sprightliness, good intentions, complete disinterestedness, and an incredible easiness of manners; but that, with all these qualities, he acted a most contemptible part for the want of resolution; that he came into all the factions of his time, because he wanted power to resist those who drew him in for their own interests; but that he never came out of any but with shame, because he wanted resolution to support himself whilst he was in them.

It is owing to the want of resolution, more than to the want of sound sense, that a great many persons have run into imprudences, injurious, and sometimes fatal to their worldly interests. Numerous instances of this might be named, but I shall content myself with naming only one—and that is, rash and hazardous suretiship. The pit stands uncovered, and yet men of good sense, as well as of amiable dispositions, plunge themselves into it, with their eyes wide open. Notwithstanding the solemn warnings in the Proverbs of the Wise Man, and notwithstanding the examples of the fate of so many that have gone before them, they make the hazardous leap. And why? Not from inclination, or with a willing mind, but because being solicited, urged, and entreated, they know not how to say, No. If they had learned not only to pronounce that monosyllable, but to make use of it on all proper occasions, it might have saved from ruin themselves, and their wives and children.

But the worst of it is still behind. The ruin of character, of morals, and of the very heart and soul of man, originates often in a passive yieldingness of temper and disposition, or in the want of the resolution to say No. Thousands and many thousands, through this weakness, have been the victims of craft and deceit. Thousands and many thousands, once of fair promise, but now sunk in depravity and wretchedness, owe their ruin to the act of consenting, against their better judgments, to the enticement of evil companions and familiars. Had they said No, when duty, when honor, when conscience, when every thing sacred demanded it of them,—happy might they now have been—the solace of their kindred, and the ornaments of society.

Sweetness of temper, charitableness of heart, gentleness of demeanor, together with a strong disposition to act obligingly, and even to be yielding in things indifferent, or of trifling moment—are amiable and estimable traits of the human character: but there must be withal, and as the ground-work of the whole, such a firmness of resolution as will guarantee it against yielding, either *imprudently* or *immorally*, to solicitations and enticements. Else one has very little chance, in passing down the current of life, of escaping the eddies and quicksands that lie in his way.

Firmness of purpose is one of the most necessary sinews of character, and one of the best instruments of success; without it, genius wastes its efforts in a maze of inconsistencies, and brings to its possessor disgrace rather than honor.

NUMBER XLI.

OF THE CALAMITIES OF HEREDITARY IDLENESS.

WE cannot, if we will, make ourselves torpid, like an oyster. We must needs be doing something with our existence, or endure else a wearisome load, as undescribable as it is intolerable. Indeed, occupation of one kind or other is so necessary to human quiet, that life itself is burdensome without it. For short as life is, there are but few who never complain at heart of the superfluity of their time. Whereas the wights, great and small, who have nothing at all to do, are, for the most part, perpetually uttering this most dolorous kind of complaint, or, at least, manifest no ordinary degree of restlessness—being burdened with their time much more than the most busy are burdened with their business.

The misery of idleness is to be seen nearly as much in high life, as in the rags and filth of extreme poverty. In Europe there are classes of people who are idle, as it were, out of necessity: not that they are unable to find employ, but they are unable to find *such* employ as they think comports with their dignity. Manual labor of any kind would degrade them; nor does the condition of their rank allow them to enter into trade, or even to embrace any of the learned professions. In fact, save those few who are selected to take part in the administration of government, or who are placed in high military stations, they are condemned, by the exalted condition of their birth, to perpetual idleness. And what is the result? It is that this very exaltation of birth, which places them so far above all ordinary business, makes them doubly wretched.

"There is scarcely any truth more certain or more evident," says a writer who was possessed of a personal knowledge of the splendid group whose picture he has delineated, "than that the noblesse of Europe are, in general, less happy than the common people. There is one irrefragable proof of it, which is, that they do not maintain their own population. Families, like stars or candles, which you will, are going out continually; and without fresh recruits from the plebeians, the nobility would in time be extinct. If you make allowances for the state, which they are condemned by themselves to support, they are poorer than the poor—deeply in debt—and tributary to usurious capitalists, as greedy as the Jews."

Persons in the intermediate grades between the *very* top and the *very* bottom of the scale of life, have precious advantages over those who are placed in either extreme. That they have advantages over the lowest, all will readily admit; and that they have some important advantages over the highest, is a position equally true. In point of real, solid comfort and happiness, the condition of the farmer or mechanic, who supplies his daily wants by the labor of his own hands, is infinitely preferable to that of the noblesse, above described; who, for want of regular occupation, are under the hard necessity of taking a deal of pains, and of resorting to numberless expedients and devices, to wear out the tedious moments of their earthly existence. Even whilst, with utmost eagerness, they are seemingly pursuing pleasure, their chief efforts are to escape from misery, by killing the time which hangs so heavily upon their minds and hearts. For as to pleasure, they are so surfeited of it, that they seek it only as preferable to the distressing tediousness of total inaction.

Although, fortunately, in these United States, there are no hereditary ranks, that fix, as it were, by never-ending entailment, the baneful disease of sloth upon particular families; yet excessive wealth produces, not unfrequently, the like effects. "After a gatherer comes a scatterer" is a proverbial saying, which, in whatever country it originated, is nowhere, perhaps, more strikingly matter-of-fact than in our own. Indeed, nothing can be more natural than the process. The "gatherer," if he have gathered a very large heap, is, of course, a man of great worldly prudence; but so far from being able to bequeathe that quality to his children, the single circumstance of their being set up in the world with fortunes, has an almost irresistible tendency to render them imprudent and improvident. You cannot put the old head upon the young shoulders. You can hardly convince the rich-born youth, that considerable care and attention will be necessary on his part, merely to keep the fortune that falls to him. There is more than an even chance that he will be either carelessly indolent, or prodigally dissipated; that he will either waste his time in idleness, or spend it in vain, if not vicious pursuits.

The vanity of wealth will alike affect *his* children and his children's children. They will dote much upon the circumstance of their springing from an opulent stock, and, by natural consequence, will feel themselves quite above the ordinary occupations of life. Meanwhile, the family estate will have been divided and subdivided, till the share of each comes to be very small. A sort of stateliness, is, however, kept up in their narrow circumstances, and even in their poverty. They preserve, with a sort of religious reverence, old pictures, little fragments of plate, or some precious memorial or other of what *once was*. For the pride of family, founded altogether upon wealth, seldom suffers much abatement by the ruin of that foundation. Thus it is, that the needy descendants of a very rich family are in a worse condition, by far, than most others of the sons and daughters of want; since the indolence of their habits, and the magnificence of their notions, alike disable them for procuring a comfortable livelihood, and for enjoying the little they possess.

There is one kind of revolution that is perpetually going on in this country;—the revolution in fortunes. The rich families of the last age, all but a few, are utterly extinct as to fortune; and, on the other hand, the families that now figure in the magnificence of wealth, are, in general, the founders of their own fortunes; not a few of them having emerged from obscurity, and some from the deepest shades of poverty. The revolutionary wheel is still turning, and with a few turns more, it will turn down a great part of the present rich families, and will turn up, in their stead, an equal, or perhaps greater number, from the poor and the middling classes. This course has well nigh as firm a fixture, as have the changes of day and night.

NUMBER XLII.

OF THE LAMENTABLE SPECIES OF HELPLESSNESS OCCASIONED BY PRIDE AND FALSE SHAME.

Teach your children to help themselves, is a practical maxim, deserving more general notice than it ever yet has obtained, or peradventure ever will obtain, in this scornful and foolish world. The highest and most important part of the art of teaching is to train the young mind to think for itself, and to exercise and exert its faculties of judgment and understanding, as well as of memory; for these faculties grow and increase only by exercise. The less they are exercised in childhood, the more feeble they come to be in manhood. And besides, one who has been unaccustomed to the exertion of thought in the early years of life, commonly lacks all disposition to accustom himself to it afterwards; it being a kind of labor, which early habit makes pleasant, but which early neglect renders intolerably irksome.

And as children should be led to think for themselves, or to exert those faculties which pertain to the mind only; so, also, should they be inured to the exercise of those mixed faculties, that call forth the exertion of the mind and body conjointly.

This class of exercises is of more easy performance, especially in childhood, than the other. It is altogether natural too; and it tends to give vigor and alertness alike to the mental and the corporeal frame. If children be made to help themselves as soon and as much as they are able, it wonderfully conduces to the improvement of their faculties, and has, at the same time, an auspicious influence upon their dispositions. Whereas, if they are accustomed to have every thing done for them by others, that others can do, the rust of sloth and the canker of pride will be full apt to spoil whatever of excellence nature has bequeathed them.

Childhood and youth are periods of life, which materially influence all its following periods. Whether these early years be passed in torpid indolence, or in well-directed industry, is a point on which greatly depends the worth or the worthlessness of human character. What man or what woman, that has a relish for intellectual pleasure, cannot trace that relish down to the days of childhood? Where is the man who guides his affairs with discretion, or the woman that "looketh well to the ways of her household," and yet was not in some measure imbued with industrious and provident dispositions, in early life? On the other hand, who that had been treated, till the age of twenty, like a helpless infant, and had every want supplied without being put to either mental or bodily exertion, was ever good for any thing afterwards? I freely admit, indeed, that there are some honorable exceptions; but they are like the few exceptions to a well-established general rule.

It is the misfortune of high rank and great wealth, that the children of families, so distinguished, are often treated as helpless till they become so in reality. They must have waiters to do for them a multitude of little things, which it would be greatly for their benefit to do for themselves. They must be served with such assiduity as to supersede, almost, the use of their own limbs. They have feet, but they walk not; hands have they, but they use them not, except for putting their food and drink to their mouths. And are they happy? No: it is of the nature of this kind of training to render them discontented, peevish and querulous all their lives, even though fortune should never forsake them. And if they chance to fall into poverty, they are wretched indeed—no less incapable than unwilling to earn a livelihood by industry.

But the sum of the mischief would be not so great, if it were confined altogether to families of high rank or great wealth; for these are comparatively very few. It is the feverish desire of aping the stateliness of rank and the pomp of wealth, that occasions the commonness of this perverted education, and the huge mass of wretchedness which follows it.

Madam ——— is a branch of what had been called a *good* family. The estate is run out, and she is poor and dependent. She retains, however, some precious relics of former splendor. With these she feeds her vanity. Not unfrequently she boasts that never in all her lifetime did she defile her hands with labor; and she would swoon at the thought that one of her maiden daughters should descend to the business of a milliner, or that the other should marry a substantial tradesman.

Mrs. ——— has no rich ancestry or great connections to boast of, and her worldly circumstances are but indifferent; but the darling wish of her heart is, the elevation of her children. Wherefore she moils and toils day and night, gives herself no rest, impairs her constitution by overwork, for the goodly purpose of bringing up her children in *genteel* idleness, that so perchance they may obtain the notice of the *better* sort.

Not a few, but numerous are the instances of those, who voluntarily encounter dolorous straits and hardships merely through the instigation of vanity and pride. Comfortable, if not happy, might they be, if they would only discard these foes to their peace, and consumers of their substance. And what makes it the more strange, these same persons, in other respects, are in their sober senses, and some of them not only rational, but agreeable ; it is only in this one particular that they show marks of insanity.

NUMBER XLIII.

OF THE PROPER AND IMPROPER, AS DEPENDING UPON THE DIVERSE CIRCUMSTANCES AND AGES OF LIFE.

THE love of propriety, along with an accurate perception of the difference between the *proper* and the *improper*, is an estimable quality in human beings; for though it is not a virtue in its best and highest sense, it is virtue's shield and ornament. To *woman*, in particular, it is a pledge of honor, and a diadem of beauty.

There are women who, without any extraordinary strength of intellect, or advantage of education, discover a sort of intuitive or instinctive perception of propriety, on all occasions and under all circumstances—far surpassing, in that particular, most *men* of even talents and learning. Solomon, with a single stroke of his pen, has given us the portraiture of such a woman. "*She openeth her mouth with wisdom ; and in her tongue is the law of kindness.*" Here are blended two characteristic traits, of which neither would show well by itself. Discretion unaccompanied with kindness—mere selfish, cold-hearted discretion, whether found in man or woman, has very little claim to commendation. She is a woman but in name, who has no heart in her bosom. On the other hand, kindness is very liable to error, and even to fatal error, when it lacks the guidance of discretion. Whereas the union of these two qualities, crowned withal with that essential requisite, *the fear of the Lord*—renders female character alike respectable and lovely. A woman of this description, though destitute of the advantages of beauty, or youth, or wealth, or wit, is an ornament to the human family; while to her own family she is one of the first of blessings.

The laws of propriety not only comprise all the laws of morality—for nothing that is immoral can be proper—but they reach to a vast variety of things, that in themselves are indifferent:—their propriety or impropriety depending on time, place, age, circumstances or cases, without name or number. Far from attempting to explore this boundless field, I shall but mention two articles culled from it.

First. What may be quite proper for some persons, may be very improper for others. For instance, it is proper for the rich, if they choose it, to make the appearance of riches in their buildings, their furniture, the elegances of their tables, the superior quality of their apparel, or in any lawful way else, which their circumstances can well afford. If a rich man make him great works—if he build him costly houses—if he plant him fine gardens, furnished with pools of water, "to water therewith the wood that bringeth forth trees,"—or if he array his household in splendid apparel—there is no impropriety in all this, provided the clear income of his estate be fully sufficient to defray these expenses, over and above what is due to the calls of charity. It is much better than to let his gold and his silver lie and rust in moth-eaten bags; for, by giving employ to so many artists and laborers, he encourages and rewards industry, and becomes the prop and support of the industrious poor that are about him.

But—mark the difference—when a man that is not rich, affects the manner of the rich, the impropriety of his conduct is manifest to all but himself, and he is only laughed at for his pains. Would it were an uncommon case! So it is not. There are thousands of this sort; thousands that are pawning the first and essential necessaries of life, and sinking themselves into debt and pitiless poverty;—and all for mere show. What a mass of wretchedness and misery might be prevented by a timely cure of this single folly! No kind of fascination is more generally prevalent, and there is scarcely any one that draws after it more ruinous consequences.

Second. The other of the two points that I proposed to notice, is, that certain things, which are proper at one time of life, are improper at another. In a qualified sense, "to every thing there is a season." Childhood is the season for childish things, which, in the succeeding periods of life, must be put away. Youth, also, is the season for certain things which peculiarly belong to that age. It is the spring-time of life; and there is in it a certain indescribable hilarity of look, air, and manner, that exactly befits it, but which ill suits the season of old age. A boyish old man, or a girlish old woman, is as unnatural a phenomenon as the flowers of May in the month of December.

Few things are more difficult than to grow old with a good grace; and, perhaps, the burden of the difficulty lies, with a disproportioned weight, upon the female part of our race. To the vainer and more superficial part it is bitter as death to lose the youthful bloom, for which alone they had been admired, and for which they had so much admired themselves. And hence there are to be found matrons, affecting, in dress and manners, the frivolity of girlish years—in spite of obtrusive wrinkles, and silvery locks.

It is far otherwise with the women, whose minds and hearts have been properly cultivated and replenished with intellectual and moral treasure, along with the benignant dispositions which pure Christianity inspires. The decay of their youthful bloom, or personal attractions, is succeeded by self-satisfaction, and the high esteem and respect of all around them.

NUMBER XLIV.

OF KEEPING CHILDREN FROM THE COMPANY OF CHILDREN.

He that formed man, and knew best what was in him, and what he was made for, *saw that it was not good that he should be alone.* This single sentence confutes the volumes of glowing declamation in favor of solitude, or total abstraction from the world. To man the social state is the natural state: it brightens his intellect, expands his heart, strengthens his weakness, and multiplies his enjoyments; whereas, habitual solitude tends to narrowness of heart and sourness of temper. Not that it is good to be always in company. That opposite extreme, which so many have run into, is quite as bad as the other. The solitary being who shuns all company, and the empty flutterer who finds no enjoyment out of company, are alike wide of the true mark; which is a due mixture of intervals of well-spent solitude with the business and duties and enjoyments of social life.

As zoologists tell us, " It has long been observed that those races of animals which live in societies, and unite their efforts for the attainment of one common end, exhibit a great superiority of intellectual faculties over those which lead a life of solitude and seclusion: and the observation applies equally to the small as to the larger animals; although among the insect tribes the distinction is most strongly marked." It has, also, been noticed by careful observers, that the gregarious races of animals, in many instances, evidently learn of one another, and so become more sagacious, and more expert in their operations, by reason of their living in a social state. Young singing birds, for example, are known to improve in voice and skill, by listening to the notes of an old and experienced songster.

In human beings, the social affection seems to be nearly coeval with the first dawn of reason. An infant not unfrequently has been seen to leap with joy, in its mother's arms, at the sight of another infant; reaching out its little hands to embrace the stranger. Emulation, also, is of the like early growth. Infants that have small children constantly about them, if other things be equal, learn to walk and to speak earlier than those that are confined altogether to the company of full grown people. Equally true is it, that both small and large children enjoy themselves a great deal better for being much in the company of their equals. Moreover, it increases the growth and strength of their minds, improves the faculties of their bodies, and furnishes them with a sort of information highly necessary to their childish years.

How much children learn from children is beyond account. It is true, in this way they learn some things which they must be made to unlearn. But that is not so bad as to deaden their faculties and make mopes of them, by debarring them altogether from the society of those of their own age. There is a mixture of good and evil, as in all other human affairs, so also in any system of education which human wisdom can devise; that being the most eligible one, in which the good most clearly preponderates: and upon this principle, to suffer children to enjoy the company of children, and at the same time to keep a watchful eye upon them, is a much better way than wholly to immure them, as some parents have done, either from pride, or through fear of contamination.

No topics have been worn more threadbare than those relating to the comforts, and benefits, and blessings of society: topics that have been the standing dish from time immemorial; and that have been treated of so often, and in some instances so ably, as almost to preclude the possibility of adding a single thought altogether new. There is one important particular, however, which seems to have been less heeded than the rest; and that is the *salutary restraints* which well regulated society imposes upon its members: I mean not the restraints of law, but merely those of opinion.

If there be persons who care not at all what any think of them, their minds are either far above, or far below the natural feeling of humanity. Indeed it is more than doubtful whether any person of this description exists, unless among the vilest and most abandoned of the species. It is human nature to love esteem, and abhor reproach; and, for this reason, no law has so general influence over civilized man, as the law of *Decency;* inasmuch as it governs the external conduct, or the manners, even of those who have little or no regard for moral principle. A sense of shame is one of the most powerful checks upon the atrocious vices which society deems scandalous; so that decency of manners in society is owing not so much to its laws, as to public sentiment, or the authority of opinion. How happens it that they who emigrate from places where public sentiment is decidedly in favor of the virtues and the decencies of life, and settle themselves down in a solitary situation, or among neighbors of corrupted sentiments—how happens it that often they are so changed—so strangely degenerated in their morals and manners? The reason is that they have lost, or thrown off, what had been the main check upon their behavior. As they are no longer under the stern, scrutinizing eye of virtuous society, they no longer scruple to indulge freely the irregular propensities of their minds and hearts.

There are those in private life, who are capable of doing nearly, if not quite as much good as can be done by legislators and magistrates: they are persons possessed of great or considerable wealth. In *our* country, there is no one thing that confers so much weight of personal influence as riches. The rich, if they possess parts withal, have a matchless influence upon the morals and manners of society. They are looked up to; they are imitated; in things pertaining to manners they take the lead, and have considerably the direction. Happy were it, if their influence were always directed to shame vice, and to make virtue fashionable.

NUMBER XLV.

OF TEACHING CHILDREN TO LIE.

> ——— "To be branded with the name of liar
> Is ignominy fit for slaves alone."
>
> SOPHOCLES.

THIS was the sentiment of an ancient Greek poet of great and deserved fame;—a man who, unenlightened with the rays of Christianity, spoke merely from the impulse of nature.

The ancient Persians, as history informs us, were at great pains to teach and habituate their children to speak the truth, and thought this a main point in their education. The old Greeks and Romans considered lying so infamous as to degrade a freeman to a level with their slaves. Even the Turks are reported to hold a liar in the utmost contempt. And, indeed, by a sort of general consent, in most parts of the world, this vice has been reckoned a part of cowardly meanness of nature, and branded with infamy. While the laws and sanctions of Christianity most solemnly forbid lying, and threaten it with all that is awful, the laws even of *fashion* condemn and reproach it, as the offspring of a pitiful, dastardly spirit. So that a notorious liar is excluded, as by general suffrage, not only from the communion of the pious, but also from the society of the polite.

It is not to my purpose, however, to treat here of the vice itself, or of its direful consequences; but rather to suggest ways and means to prevent its going into a habit with young children. For of these two things I am confident: *first*, that few, if any, have become notorious for lying, who did not begin to learn it while young; and *second*, that few children, if any, are deeply initiated in this black art, unless through the fault, directly or indirectly, of those who have had the immediate care of their persons and their education. Truth is as easily spoken as falsehood; and the habit of speaking the truth, when once fixed, is, perhaps, nearly as hard to be broken off as the habit of lying. They both grow into habits by degrees, and most commonly according to the management and moulding of early childhood.

Tell me not that there is in some children, even in some little children, such a strong propensity to lying that the habit cannot be prevented by any human means. How many thousand *pagans* (the old Persians, for instance) took such pains with their children in this particular, that among them all a single liar was scarcely known. And it is hard to tell why *Christian* parents and instructors might not be equally successful, if they would only use the same prudence and unweariable diligence.

It is said that the children of the oppressed poor, in jolly and generous-hearted Ireland, are remarkably quick and intelligent, but almost universally addicted to lying, which they are taught even by their own mothers. The boy is sent off, by his mother, to pilfer and bring home fuel from the landlord's turf-rick. If the little urchin succeeds and returns well-laden with plunder, he is applauded. If he happens to meet with the landlord, or any of his domestics, and is asked whither he is going;—provided he brings himself off by lying, he is praised for his art and cunning. But should it bechance him to speak the truth in reply to the interrogation, he is sure of a whipping upon his return home; or, at best, of a sharp reprimand from his mother, in terms like the following:—

"Ah, ye little brat! And what made ye tell the gentleman when he met ye, ye rogue, that ye were going to the rick. And what business had ye to go and belie me to his honor, ye unnatural piece of goods! I'll teach ye to make mischief through the country! So I will. Have ye got no better sense and manners at this time o'day, than to behave, when one trusts ye abroad, so like an innocent?"

I would fain believe that, in this free and goodly country of ours, there are not very many mothers, or fathers, disposed to teach their children to lie, wittingly, directly, and even by their positive injunctions; yet I do fear there are very many who do it, either unwittingly, or indirectly, or consequentially.

Some do it unwittingly, or without consideration. The child (be it supposed) begins to lie ere it can fairly be regarded as a moral agent. In such a case,—and such cases are not uncommon—it is diverting, particularly to parents, to hear the cunning little thing *fib.*—"And where is the harm?"—So say, and so think some inconsiderate ones. But they wofully err. The harm lies here. The *fibbing* child, though only three or four years old, is now beginning to be fashioned to the awful habit of lying; and though easy to be cured at this age, the cure may, a few years hence, be very difficult, if not impossible.

Others, again, indirectly teach their little children to lie by passing deceptions upon them.—Now every deception that is passed upon the child, goes to teach the child to deceive. The deceptive arts that are played off upon himself, he is quickly prepared to put in practice upon others. Especially if his parents, to whom he looks for example, deceive him with falsehoods for whatever purpose, he, also, will not scruple to utter falsehoods to gain his ends.

Finally, some so keenly mark, and so severely punish even the petty faults of children, that they are strongly tempted to a denial of the truth, whenever they see the least chance of escape by that means;—and thus they begin to form the habit of lying, as it were, in their own defence.

To teach children to despise and detest falsehood and prevarication, and on no account to be guilty of an untruth, is one of the most essential articles in a good education. This is among the good seed that should be sown, betimes, in their minds, by their parents and instructors; so as to prevent, if possible, their ever uttering a wilful falsehood, or, at least, to cure the evil at its first budding: else the force of habit being superadded to the vicious propensities of nature, a cure will be doubly difficult, and next to hopeless.

Great care should be taken, not only that children be not led into temptation to this pernicious evil, but, also, that they be early and constantly guarded against it by all prudent means, and be made to form the habit of honestly speaking the truth on every occasion. Be not over much prying and severe in regard to the mere frailties common to childhood. Many things you must overlook, and forbear to notice, unless you would render your government over your children both odious and contemptible by your perpetual chiding. Never deceive your children by word or deed. Never fail to reprove them seriously for any, and every act of falsehood, or equivocation, that you find them guilty of; however much your parental vanity may be flattered with the dexterity of the little deceivers. Whenever they frankly own a fault, whilst you blame them for the fault, forget not to commend them for speaking the truth about it.

NUMBER XLVI.

OF HABITUAL DISCONTENT, ARISING FROM IMAGINARY WANTS.

The following short apologue of *Sadi*, an Asiatic sage, is full of valuable instruction:—"I never complained of my wretched, forlorn condition, but on one occasion, when my feet were naked, and I had not wherewithal to shoe them. Soon after, meeting a man without feet, I was thankful for the bounty of Providence to myself, and with perfect resignation submitted to my want of shoes."

The true secret of living happily, lies in the philosophy of contentment, which is of more value than the imagined stone of the alchymist, that turns every thing to gold.

It is to be lamented, however, that in this age of boasted light and improvement the philosophy of contentment is very little studied or regarded. From various corrupted sources we have learned not to be content, but dissatisfied with the ordinary conditions of life. And though neither *shoeless*, nor destitute of any essential article of raiment or food, we are ready to consume our hearts with vexation because we are not seated at the upper end of fortune's table. The semblance of happiness is more sought after than the reality; the mere phantom of it, rather than the substance. The simple plainness of former days is despised. Plain apparel, plain fare, and plain houses and furniture, such as our worthy progenitors were quite contented with, and very thankful for, our fastidious delicacy regards with scorn, and we must needs be fine and fashionable, or pine our lives away in grief and shame. Nor would it be either so alarming, or so lamentable, were this the folly of only a few. But the worst of it is, it has spread, like an epidemic, over the whole land, and throughout almost every class of society. Tens and even hundreds of thousands, embracing both sexes alike, are the miserable victims of a morbid sensibility, and squeamishly dash from their lips the cup of ordinary comfort, which is presented to them, because it is not filled to the brim, or because it is not spiced and sweetened exactly to their taste.

And where lies the remedy? It is not within the art of the apothecary, or in the power of any nostrums of partial and limited effect. No, the people must be wise for themselves. The great body of the people, coming once more to their sober senses, must agree to return to the plain, frugal, uncostly habits of other times; and must strive, with general accord, to bring those long-discarded habits into fashion again, and to render them honorable by the suffrage of public opinion.

As the want of contentment is one of the most grievous wants that affect human life, it ought to be provided against with the utmost care, and particularly in the following ways.

1st. In training up children, scarcely anything is of greater importance than guarding them against the intrusion of too many artificial wants. I say *too many*, because *some* wants of this sort do naturally and necessarily grow out of civilization, and it is only their excess that tends to discontent and wretchedness. Of that excess the danger is great, inasmuch as the effects are always deplorable. What multitudes, at this very instant, are discontented and wretched, who might enjoy life comfortably, had they been early taught to conform their desires to their conditions, and to act upon the principles of sober and rational economy. Nor is it of small importance in training up children, to accustom them to useful employment. A useless life is seldom found to be a contented one. Occupation is so necessary to human quiet, that to bring up children in idleness, is the way to make them a burden to themselves, as well as to the community.

From this twofold cause, the excess of artificial wants and the neglect of forming habits of useful industry in the early period of life, has sprung, perhaps, full half of the discontent that secretly preys upon so many bosoms. In short, important as it is to teach children reading and writing and the use of figures, it is of still greater importance to regulate their tempers, to curb their wayward desires, and to fix them in habits of industry, temperance, and frugality, without which the acquisition of learning could be but of little benefit to them.

2d. The self-discipline of adult age is an essential requisite towards leading and enjoying a contented life. A well disciplined mind studies to be content, and most commonly is so. It attains its desires by moderating and limiting them, and thus bringing them within the compass of its means. It accustoms itself to view without envy the wealth and grandeur which fall not to its lot, and which seldom render their possessors more happy; and to be satisfied with, and thankful for, the mere necessary and common accommodations of the journey of life. In short, it depends much less upon our circumstances, whether we shall be happy or miserable in life, than on our tempers, and our view of things. Many enjoy themselves well in narrow circumstances, because they bring their minds to their situations. But when to narrow circumstances are added, large desires and magnificent notions, it is then, and only then, that unhappiness results from the want of a fortune.

NUMBER XLVII.

OF SEVERAL OF THE PREDISPOSING CAUSES OF UNHAPPY MARRIAGES.

It is a common saying in the world, that there are but few happy marriages; and doubly deplorable would be the condition of mankind were it wholly true. It is true, however, only in a qualified or limited sense.

What! is marriage, in itself considered, a source of wretchedness rather than of weal? Do they who marry, change their condition *generally* for the worse? Are the married, for the most part, less happy than the unmarried? So it is not; nor will any assert it but the profane and licentious, or the inconsiderate. Yet, after all, but few marriages are exceeding happy. And why? It is not for lack of excellence in the institution, nor because the connubial state is not, in itself, conducive to human comfort and weal. Elsewhere lie the reasons; of which some will be included in the following particulars.

1st. It often happens that too much is expected beforehand. In none of the conditions or relations of this life is unalloyed happiness the lot of man; and, by consequence, those who indulge the unreasonable expectation of finding it in marriage, must inevitably drink of the bitter cup of disappointment.

2d. Since the fall, the intercourse of married life has never been (such as it primitively was) between persons of perfect innocence and virtue; but it is in all cases between those who are frail, infirm of mind, and more or less defective in heart. Now it is for want of duly considering this matter before their marriage, that a great many couples are unreasonably vexed at the infirmities, failings, and petty faults, which they perceive in each other afterwards; charging upon wedlock the disappointment that originated in the illusions of their own fancies.

3d. As in other contracts, so in that of marriage the parties too often deal unfairly with one another, by artfully concealing their personal defects and affecting qualities of which they are devoid.

That ornament of human nature, as well as of the society of Friends, to which he belonged, namely, Dr. Fothergill, of London—a man alike distinguished for parts and learning, for benevolence and piety—being informed that a gentleman, at a house where he visited, was paying his addresses to a young lady, desired leave to offer him a piece of advice. The gentleman making a bow of submission—"Friend," said the shrewd physician, "my advice is this—*that thou shouldst court in thy every-day clothes.*"

What a deal of matrimonial disappointment and strife might be prevented if, while the treaty was going on, both the wooers and the wooed would appear in their *every-day clothes*;—or in no better character for temper and disposition, or for any attractive and estimable quality, than such as they were determined to maintain, after marriage, constantly, throughout the whole of their lives.

4th. The little obliging attentions which are the food of friendship, and without which close and ardent friendship can hardly be kept alive for any long while, are too often remitted after marriage, and even discontinued. And hence, without any flagrant fault on either side, coolness arises, then indifference, and finally alienation.

5th. Among the higher classes, marriage, in too many instances, is the old, calculating chaffery of avarice and ambition for money or for rank. And as neither love nor friendship has any concern in the contract, it is no wonder that neither love nor friendship should ever after spring up and bless the union.

6th. Amongst the lower classes many rush into marriage improvidently, or without being furnished with any competent means of supporting a family. Poverty and want follow of course. Their own suffering is aggravated by the sufferings of their little ones; and they look back, with deep regret, to the comparative comforts of their single life.

Lastly, there are those of the baser sort, who, by reason of the perverseness of their tempers, or the pravity of their hearts, and the viciousness of their lives, would needs be wretched in any condition. As husbands and wives, they mutually are fiendlike tormentors, if equally matched; or if they are yoked together unequally, the connection proves the sorest of calamities to the better party.

And yet, after making all these deductions, it is unquestionably true that more than a full moiety of the social comfort enjoyed in this world, is the fruit of marriage. In it the extreme cases either way are comparatively few. Of married men and women, the most, by far, are made neither *very* happy, nor *very* wretched by this connection. Between these two extremes there is an intermediate class, immense in number, who, though they constantly experience a mixture of good and evil in the married state, will perceive, nevertheless, upon a fair estimate, that the good considerably preponderates.

One observation more and I shall conclude. The surest basis of connubial happiness is genuine piety. "Wisdom," as observes a venerable sage in the Apocrypha, "is a loving spirit." The wisdom that is from above is peaceable, gentle, and easy to be entreated. The humility, the meekness, the benevolence, the gentleness of real Christianity, and indeed the whole body of the Christian virtues, when heart-felt and acted out in sincerity, do directly and powerfully tend to sweeten the trials and multiply the comforts of those who are partners together in marriage, while the hope of meeting in a better world "strews their path to the grave with flowers."

NUMBER XLVIII.

OF FAVORITISM IN THE DEALING OF PARENTS WITH THEIR CHILDREN.

As parents naturally love their children, so they naturally wish to be loved by them; and yet, very often, this darling wish of their hearts is defeated by their own imprudence. Upon this point it would be easy to enumerate facts or instances; but I shall mention only one—and that is, the partial favor and disfavor of parents towards their offspring. Parental favoritism springs, sometimes, from motives that are seemingly reasonable, as some children are possessed of dispositions much more attractive than those of others. But even where this difference is clearly seen, it concerns the parents to take heed that the bias of their hearts becomes not too visible in their conduct. It is no wonder that the venerable patriarch felt a superior degree of affection for the son, who, in regard to every thing morally excellent and lovely, was so manifestly above his brethren: nevertheless, the manifestation of the partiality, so reasonable in itself—*the coat of many colors*, for instance—led to consequences of the most tragical nature.

Happy would it be, however, if there were no parental bias but such as is founded on merit, as in the instance just mentioned: whereas it sometimes springs from causes that can afford it not the least shadow of excuse.—Of these I will name only two.

1st. Personal beauty, and especially female beauty, is frequently the ground of parental partiality. Notwithstanding that the mere possession of beauty neither implies merit nor gives promise of any real exellence, yet it often happens that the most beautiful of the daughters is, for that single reason, the most caressed by the ill-judging parents, who, on the same wretched principle, are the most negligent of the one that has the least personal comeliness. The unfeeling cruelty of this species of domestic favoritism is too obvious to need remark: its results are unhappy every way. Even the favorite herself is a great loser, for in proportion as her vanity is fostered, and by *such* hands, every estimable quality, that might grow up in her mind under proper culture, is stifled. On the other hand, the smothered discontents and heart-burnings of the children who lie under unmerited neglect, and their feelings of envy toward the favorite, are the seeds which often burst up finally into violent and interminable contentions.

Parental discretion acts a part quite different from that which has now been described. It warns and admonishes her to whom nature has been lavish in personal attractions, and teaches her betimes not to value herself upon them; while it encourages those of the family that possess the least of personal comeliness, by imprinting it upon them that the due cultivation of their intellectual and moral faculties will make them respectable and respected.

2d. There is another species of favoritism practised by

parents, which, if not so common, is yet more reprehensible: it is treating the prosperous child with fond attention, and the unprosperous one with cold neglect. Worldly prosperity is no evidence of merit, nor adversity of demerit. It often happens that of the members of the same family, having in their outset in life the like prospects—it often happens that some come to wealth, whilst others are cast into the shades of poverty, through misfortune rather than from any faultiness in their own conduct. In cases of this sort, the partiality of parents, if it be allowable at all, should lean to the unfortunate child: at least, they are bound by the ties of nature and duty to show quite as much attention to the unfortunate, as to the fortunate part of their offspring. And it would be a libel upon parents to say, that, in general, the tide of their affection flows or ebbs according as their children make out well or ill in the world. The thing is not common, nor yet is it very rare. There are few persons of considerable age and observation, who have not witnessed it in more than one instance. And whenever and wherever this happens, it excites emotions of disgust and abhorrence. When the unfortunate son is treated with coldness, because he has been unfortunate, and is poor; when the unfortunate daughter, along with her needy little ones, is neglected and in a manner forsaken—not by the world only, but by father and mother—when persons bearing the sacred name of parents, are kind only to those of their children who need not their kindness, and forsake those who need it most—when such a horrible thing is seen in the land, it is seen to be detested.

NUMBER XLIX.

OF THE INESTIMABLE BENEFITS OF LAW.

Of all human institutions, that of *Law* is of primary importance. The benefit of government consists not so much in its being a guard against external, as against internal violence. For it is not certain that a people living without government would be invaded from abroad; but it is quite certain that they would invade, pillage, and murder one another at home. In every age, and in every country, man, unfettered by law, has been a tiger to man. Not that, at all times and in all countries, there have not been some persons, inclined of their own free will to do aright, but their number and strength have never been sufficient to stem the torrent of violence without aids from the arm of civil government. So far from it, where anarchy has prevailed, the more virtuous have ever been its marked victims.

If we trace back the stream of time as far towards the source as there are any lights furnished us from history, we shall find that no tyranny has been so horrible as that of anarchy. In the antediluvian ages, in which no regular government of general extent was, perhaps, known, " the earth was filled with violence." Those *giants*, those *men of renown*, so termed by the sacred penman, were, there is reason to think, daring and mighty robbers, who, at the head of their companies of bandits, traversed the countries, committing pillages, murders, and violence wherever they went.

In the patriarchal ages there were men of exalted piety, who ruled well their own children and domestics. But even then, well-regulated civil government was scarcely known any where: else the most venerable patriarch could hardly have been so distressed with fear for the honor of his wife, and lest he should, himself, be murdered on her account, when they were journeying together to Egypt, which at that time was the most renowned for arts and sciences of any country in the world. There were periods of the like anarchy and its horrible concomitants in the history of the tribes of Israel; when "every man did that which was right in his own eyes;" when "the highways were unoccupied, and the travellers walked through by-ways," for fear of the swarms of robbers and murderers that infested the country.

In the *Heroic Ages* of ancient Greece, there was very little of government or law; mere brutal strength, united with ferocious courage, being the only passport to eminence. Theseus and Hercules were renowned and deified for their valorous exploits against robbers. Not that they themselves were scrupulous of committing robbery and murder every now and then; but they were renowned and deified, because they had been the means of extirpating a race of banditti, more execrable than themselves.

The age of chivalry, in modern Europe, bore a considerable resemblance to the heroic ages of Greece. Chivalry, or knight-errantry, had its origin in the deplorable condition in which the countries of Europe were placed. The knights-errant, or roving knights, were professedly the protectors of the weaker part of the community, and particularly of the fair sex, whose champions they pretended to be, and whose ravishers they very often were. The licentiousness of manners, during the anarchical age of chivalry, was, if we may credit the fragments of its history, both general, and shockingly enormous.

Even so far forward as the ninth century, there was no public maritime law in Europe; and in consequence of this lawless condition of the seas, piracy was not only tolerated, but held in honor. The petty sovereigns of the nations upon the Baltic, provided each of their sons with a ship or ships, and enjoined it upon them to make their fortunes by piracy and plunder.

There is an instance comparatively recent, and yet bearing an affinity to those that have been adduced above. Scotland, it is well known, is at present, and long has been, one of the most moral countries in the world: yet, only three centuries ago, for want of a stable government, it was a land of robbers and ruffians.

Camden, in his Britannia, speaking of the robberies committed by the Scotch Borderers, in the sixteenth century, says: "They sally out of their own borders, in the night, in troops, through unfrequented by-ways, and many intricate windings.—All the day-time, refresh themselves and their horses in lurking-holes they had pitched upon before, till they arrive, in the dark, at those places they have a design upon. As soon as they have seized upon the booty, they, in like manner, return home in the night, through blind ways, and fetching many a compass. The more skilful any captain is to pass through those wild deserts, crooked turnings, and deep precipices, in the thickest mists and darkness, his reputation is the greater, and he is looked upon as a man of an excellent head. And they are so very cunning, that they seldom have their booty taken from them, unless sometimes, when, by the help of bloodhounds, following them exactly upon their tracks, they may chance to fall into the hands of their adversaries. When, being taken, they have so much persuasive eloquence, and so many smooth and insinuating words at command, that if they do not move their judges, nay, even their adversaries (notwithstanding the severity of their natures), to have mercy, yet, they incite them to admiration and compassion."

Two important particulars clearly follow from these historical sketches. The one is, that since we live in an age of regulated government and superior civilization, in which life, character and property are well secured by law, we cannot too highly prize those blessings: and the other, that it behooves all persons, possessing any regard for religion, or morals, or even for their own personal interests, to use their best endeavors to preserve social order, and to set their faces steadfastly against all wanton violations of good and wholesome laws. Neither is it an unimportant part of *Christian* education, to teach and habituate children to prize and venerate the wholesome institutions of government and law.

In a free republican government, such as ours, the laws are not only *for* but *from* the people, and it is indispensably requisite that its youth should have a general knowledge of its constitution, and of the most interesting parts of its code of civil and criminal law; since without it they will be poorly qualified to act their parts properly as freemen, either in a public or even in a private capacity. Not to mention that some hapless youth, now in vile confinement, might have been deterred from the transgressions which brought them thither, had they been seasonably and fully aware of the penalties that would be incurred by such transgressions.

The Prussian Frederick the Great is said to have remarked, that the laws of a whole realm might be comprised in a pocket volume. And so it might be in an absolute despotism; but in a free, and rich commercial country, the laws must needs be voluminous, and the professors of law numerous. This body of men, whatever be their aberrations in any other respects, have ever been found the strenuous advocates and powerful defenders of civil liberty. The reason is obvious, and a cogent one: it is only in a free country that the lawyers can obtain wealth and consequence; for where the judges are the creatures of a despot, it is not the pleading of the advocate that avails, but the bribe of the client.

Before I end, it is proper to mention the absolute necessity of an impartial and a vigilant administration of the laws, without which they are useless, and sometimes worse than useless. And here, instead of argument, I will merely transcribe a wholesome anecdote from Malcom's History of Persia.

From the year 1757 until the period of his death in 1778, Carim Khan reigned, with great reputation, over the whole of Persia, with the exception of two provinces. Carim one day was on the point of retiring from his judgment seat, harassed and fatigued with a long attendance, when a man rushed forward in apparent distraction, calling out in a loud voice for justice.—

"Who are you?" said Carim. "I am a merchant," replied the man, "and have been robbed and plundered, by thieves, of all I possess."—"What were you about," said the prince, "when you were robbed?—"I was asleep," answered the man.—"And why did you sleep?" exclaimed Carim, in a peevish and impatient tone.—"Because," said the undaunted Persian, "I made a mistake, *and thought you were awake.*"

NUMBER L.

OF A DISPUTATIOUS TEMPER AND HABIT.

It is a saying often quoted as Dr. Franklin's, that "by the collision of different sentiments, sparks of truth are struck out, and light is obtained." But it seems to have been current, though in another manner of phrase, before it came from the pen of the justly celebrated Doctor. In an Almanac, dated one hundred and fourteen years back, I have met with the following homely but pithy verse:

> "But quill to quill, like flints on steel do smite,
> Which kindle sparks, and those sparks give us light."

On the other hand, a writer possessed of masterly powers of reasoning, who flourished in the beginning of the last century, appears to have thought that disputing, whether by means of the quill or otherwise, is apt to produce a great deal less of light than of heat and smoke.

Mr. Locke, in his Treatise on Education, observes, "If the use and end of right reasoning be to have right notions and a right judgment of things; to distinguish betwixt truth and falsehood, right and wrong, and to act accordingly, be careful not to let your son be bred up in the art and formality of disputing."— And, as a reason for that conclusion, he goes on to describe the wretched manner in which disputes were generally managed:— "Whether pertinent or impertinent, sense or nonsense, agreeing with or contrary thereto, what he had said before it matters not: for this, in short, is the way and perfection of logical disputes, that the opponent never takes any answer, nor the respondent ever yields to any argument. This, neither of them must do, whatever becomes of truth or knowledge, unless he would pass for a poor, baffled wretch, and lie under the disgrace of not being able to maintain whatever he has once affirmed, which is the great aim and glory of disputing."

Here we find a "collision of different sentiments" on the very question whether disputing tends to advance correct knowledge or to retard it.

Now, to do justice to both sides, it must, I think, be granted that each is in the right, provided allowance be made for the opposite views in which the subject presents itself. Were disputing conducted as it ought to be, with sincere and paramount love of truth, and a benignity of temper, there might spring from it much good, without any considerable mixture of evil. But conducted as it most commonly has been, with acrimonious feeling, and the fierceness and obstinacy of pugilists, rather than with the honest candor that is willing in all cases to yield to evidence, it too often serves but to exasperate and mislead; so that nothing is less desirable in youth, or less to be encouraged, than a disputatious or cavilling temper.

In certain memoirs of the life of Frederick the Great, it is related that, aspiring after the fame of a philosophical reasoner, he was much inclined to exercise his talents, now and then, in disputing with the learned men of his court. Accordingly, he used, at his leisure, to send for the philosophers whom he kept in waiting, to reason with them; professing, the meanwhile, that he laid by the monarch, and put himself on an equal footing with them, and encouraging them to be free and do their best. But if any one of them happened to invalidate his arguments, or to get the better of him in any way, he instantly flew into a violent passion, and bestowed upon the offender the most scurrilous epithets. The memoirs further relate, that at one of his literary entertainments, when, in order to promote free conversation, he reminded the circle that there was *no monarch present*, the conversation chanced to turn upon the faults of different governments and rulers. General censures were passing from mouth to mouth, with a kind of freedom which such hints were calculated, and apparently intended, to inspire. But Frederick presently put a stop to the topic, exclaiming, "Hold your peace, gentlemen, be upon your guard, *else the king will be among you.*" This instance, while it speaks the imperious, insolent despot, is characteristical of our general nature. Of disputants, in all ages of the world, there have been but few that were scrupulous of using all the means in their power to baffle, bear down, and silence their opponents; but few, whose unfairness of manner and bitterness of temper have not furnished clear proof that they were more actuated by the proud desire of victory, than by a sincere regard to truth; very few, who have shown themselves willing, in all cases, to give truth fair play. Contrariwise, men, that are naturally, or by custom, of a disputatious temper, seldom are so for truth's sake. Generally, something else than the love of truth has the strongest hold of their hearts.

Perilous, in this respect, is the moral condition of that class of men, whose professional business of disputing, and whose fame and renown, depend upon success in gaining their causes, just or unjust.

"*An indiscriminate defence of right and wrong, contracts the understanding, while it corrupts the heart.*" This short sentence of the celebrated Junius, is deserving of the serious attention of young men of ingenuous dispositions, who have recently entered, or are about entering, upon the profession of the law. One, accustomed to argue indiscriminately for and against truth and right, and whose main road to distinction lies in his talent "to make the worse appear the better reason," needs, of all men, to keep a careful watch over his moral frame.

Theological disputes are of a nature, that would seem to secure them from the aberrations incidental to those of worldly men. The theologian stands upon hallowed ground. Truth, *Divine Truth*, is his pole-star. The inspired volume is his directory; of which he must not wittingly misconstrue any part for the sake of gaining his argument, or even though he might gain by it the whole world. His case is similar to that of the Persian judges, who were made to interpret the laws of the realm with ropes about their necks, as indicative of the punishment that awaited them if found guilty of any wilful misinterpretation. And besides, as truth must be his sole aim, so his manner of defending it must be consonant to the spirit of Him, who was "meek and lowly in heart"—who, "when he was reviled, reviled not again." Wherefore, in that sacred department, if any where, it might be expected that disputes would be conducted with the utmost fairness, and with exemplary benignity of temper. Would it were always so!

"The man who, in controversy, pays a strict regard to truth and candor, gives clear evidence of the excellence of his understanding and the uprightness of his heart; whereas, sophistry and quibble, rancorous invective and scurrilous abuse, warrant a suspicion of the advocate, however righteous be his cause."

NUMBER LI.

OF OVERDOING IN GOVERNING CHILDREN.

As nothing more clearly evidences the weakness of a legislature than a strong propensity to multiply laws beyond what real and absolute need requires, so also is it in regard to domestic government. In families, as well as in larger communities, there often is too much Law. A few rules are necessary for the government of children, and but a few. These should be too plain to be misunderstood; too reasonable to admit of any dispute or doubt; and too important to be violated or neglected. They should be engraven early upon the memories of the children, and enforced, when need requires, with steady and inflexible firmness;—and, by and by, they will grow into habits. Submission and obedience will become natural and spontaneous.

Children managed in this manner from infancy, and by parents, too, whose examples comport with their rules and injunctions, and whose exercise of authority carries along with it evident marks of tender affection ;—children reared up under this steady, mild, and yet firm discipline, soon become tractable, except in extraordinary instances of perverseness. They feel the yoke to be easy, and are withheld from acts of disobedience, more out of filial love and respect, than from the dread of chastisement. Hence it is, that in some houses, family government goes on with singular regularity, though so silent as to be scarcely perceived. There is no violent scolding; no boisterous threats; no fierce looks. Both the father and the mother are so mild and even in temper and behavior, that they seem scarcely to display any authority at all; and yet, their children are orderly, submissive, and dutiful, in a very uncommon degree. A single word, or a mere glance of the eye, from either parent, they mind more than the children of some families do the pelting of hard blows.

Neither is it the only advantage of this method of family government, that it accomplishes its object the most effectually, and with the least trouble;—there is another of equal, if not of greater moment. Children thus managed are led to delight in the company and conversation of their parents, and to receive counsel readily from their lips: and when they come of age to act for themselves, the transition from the state of subjection to that of personal independence is easy and scarcely perceivable. They don't feel like emancipated slaves. They are not intoxicated with liberty, but enjoy it soberly; still looking back, with mixed emotions of respect and love, to the salutary discipline they had been under, and still accustoming themselves to consult their parents, and to receive their advice with deference.

Nothing, indeed, is more clear, than that the simplest government is the best for children; and yet this plain matter of fact is often overlooked, and that too, by some of excellent minds and hearts. Many parents of good sense and great moral worth, fearful of failing in their duty by not governing enough, run into the opposite extreme. They maintain a reservedness, a distance, a stateliness toward their children, who hardly dare to speak in their presence, and much less to manifest before them any symptoms of the gayety of their youthful hearts. They encumber them with a multitude of regulations; they tire them with long lessons of stern monition; they disgust and alienate them with a superabundance of sharp reproof; they treat their little levities as if they were heinous crimes. Instead of drawing them with "the cords of love," they bind them fast with cords that are galling and painful.

This mistaken, though well-intentioned manner of family government, is very apt to draw after it several unhappy consequences. Children so brought up, how much soever they fear their parents, do rarely love them very much. However much they respect their virtues, they seldom yield them the warm affection of their hearts. Of some, it breaks the spirits, and renders them unenterprising, tame and servile, in all the succeeding periods of their lives. Others, who have more native energy of mind and stiffness of heart, it makes exceedingly restless; and whenever these can get aside from parental inspection, they are particularly rude and extravagant in their conduct. With longing eyes, they look forward to the day of emancipation from parental authority, as to a jubilee; and when the wished for time has come, they are like calves let loose from their stalls. The transition is so great and so sudden, that it wilders them;

and it often happens that their ruin is involved in the first use they make of their freedom.

They are wide of the true mark in family government, who make a mighty bustle about it. In their laudable attempts to excel in that way, they spoil all by overdoing.

NUMBER LII.

OF PROCRASTINATION.

THE nation from which we derive our language, has been distinguished, perhaps above all others, for steady, persevering industry; and several English old sayings, or proverbs, correspond with this prominent feature of national character. One of these ancient sayings of English origin, is, " Never put off till to-morrow what may be done to-day." On the contrary, sluggishness and procrastination are national attributes of the Spaniards, who, though acting with great spirit and vigor whenever roused to action, continue slothful and dilatory at all other times. Nor is it a little remarkable, that there is a Spanish proverb directly of opposite meaning to the English one, just now mentioned. Laborde, in his View of Spain, affirms it to be a Spanish proverbial maxim, " That one should never do to-day what may be put off till to-morrow."

Whether it be owing to nature, or to education and habit, or from whatever cause else it may spring, there is, in this goodly country, a prevailing disposition to follow the last of these two opposite maxims; though we are all ready to admit the reasonableness of its contrast. No infatuation is more deplorable, nor yet more general, the whole Christianized world over, than the vain hope that leads us to put off, from day to day, the great work which must be done, or ourselves be for ever undone. But I am now to speak not of the common and most deplorable infatuation which relates to the concerns of immortality, but of that which concerns our temporal interests.—Of the fatal error of the former, the Holy Volume and the Pulpit give solemn warning; —of some of the mischiefs of the latter, it is mine to treat in this short essay.

Few things are more ruinous, even to our secular affairs, than customary procrastination. It confuses and blights every kind of worldly business; for business not attended to in the proper time and season, is either not done at all, or done with more labor and difficulty, and to less purpose.

Some men are in the practice of letting their accounts lie unsettled for several years together. It is no matter, forsooth; they are near neighbors and close friends, and can come to a reckoning at any time. At length, a settlement between them commences. The accounts of each, however honest, are swelled beyond the expectation of the other. On both sides, several items have vanished from the remembrance of him who is charged with them. A warm dispute ensues; perhaps an arbitration; peradventure an expensive lawsuit; and these close friends are severed for ever.

Some men neglect to make their *Wills*, though they know their estates would be inherited contrary to their own minds and to the rule of equity, if they should chance to die intestate. Knowing this, and sincerely wishing that right may be done to their heirs, they are fully determined to perform the necessary act and deed, some time or other. "But why just now? Another time will do as well." And thus they delay the thing from year to year, till, at the last, the time of doing it is gone by; a precious widow, or a beloved and deserving child, is left to suffer, through life, the bitter consequences of this default.

Some farmers double their labor, and lose half their profits, for want of doing things in the proper season. Their fields are overgrown with bushes and thorns, all which a little *seasonable* labor might have prevented. Their fences, and even their buildings, are neglected, till the cost of repairs becomes increased several fold; besides their sustaining a train of inconveniences, and of serious injuries from the neglect.—And so, also, their crops cost more labor, and at the same time are leaner in bulk, or inferior in quality, by reason that much of the labor that had been bestowed upon them, was out of season. Nor is it uncommon to see farmers of this sort in a mighty hurry and bustle. They are behind their business, and running to overtake it, which is the cause of their being so often in a greater hurry than their neighbors.

Many a one loses his custom, as a mechanic, by not doing his work in season. It makes no odds, he thinks, whether the thing be done precisely at the time agreed upon—but so think not his customers.

What does not a merchant lose in custom, in credit, and in cash, by neglecting his books, though it be only for a few months or for a few weeks? How hard does he find it to set to rights what might easily have been kept right, if he had done the work of each day within the day.

Honest Jonathan borrows a sum of money of his particular friend, on the express promise of scrupulous punctuality in repaying it. He gets the money by the day of payment, but being busy here and there, he delays to carry or send it. The money happens to be sorely wanted the very day it becomes due;—and, with that particular friend, Jonathan's borrowing credit is utterly lost.

His Reverence,—a clergyman of no mean abilities, appears below himself in the pulpit, merely from his having got into the practice of delaying preparations for the Sabbath to the very last of the week, when, not unfrequently, company unexpectedly falls in, or he unexpectedly is called out: so that a considerable proportion of his sermons, composed in the hurry of his spirits, bear no great analogy to the "*beaten oil*" of the sanctuary. A reversal of merely *timing* his preparations, would contribute as well to the comfort of the respectable gentleman himself, as to the edification of his hearers.

Doctor —— possesses undoubted skill in his profession, but loves talk better than practice. Called away in a case of pressing emergency, he sets out with speed; but meets an old acquaintance, to whom he opens a budget of news and politics, which takes up half an hour in the relation; and by the time he arrives, all is over. Half an hour sooner, and his patient might have been saved.

Violent pains and feverish chills seize us. If they go not off, we will send for a physician to-morrow. Ere to-morrow arrives the distemper gains a firmness of fixture that baffles the physician's skill.

One instance more, and a common one.—" Not *ready*," says the sharp-eyed lawyer, when the court is in waiting, and the patience of the witnesses is tired with long attendance.—And why not ready? Procrastination lies at the bottom. Here, however, procrastination itself turns to good account. The case is laid over, and the fees are augmented,—it is only the pigeons that are plucked.

NUMBER LIII.

OF THE WELL-INFORMED.

What has been commonly termed the Republic of Letters, till a late period had been no other than a monopolizing and an overbearing aristocracy. The precious treasure was in the possession of only a few, who, with miserly feeling, locked it up from the mass of the people; communicating of it merely to one another, and to their select pupils.

"Knowledge that is hid, and treasure that is locked up, what profit is in them both?" This question of the ancient sage, that penned the book of Ecclesiasticus, carries its own answer along with it.

Of very little profit indeed to the world, were those philosophers of antiquity, whose philosophy was either wrapped up in mystery, or withheld from all but the initiated few. For as gold is of no service while it remains hoarded, and is made serviceable only when put in circulation, so also intellectual treasure can benefit mankind only in so far as it is generally diffused.

The *Art of Printing* produced an astonishing change in this important respect; a change that is still progressing, and that promises a most happy consummation. Ere its discovery, the whole rational world consisted of only two classes; namely, learned scholars and an illiterate vulgar; between which there was very little of fellowship, or of any thing in common. Whereas printing, by multiplying copies with so much ease, and furnishing books in such plenty and cheapness, soon began to break away that "middle wall of partition." Yet it was not till a considerably late period, that the tree of knowledge was brought fairly within the reach of the multitude.

From the beginning of the last century, and thence up to the present day, literature and science have advanced chiefly by *diffusion*. In the former ages, there were giants in the literary departments; men of iron constitutions of body and mind, who, by indefatigable industry and patience of toil, treasured up in their minds and memories such a prodigious abundance of learning as would now seem incredible. This race of *Anakim* is well nigh extinct, and of learning there are no living prodigies comparable to those of earlier time. Nevertheless, knowledge has rapidly progressed by the general spread of it. It being no longer confined to scholars by profession, or inherited exclusively by the lordly sex, there now are of both sexes very many readers, who without any pretensions to deep scholarship, have arrived to respectable degrees of information. The truth of it is, among those especially who speak the English tongue, there has risen up a *middle class*, aptly denominated *the Well-Informed*.

And who are *These*? These are persons who, though not to be ranked with men of deep scholastic lore, nor by any means affecting such distinction, are, notwithstanding, possessed of a fund of useful knowledge, whether for conversation, or for the various practical purposes of life. They are often found, in short, to have a great deal more of *general practical* knowledge than commonly falls to the lot of men of profound science or literature. For one who devotes himself to science alone, or to literature alone, however deeply intelligent in that single respect, must needs be ignorant as to most other things.

But the class of the Well-Informed requires a more particular description. By no means does it include all readers, and much less all that *can* read.

Of those who *can* read, the greater part make very little use of this inestimable advantage, and are very little the wiser for it. Again, of those who *do* read, a large proportion choose rather to be diverted or amused than instructed. They *are* diverted; they *are* amused; but enlightened or informed in any respectable measure they are not. There are great readers both male and female, who in no wise are well informed. Either their reading is chaffy and uninstructive, or they neglect to join with it the close exercise of their intellectual faculties; so that their judgments are not strengthened, nor their understandings enlarged, though an abundance of truths and facts are confusedly heaped together in their memories.

To attain the character of *well-informed*, one must read with prudent selection as to books; with an attentive exercise of one's own reason and judgment; with close application of thought;—and one must improve one's own mind, not by reading only, but also by a living intercourse with intelligent society. For it is not in abstraction from the world, but in the bosom of society—of well-regulated and well-informed society—that the mind enjoys the best opportunities for obtaining expansion and vigor. Here alone, it experiences a genial warmth, and powerful stimulations to laudable exertions. Here alone is it, also, that the fallacies and errors of its own crude conceptions are corrected by means of their frequent contact, comparison, and collision, with the conceptions of kindred minds.

The road is open. The means of information are so ample and so easy of access, that the reading youths of the present day seem to have it fairly in their power to become well-informed men and women. Two hours in the twenty-four, employed in well-directed intellectual industry, might suffice, in no very long course of years, for gathering a respectable treasure of valuable knowledge. A person who should walk only one hour, or three miles and a half, every day, would in the course of twenty years have travelled as many steps as would reach round the globe.

NUMBER LIV.

OF THE VAINNESS OF TRYING TO PLEASE EVERY BODY.

There is a happy medium betwixt the heartless disposition to please nobody, and the absurd aim to please everybody; and fortunate are they who find this middle line, and keep to it so steadily as seldom to run into the extreme on either side.

It is no good sign to be indifferent with respect to what the world thinks or says of us, since it would argue either a fulness of pride, or a total lack of sensibility. This would be the character of such indifference, were it real; but, in truth, it is mere affectation or pretence. If we except those that are at the very bottom of the scale of human life, and only a small proportion even of them, it may be fairly concluded that no man nor woman is altogether indifferent about the good or bad opinion of fellow beings. So far from it, the few, who lay claim to this unamiable distinction, have been found, generally speaking, peculiarly rancorous and vindictive toward such as had made free with their characters, or had merely spoken disrespectfully of their talents. No authors, for example, have writhed with more agony under the merited lash of criticism, or have been more jealous and vindictive, than some of those who pretended to look down with cold scorn upon the whole fraternity of critics.

Social qualities and feelings are among the primitive ingredients of our nature, and to divest ourselves of them would be to divest ourselves of humanity itself. They are rather to be cherished and cultivated, in every way, and by all lawful means. It is not only right, but laudable, to wish to be generally esteemed and beloved—to cultivate friendships—to avoid giving unnecessary offence—and to conform to the feelings and customs of those about us, so far as may be done with a good conscience, and consistently with one's personal circumstances. It is not only right, but laudable, to make it a part of our own pleasure to please others; and, when we are compelled to differ from them, to do it, if possible, without rancor or bitterness.

There is such a thing as a union of condescension and firmness, and a happy thing it is. To condescend in things indifferent, in things trivial, in things that touch not the conscience, nor seriously damage or endanger one's earthly interest and welfare; and meanwhile to go not a step farther for any persuasion whatever—no, not to please one's nearest friends—*that* is the golden mean. As some pretend to care for none, there are those, who, on the other hand, try to please all by becoming—not in the best sense—" all things to all men." Some do it from selfish designs altogether; and others from a too great persuadableness of temper and yieldingness of heart. The last can't bear, in any case, to be opposed or to oppose; and so they readily fall in with the sentiments and views of their present company, and side with every man they meet. Often this pliability of mind or temper is owing to a sort of amiable weakness, but it is destructive of all respectability of character.

I know not how to illustrate this point better than by the following story, which as to substance and pith may be regarded as undoubtedly true.

Some very long time since, Parson M——, of Massachusetts, (then a British colony,) happening at Boston, bought him a wig there, and returning home, wore it at church the next Sabbath. As a wig of such size and shape was quite a novelty in that obscure place, it gave offence to almost the whole congregation, who, both male and female, repaired the next day to their minister's house, and stated their complaint, the burden of which was, that the wig was one of the Boston *notions*, and had the look of fashion and pride. The good-natured minister, thereupon, brought it forth, and bade them fashion it to their own liking. This task they set about in good earnest, and with the help of scissors cropped off lock after lock, till, at last, they all declared themselves satisfied, save one—who alleged, that wearing any wig at all was, in his opinion, a breach of the commandment, which saith, "Thou shalt not make unto thee any graven image, or any likeness of any thing that is in heaven above, or that is in the earth beneath." This last objector Mr. M—— silenced, by convincing him that the wig, in the condition in which it then was, did not resemble any thing either above or below.

Even so fares it with the characters that make it their aim to please every body. Slashed on this side and on that, and twisted into every shape and out of all shape, they finally come to the condition of his Reverence's wig.

NUMBER LV.

ON THE EASINESS OF THE TRANSITION FROM CHRISTIAN CIVILIZATION TO COMPARATIVE BARBARISM.

THE philosophers of the last age expatiated often and largely on the felicitous condition of savages. Those simple children of nature, they held up to view as models of human excellence, and as possessing the greatest sum of human enjoyment. With minds unwarped by prejudice, and with hearts unsophisticated, and true to the genuine impulses of nature, their lives reflect, forsooth, the express image of primeval innocence. Knowing neither the galling fetters of law, nor the unnatural and odious distinctions of civilization, they, free as the air they breathe, roam their forests, or together enjoy the sports and pastimes of social intercourse, without obstacle or hinderance. And what though their dwellings are smoky cabins, or nothing better than dens and caves of the earth? What though their raiment, if raiment they have, is foul and squalid? And what though their scanty food is rancid and loathsome? No matter.

Being always accustomed to this way of living, they desire nothing better, and, without any repinings or discontent, they joyfully receive what nature gives. Happy savage! happy in comparison with civilized man, pining under the cruel power of prohibition, doomed to delve the earth or plough the ocean, the slave of artificial wants, the prey of ambition and avarice. Thrice happy savage! Threefold more happy than the child of restraint, of labor and of care; threefold more happy than the slavish muck-worm of civil society, maugre all his superfluous wealth, and his boasted arts and institutions.

Such were the dreams of former days—even of days not long past. But they are known now to be *but* dreams. Subsequent discoveries have confounded the philosophism of Rousseau, and put to shame the disciples of his school. *Many have run to and ro, and knowledge has been increased.* Great indeed, and far beyond all former example, has been the accession of knowledge, within the last forty years, respecting the habitants of our globe. Travellers and voyagers have traversed, as it were, the whole living world in every direction. New regions have been explored. Nations and tribes, formerly unknown or scarcely known, have been closely inspected; their morals, their manners, and their modes of living, carefully noted and accurately described.—And the results are unfavorable alike to the condition, and to the character of the mere child of nature. It is found that the dim lights, which are beheld here and there amidst the thick darkness of the pagan world, sprang from patriarchal tradition; that even in *civilized* countries, in no wise illumined with the rays of the gospel, the most abominable idolatries, and the most horrible practices in social and domestic life, are sanctioned by long and immemorial custom; and that the child of nature, the mere savage, "is every where found to be a restless, unfeeling, treacherous and ferocious animal."

There is one respect, however, in which philosophism has been not altogether in the wrong. It is, that the savage state is the most *natural*, that is to say, the most congenial with the depraved feelings and propensities of the human kind. Well-ordered, social institutions are mounds which virtue erects against vice, and which vice is ever struggling to demolish. Whereas, in what is called the state of nature, every man does what seemeth him good; indulging with little or no restraint in whatever his heart inclines him to. And of all things in the world, this is the sweetest; more gratifying than to be "clothed in purple, to drink in gold, and to sleep upon gold." Nothing is more natural to man than the love of liberty, or more delicious to his heart than the uncontrolled enjoyment of it;—of the liberty of doing as he pleases; of openly acting, in every way, and in all cases, according to his inclinations, without dread of punishment or fear of shame. Upon this liberty—which indeed is the only liberty for which our fallen nature has a sincere and an unreserved liking—the laws of regular government, the customs and opinions of virtuous society, and, above all, the institutes of a most holy religion, are galling checks.

Hence it is, in a considerable part, that the transition from civilization to savageness is much easier than from the latter condition to the former. Almost always, a savage feels a decided preference for his own way of life, and looks down upon the accumulated conveniences of civilized man, not with a cold indifference, but with utter disgust and contempt. Not for all the wealth that the world could confer, would he barter his liberty. If you take away a savage boy, and bring him into the bosom of civilized society, he pines for his native wilds. Though you feed, and clothe, and instruct him, and even caress him as your own child, he still pines with discontent. Or even if, perchance, you get him to be apparently satisfied with his new situation, after a short sojourn with savages, he becomes as much a savage as ever. But though the ascent is hard and painful, the descent is easy. A boy taken from civilized life, and made to live with savages, how soon he is identified with them, in feeling as well as in manners!—When brought back, after a few years, to his native home, how difficult, how next to impossible it is, to dissolve the charm that had fastened itself upon him; to cure him of his wildness; to make him steady, and industrious, and satisfied under the wholesome restraints of law and religion. It is not theory, but experience that speaks in this wise.

Nor are these the only instances with which experience furnishes us. There is one of much greater importance, and of far deeper interest; it is the apparent unconcern, not to say eagerness, with which multitudes of our countrymen recede from civilized life.—Look! what perpetual streams of emigration from the bosom of a civilized and religious society to the outskirts of the living world. Look! how new levies of the *forlorn hope* eagerly advance forward, year by year, beyond the last ulterior limits; leaving behind them regions of wilderness, thinly checkered, here and there, with marks of cultivation.

"The world is all before them where to choose."

See the population of an immense frontier,—a population of

millions "of our own color, flesh and blood,"—nearly as destitute of the means of moral and religious improvement as the savage "who yells on the banks of the Missouri"—without schools, without a ministry, without religious institutions, without the Sabbath, without Bibles; sunk and still sinking into the depths of moral debasement; their children growing up under the blasting influence of an unchristian culture, with scarcely any sense of moral or religious obligation!

Not that no part of the spectacle is cheering. The sight of so many frightful wilds, the dreary haunts of ravening beasts, turned into fruitful fields, is delightful, at the same time that it reflects credit upon the industry, the enterprise, the hardihood, and the perseverance of our countrymen. But it is advancing too fast. There are few, if any, even of those old settlements whose population is yearly drained away by thousands, which might not, by improved cultivation, by husbanding all their resources, and by returning to the plain living of former times, be made to support even a great increase of population, while their superior intellectual, social, moral, and religious advantages would much more than countervail any advantage obtainable by emigrating into foreign deserts. The emigrations are not, however, from the old settlements only. The roving spirit of the Tartar and the Arab, seems to have seized the Americans. Even when a recent frontier is scarcely populated in the proportion of the twentieth part of it, they begin to remove further out; as if it were the object nearest their hearts to recede as far as possible from the very appearance of civilization.

NUMBER LVI.

A COMMENT UPON A CELEBRATED ALLEGORY OF ANTIQUITY.

A celebrated ancient philosopher of the pagan school, has represented human nature under the similitude or analogy of a chariot drawn by two horses; the one of excellent mettle and lively motion; and the other sluggish and obstinate; so that while the former sprung forward, his mate hung back. And it must be owned that there is a striking aptness in this little allegory.

Of all the animals in the whole living world, none are seen to act inconsistently but those of Adam's race. The lower animals, acting from what we call blind instinct, are, nevertheless, uniform and consistent in their conduct; while we, who proudly lay claim to the high endowments of reason, run into inconsistencies and absurdities every day of our lives. We know the right, and approve it; we see the wrong, and condemn it; and after all, very often the right we reject or forsake, and the wrong we pursue.

This marvellous phenomenon, namely, the disjointed condition of human nature and the perpetual variance of man with himself, has been plainly visible in all ages; and oft and many a time, has mole-eyed philosophy puzzled herself in vain to account for it. It used to be thought by the engrossers of the wisdom of this world, that the mind and the body were unequally yoked together; that the former, being of celestial mould, was naturally inclined to mount upward, and that the latter ever checked the noble flights of its yoke-fellow, forcing it back to kindred earth. The wise son of Sirach seems to have been tinctured by this fashionable philosophy, when he remarked, "*The corruptible body weigheth down the soul.*"

For which reason, the body has met with hard usage among the religionists of different schools. The bigots of paganism, and the bigots of popery in the dark age, regarding their bodies as clogs to, and polluters of their nobler part, proceeded to treat these unworthy co-partners with unmerited scorn and cruelty.

Revelation, fairly understood, sets this whole matter in a clear light. In it we see whence sprang the strange inconsistency in human nature, and from it we learn that, as neither the soul can subsist in the present state without the body, nor the body without the soul, so they should live together in harmony—provided that the inferior be never permitted to get the upper hand, but be kept at all times in due subjection to its superior.

This allegory of Plato, aptly represents the strange disparity of the *Mind* and *Heart*, and the unnatural discord and strife so often existing between these two neighboring powers. And here I must premise that by the *mind* is meant the intellectual faculties, and by the *heart*, the turbulent tribe of appetites, passions, prejudices, and wayward volitions, as well as the benign family of moral virtues. The subject is no less prolific than interesting;—but here it must suffice barely to mention two prominent particulars.

1. Not unfrequently there are yoked together minds and hearts, very unequal as respects *natural* strength. Some have stout hearts, but feeble minds; what is called valor they possess in a high degree, but their understandings are dwarfish.

On the other hand, some men of large and powerful understandings, are devoid of valor, and even remarkable for their timidity.—Horace, the first of geniuses, threw away his shield in battle, and took to his heels. And Cicero, a man of a most luminous mind, had far less active courage than Pompey, who was many degrees below him on the intellectual scale.

2. There are some persons, strong in understanding, and yet weak to resist the impulses of passion and appetite; and this moral defect is fatal to their character and ruinous to their happiness. A firmness of *Will* to obey the dictates of reason, in despite of the din of clamorous appetites and passions, is the parent of every thing morally good and noble. On the contrary, if this strength be wanting to the heart, the highest degree of intellectual strength and brightness may be associated with the lowest degree of moral debasement.

How powerful, and almost seraphic the mind of Bacon! How pitifully weak the fortress of his heart! The reverse of this appalling picture may be seen in the life of him, whose memory we so delight to honor. A biographer of Washington remarks;—"Possessing strong natural passions, and having the nicest sense of honor, he was in early life prone keenly to resent practices which carried the intention of injury or insult, but the reflections of maturer age gave him the most perfect government of himself." His characteristic feature was a persevering resolution to act, on every emergency, according to his sense of right and duty.—And it is probable that there is no man, either among the living, or mentioned on the page of history, who followed more unswervingly the dictates of his profound and discriminating judgment, and of his enlightened conscience; and it is *that* which makes his character so peculiarly venerable.

"Illustrious man! deriving honor less from the splendor of his situation than from the dignity of his mind; before whom all borrowed greatness sinks into insignificance, and all the princes and potentates of Europe become little and insignificant. He has no occasion to have recourse to any tricks of policy or arts of alarm; his authority has been supported by the same means by which it was acquired, and his conduct has uniformly been characterized by wisdom, moderation and firmness."

Resolutely to deny, in all cases, one's appetites, passions and desires, when they are inconsistent with reason and duty, is a cardinal virtue in human character, which, however, is rarely seen in persons who were not disciplined to it in their early years. Wherefore, to lead its pupils to master their appetites and passions, is one of the essential arts of a good education; nor is any thing more necessary through the whole course of life, than to suppress and to subdue those rebellious emotions of the heart, which war against the law of the mind.

The goodness and wisdom of Providence, directed to the production of human happiness, puts the means, in a great measure, within our reach. "The efficacy of conduct of every sort does not depend so much on *force of understanding*, which is not in our power, as on *integrity of Will*, which is in our power."

NUMBER LVII.

OF FORGETTING OLD DEBTS, AND SHUFFLING OFF THE PAYMENT OF SMALL ONES.

There is a pretty large number of men in this country, who, though not of the Hebrew stock, do, nevertheless, cleave fast to that part of the old Mosaical law, which enjoins a *Release.* They think, or seem too think, that the debts owed by them are by so much the less binding, by how much the older they have grown; and that when they come to be *seven years* of age, they are of course cancelled in the chancery of equity and conscience. This is more particularly the case as respects *small* debts; about which a great many, otherwise of good memories, have a convenient lack of recollection.

The following story I have heard related as matter of fact.—No very long while since, A. lent his neighbor B. a small sum of money, to be repaid in one week. However, without any thing being said about it on either side, it ran on a whole year, when the lender asked for the money, and got a prompt renewal of the old promise of payment in a week's time. In the same way it was permitted to run on another year, when the loan was craved again, and again was the same promise renewed. At the end of the third year, A. solicited payment for the third time, and in the presence of a third person; and receiving naught but a new edition of the same fair promises, he expressed his determination of speedily doing himself justice, and went his way in a pet. B. was amazed at this uncourteous behavior—for they had ever before been loving friends—he was struck with amazement, and addressing himself to the said third person, remarked: "That neighbor of mine, sir, I must needs say, is a worthy man in the main, but, after all, he is an oddity. The trifling debt, do you see, is an old affair, an affair of several years' standing, and yet he duns me as hard as if I had borrowed the money but a month ago!"

It is a curious fact, of no very auspicious omen, that, while most other things have been growing dearer, promises have been growing cheaper. They have come to be like that kind of drug that operates speedily, or not at all. They become stale, as it were, by time; so that the longer the exaction of performance is forborne, the more difficult it is to obtain it. Hence small debts that have waxen old, are as bad as lost, being scarcely worth the trouble of collecting.

Nor is it altogether among the baser sort that this delinquency is found. You may find it among men of high standing, and of honorable feelings in most other respects. They would scorn the imputation of meanness, or falsehood, or roguery; but, nevertheless, permit themselves to forget their promises, especially in little matters, and the rather, perhaps, from thinking that their creditors, out of respect or fear, would as lief lose the debt as urge for payment in good earnest. It is found, often found, among men, mild in temper, courteous in their manners, kind and neighborly, hospitable in their houses, and, in short, of excellent reputations, save in this single particular. If you are in distress and need their charity, they will *give ;* but if they owe you, they will shuffle off payment without any regard to your interest or feelings.

Marvellous inconsistency ! Are they so blind as not to see that withholding just dues, of however small amount, is positive injustice ? That it scarce makes any difference on the moral scale, whether one filches from his neighbor, or intentionally withholds what belongs to him ? Are they unaware that it destroys their credit, and blots their reputation ? That it attaches to them a general suspicion of want of principle, or rather of wilful falsehood and dishonesty ? Are they unaware of the smothered indignation that burns in the bosoms of those they so lightly disappoint ? Of the hard and bitter things that are privately said of them, on this account, even by their friends ? Or, finally, are they unaware that the public interest suffers more from this species of evil than from all the theft and robbery committed in the land ; and that, if all men acted in this respect like them, there would be an end to private credit and mutual confidence ?

Small debts are entitled to be regarded as debts of honor. A man of strict honor, and competent means, will be particularly careful to discharge, spontaneously and punctually, those trifling debts, which it is so unpleasant even to ask for, and much more to *dun* for over and over again. A man of strict honesty will say not to his neighbor, " Go, and come again, and to-morrow I will pay," when he has it by him. Instead of which, it is his settled rule, as far as his circumstances will permit, to pay without delay, without hesitation, without grudging, without giving his neighbor the trouble and pain of repeated requisition and importunate solicitations.

NUMBER LVIII.

OF DEVOTEDNESS TO PLEASURE.

It is an irrefragable maxim, as well of experience as of revelation, that *He that loveth pleasure shall be a poor man.* Indeed scarce any maxim is so fully sanctioned by experience; since, in all ages, and among all ranks and classes, an inordinate love of pleasure has proved the certain road to want and ruin.

Most strikingly verified is this sacred text in the instances of drunkards and debauchees, who give up themselves, soul and body, to the embraces of pleasure, in her grossest and most disgusting forms. Always and every where, those profligates, after a short run, come out not merely poor men, but poor *creatures.* Inevitably, and very shortly, they become the poorest of the poor, alike destitute in circumstances, and contemptible in character; a burden to their friends, and a heavier burden to themselves.

Mark the young beginner in the career of profligacy; one not of the baser nor even of the commoner sort—a child of fortune. How accomplished! how blithe and jovial!

Mark him again in his next stage, when youth is just ripened into the maturity of manhood.

"If thou beest he, but O how fallen! how changed!"

See his bloated countenance, his livid cheek, his beamless eyes!

Once more, mark his mid-age. The crop is now fully ripe. See what it is!—squalid poverty, loathsome disease; bodily decrepitude and mental imbecility; alike loathsome and self-loathing.

Finally, mark his end. "This man of pleasure, when, after a wretched scene of vanity and woe, his animal nature is worn to the stumps, wishes and dreads death, by turns."—Now he is sick of life, and bitterly chides the tardiness of time:—anon he starts back with horror, lest the grave should not prove a "dreamless bed." The classes of downright drunkards and debauchees include, however, but a small proportion of the hapless mortals, whom the siren *Pleasure* allures to their ruin and destruction.

"Come on, let us enjoy the good things that are present. Let us crown ourselves with rose buds, before they be withered." With such language it is that the sorceress persuades and prompts the youthful heart · nor does she persuade and prompt in vain. The delicious poison insinuates itself, and spreads over the whole frame. The youth, thus infected, becomes unstable in all his ways. All close and steady application, whether to study or to business, he heartily loathes. Plodding industry of every kind, he regards with scorn. To make, as it were, a holiday of the whole year round, is the object of his desire, and the summit of his ambition. As years multiply upon him, his habits of fickleness are but the more riveted. He is within the circumference of a whirlpool, with a heart and mind too enervated to force his way back. Perhaps he remains, however, on the extremity, and never, in his whole lifetime, is drawn to the fatal centre, where is utter wreck of reputation, and of the whole moral frame. Perhaps he escapes the grosser vices. Perhaps no foul blot cleaves to his character, and the worst that can be said of him is, that he is a careless, imprudent, and improvident man, a devoted lover of jolly company; that he is here, and there, and every where, except at home and about his own proper business.

Lucky indeed, if he be no worse off; but lucky as he is, he must needs be *a poor man;* poor in worldly circumstances, and of a character almost worthless at the best. If he is left with a fortune, it melts away in his improvident hands. If he begins the world without fortune, he lays up nothing for sickness and old age; instead of which, he ever lives beyond his income by leeching his friends, and abusing the confidence of his creditors. If he have a family, his wife mingles her scanty meal with her tears, while their children receive little from him but an example that powerfully tends to lead them astray. In short, he is exactly such as no downright honest and honorable man would choose to be. If all were like him, poverty, wretchedness and misery, would pervade the whole fabric of human society.

It need scarcely be added, that a lover of pleasure (even one of the comparatively innocuous sort last mentioned) seldom enjoys his proportionable share of that commodity. At best, his empty pleasure is so mixed up with vexation of spirit, that he more abundantly feels the one than enjoys the other. Not to mention that an idle, useless life, however free from gross immorality, is in the sight of heaven a criminal life; it is burying the talent that ought to have been employed diligently, and to useful purposes.

We have received our earthly existence, not on conditions of our own prescribing, but on the conditions prescribed by Him who made us. With respect to the present life as well as the future one, it is to be expected that the quality of the harvest will be the same as that of the seed. If we eat up the seed, we prevent the crop. If we sow the tares of idleness and prodigality, we shall reap the tares of poverty and shame.—There is no such thing as abolishing, or bending, or evading the fixed laws of nature; whether we like them or not, they will go steadily into effect.

See you a young man diligent in his business, frugal, provident and sober? you see one who will be respected and respectable; who, in all probability, will enjoy, through life, at least a competence; and who will be a blessing to his family, to his friends, and to society at large. On the other hand, when you see young men idle, improvident, extravagant, averse from all regular and close attention to useful business, and practically saying in the general course of their lives, "Go to now, let us enjoy pleasure;"—you then see such as are speeding, if not into atrocious crimes, at least into the condition of beggarly want; such as will wring the hearts of fathers, mothers, wives, and children; such as will be *moths* upon society, rather than its useful and worthy members.

Even *worldly* interest imperiously requires self-denial. One who can deny himself nothing, will be good for nothing, however excellent be his talents, and however great his advantages. To teach youths the art of self-denial, is one of the essential branches of good education. That is best done by storing their minds, seasonably, with the precepts, prohibitions, and warnings contained in the Holy Bible. Next to this, they should, by all means, be kept from contracting habits of idleness and dissipation, and be so inured to some kind or other of laudable industry, that their very toil, whether of business or of study, will be at length a pleasure.

NUMBER LIX.

OF VANITY, AS MAKING PART OF THE WARP OF OUR GENERAL NATURE.

VANITY, or the undefinable human quality called by that name, being the subject now under consideration, the following plain little story is somewhat proper to open with.

The Baron de Tott, happening to come of a sudden into the company of a knot of Turkish ladies, who, from the usage of their country and the precepts of their religion, were in duty bound to be veiled always in the presence of strangers of the other sex ; he remarks in the book of his travels, that the elderly matrons made haste to veil themselves, but the young and the handsome remained with their faces uncovered for some time after his entrance.

Now, if this be a notable instance of *female* nature, it springs, nevertheless, from a principle belonging to the general nature of our species, and which operates with nearly equal force in both sexes. It is not Woman alone that is vain.—" Surely every *Man* walketh in a vain show"—at least in some one respect or other.

There is scarcely any single ingredient that more thoroughly pervades human nature, than the one that goes by the general name of Vanity. Hence it was to vanity that the cunning tempter addressed his temptations in the garden, with such deplorable success; and to vanity he addressed his temptations in the wilderness, where he was so signally foiled. He knew the weakest side of humanity, and there made his attacks.

The strange quality called vanity, is a particular modification of the general principle of selfishness, and is exactly the reverse of the scriptural precept, *Let each esteem other better than himself.* It would be difficult to define it, and still more difficult to describe it, in all its symptoms, and trace it throughout all its numerous branches: and yet, if you observe with a close and discriminating eye, it is impossible to mistake it; for to the mind's ken it is clearly visible, in its every shape, however undefinable and indescribable. Vanity is, as it were, "the froth of pride," and is distinguishable from downright, unmixed pride, which is stiff and unbending: whereas vanity is flexible, and bends any way, and every way, to set itself off. But though vanity is different in some respects from pride, it has in its nature, perhaps, quite as much selfishness; self-display being its constant and invariable object, or rather the pole star, towards which its every thought and every action tend.

Although the principal food of vanity is wealth, rank, learning, wit, beauty, eloquence, strength, valor, or the whatever something that distinguishes the individual from the multitude; yet it can live and thrive on food of almost every kind and nature. "We may see vanity living in a hovel, vanity clothed in rags, vanity begging by the way, vanity conjoined with bodily ugliness and deformity:" it is to be found as well in savage, as in civilized life; as well amongst the squalid and beggarly race of gypsies, as in polished society. In a word, it can find nourishment and gratification in all extremes; in the haggard looks and squalid habiliments of a hermit—provided they confer distinction—as much as in brocades, pearls and diamonds. It is quite as much gratified with the distinction of *humility*, as with that of loftiness and splendor. If a Cardinal of the Romish church is vain of the lofty title, *His Eminence*, the Greek Patriarch of Constantinople is, probably, no less vain of the humble title, *His Lowliness.* Nor was the vanity of the most lordly and aspiring of all the Popes of Rome, ever more gratified, perhaps, than when, under the gaze of the public, they were employed, upon their knees, in washing the feet of some of their beggarly vassals. In sober truth, vanity is never more conveniently lodged, than when she lies concealed under the disguise of extreme humility.

Sometimes, Vanity, to gain her point, disclaims even her own existence. *I say it without vanity—I speak it without the least ostentation*—is often made the prelude to self-commendation.

It is questionable whether man would be a *laughing* animal, if he were not a *vain* one But, without all question, it is vanity that most generally affects his risibles, when he laughs at his fellow-man.

In many instances, Public Virtue would never have gone so far, if Vanity had not borne it company. Jehu, for example, never had driven so furiously to carry forward a holy cause, had not Vanity ridden with him—" Come, see my zeal."

What is called liberality, frequently is nothing more than the vanity of giving. We are exceedingly prone to give (whenever we give at all), hoping to receive—if not in kind—at least in credit and honor. So, also, Vanity gives praise, in hope of receiving it back again with interest.

It is owing to vanity that we voluntarily endure unhappiness to appear happy; that we rob ourselves of necessaries, to appear as if our circumstances were plentiful and affluent. Many a one is at more expense in maintaining Vanity's brood than it would cost him to bring up, in a plain way, a family of children.

Vanity undervalues itself with a view to extort praise. "When any one," says Dr. Johnson, "complains of the want of what he is known to possess in an eminent degree, he waits with impatience to be contradicted."

Reproof is often given, not so much to mend the reproved, as to show that the reprover is free from the faults himself. Advice is often offered, rather to give the adviser the air of wisdom than to benefit the advised.

Secrets, oftentimes, are divulged more from the vanity of one's having been intrusted with them, than from any other motive.

As vanity, in different proportions, variously directed, mixed up with different elements, and displaying itself in different forms, is a universal quality or principle in mankind, so it belongs to our species exclusively perhaps. For we have no reason to think that, either above or below us, in the whole universe of God, there is any other race or order of creatures fully like to man in this respect. Nor man, nor woman, is there, who hath not so much as a little *spice* of vanity, either in external conduct, or in the secret folds of the mind and heart. In a moderate degree, this marvellous quality of our species, is not inconsistent with real and great moral excellence ; but in the extreme, or when it is the *master-principle*, it is *that plague* of the heart, which taints all the springs of action. Neither is there any thing more carefully to be guarded against, and nipped in the bud, in the course of early education. Because the extreme of vanity is of near kin to the extreme of avarice. The very vain person, like the very avaricious one, makes every thing centre in self, and will use as many low and vile tricks for applause, as does the other for wealth. Moreover, vanity, like avarice, commonly increases with age, and like that, the more plenteously it is fed, the more voracious grows its appetite.

NUMBER LX.

OF THE RUEFUL CONSEQUENCES OF LIVING TOO FAST.

FEW practical errors of a secular nature are of so innocent intention, and yet of so direful consequence, as that of *over living*, for the special sake of making a figure. The men and women, who are first the subjects of this error and then its victims, are not usually of the baser sort. This path, bordered on every side with precipices, is often gone into unawares at first. It is indiscretion mixed up with vanity, and that without a single particle of the corrupt leaven of intentional dishonesty, that leads men into it. But though overliving may, in its commencement, be owing to mere indiscretion combined with vanity, yet in its progress it becomes deserving of a far worse name. That is indeed a pernicious and mortal error, by which one puts himself into circumstances which, as it were, compel him to commit new errors increasing in magnitude as fast as in number.

The error I have been describing, would be not so direful if it admitted of an easy cure; but though there is an obvious remedy, yet, in some cases, to apply it in season requires uncommon fortitude. Indeed in the single state, or even in the married state while the children of the family are in their infancy, it is not very difficult to retrench inordinate expenses, provided the *twain* happen to be *one* as to opinion of the expediency of it;—a thing that might be as common, perhaps, as it now is rare, if husbands would only inform their wives in good season of the unprosperous condition of their worldly affairs. But through pride, false delicacy, or whatever motive else, wives are often held in ignorance of the true state of their family circumstances, till the moment that ruin breaks upon them; and then are they upbraided by the world for an extravagance, which they had not run into but for the bandage upon their eyes.

In families where the children, and particularly the daughters, are grown up, or nearly grown up, the impediments to a prudent retrenchment of expenses are multiplied. For though both father and mother see the absolute need of it, it is no easy matter to convince the youthful gentry of it, or to dispose them, if convinced, to sink, of their own free wills, from splendid young ladies, into plain, industrious, frugal girls. Their remonstrances, their entreaties, and especially their tears, it is hard to resist:—and so it happens that a great many continue to steer toward the fatal gulf, though it be clearly in their view.

When a man is once resolved to keep up expensive appearances till he can hold out no longer, his moral frame goes to wreck as fast as his circumstances. However honest, however trustworthy he may have been in his better days, he no longer possesses these estimable qualities, nor any just sense of honor. He casts about him for arts of shift and evasion. The perpetual duns at his door, he tries to satisfy with fair promises, which he has no expectation or intention of performing. His heart becomes callous toward his creditors, and he grows quite regardless of their feelings, however deplorably they have to suffer by him. Like a drowning man he catches at every thing. To gain a little respite, he will inveigle his near friend into suretiship for him, and will drag his friend along with him to ruin.

Poor human nature is seldom proof against strong temptations *voluntarily* run into; and as seldom, perhaps, in the instance under consideration as in any other. Nor are there any who are fairly entitled to promise themselves beforehand, that their integrity can stem the moral whirlpool, in which so many characters, once fair, have been overwhelmed.

An excellent rule has been laid down by the eminent moralist, Dr. Johnson; and it were to be wished, that young men, in particular, would remember it, and make a practical use of it at the outset of active life. The rule is this—" A man's *voluntary* expenses should not exceed his income." A huge mass of misery and mischief might be prevented, were it the general custom to adhere to this maxim.

Honest young householders, ye that are now beginning life together in the wedded state, guard with particular care against *the lust of the eye.* Of all our senses, that of eye-sight seems to have the nearest affinity with the heart, and the most often to lead it astray. The philosophers of antiquity were so sensible of this, that, to concentrate and rectify their ideas, one of them, *Democritus*, was said to put out his eyes, and another, *Pythagoras*, to shut himself up a whole winter in a subterraneous cave.

Now though, fortunately for our age and country, these examples are as destitute of admirers as of followers, yet the exercise of constant watchfulness over the eyes was never, and nowhere, more needful; the common folly of large expenses where there is but small income, being committed, for the most part, rather to please the eye than from any other motive—and not so much for the sake of the spender's eyes, as to attract the eyes of others.

NUMBER LXI.

OF BANQUETING UPON BORROWING.

"Be not made a beggar by banqueting upon borrowing, when thou hast nothing in thy purse."—ECCLES. xviii. 38.

THE moral philosopher of old Jewry, who penned this admirable book, is *practical* in his observations, and, at the same time, acute and discriminating. He dips not into the incomprehensible subtleties of abstract science, relative to the mysterious frame and texture of humanity, but describes the wonderful creature, *Man*, such as he is shown to be by his actions, and adapts his moral and prudential cautions and precepts to man, *as he is*—to his condition and conduct in real life.

Whether the sage had himself been taken in by some of them, or from whatever cause, he hits off certain borrowers of his own time with a peculiar keenness of description, in the passage that here follows.

" Many, when a thing was lent them, reckoned it to be found, and put them to trouble that helped them. Till he hath received, he will kiss a man's hand; for his neigbor's money he will speak submissively; but when he should repay, he will prolong the time, and return words of grief, and complain of the time. If he prevail, he shall hardly receive the half, and shall count as if he had found it: if not, he hath deprived him of his money, and he hath gotten him an enemy without cause: he payeth him with cursings and railings; and for honor he will pay him disgrace."

The sage next proceeds to relate how the aforesaid conduct of some certain borrowers went to discourage all liberality in lending. "Many therefore have refused to lend for other men's ill-dealing, fearing to be defrauded."

And here one might amuse himself not a little with comparing the past with the present—things relative to borrowing and lending, as they stood some thousand years ago, with what they are now-a-days, in this goodly country of ours.

But to proceed: our venerable author is not as a cold-blooded satirist, who rather labors to excite the feelings of scorn and hatred, than of compassion. He gives, on the contrary, no countenance to covetous hoarding;—much less to griping extortion. He saith not, "Since things are so, it is best to trust nobody." No. So far was this ungracious sentiment from the heart of the son of Sirach, that he warmly inculcates a noble liberality, a disinterested benevolence. For after having observed, that *many refused to lend for other men's ill-dealing, fearing to be defrauded*, he immediately adds, "Yet have thou patience with a man in poor estate, and delay not to show him mercy. Help the poor, for the commandment's sake, and turn him not away, because of his poverty. *Lose thy money for thy brother and thy friend, and let it not rust under a stone to be lost.*" Again, in the same chapter he says, "He that is merciful will lend unto his neighbor."—"Lend to thy neighbor in the time of his need." And elsewhere, he cautions against a churlishness of expression and manner in the act of giving, and by parity of reason, in lending. " My son, blemish not thy good deeds, neither use uncomfortable words when thou givest." All which is accompanied with this wholesome injunction to the other party. " Pay thou thy neighbor again in due season. Keep thy word, and deal faithfully with him, and thou shalt always find the thing that is necessary for thee."

Upon the whole, then, it may be fairly concluded, that the precious book now under consideration—which indeed possesses every venerable attribute, with the exception of inspiration alone —is very far from altogether discouraging the neighborly intercourse of borrowing and lending; seeing that the scope of its lessons on this subject, is to recommend moderation and scrupulous punctuality to the one class, and a humane and generous line of conduct to the other.

One may borrow occasionally, and be the better for it, and, at the same time, the lender suffer no injury or inconvenience: but to *banquet* upon borrowing, is a beggarly way of living. *If thou hast nothing in thy purse*, replenish it, if possible, with thy own earnings, rather than by borrowing; or if that be impossible for the present, yet be cautious against borrowing more than is needful, and ever be careful to pay it back in due time. For— to repeat the admonition before cited—" Pay thou thy neighbor again in due season. Keep thy word, and deal faithfully with him, and thou shalt always find the thing that is necessary for thee."

I entreat the reader's particular attention to the matter which I have just now rehearsed, since it comes from no ordinary authority, and is of superior excellence in itself. For the rest, the few observations that will follow, must suffice.

In the simple old times of our author, borrowing for a premium, or on interest, was scarcely known. So that they who, in those days, banqueted on borrowing, must have done it only in a small way, which bears no sort of comparison with the every day's experience of the present age. This thing has, with us, been carried to a wild extreme, utterly unknown to any former age, or in any other country; and a frightful mass of wretchedness has been the natural consequence. But passing this over, what remains is to consider the subject of borrowing, on the small scale, and according to the most general acceptation of the word.

In this sense of the term, one who borrows, contracts a debt, with respect to which every principle of honesty and honor binds him to observe the utmost punctuality. For the lender gives up the use of his property without fee or reward. All he demands or expects is, that the thing be returned in good condition, and punctually, according to promise. Wherefore, a loan is a sort of *sacred* debt; and to delay payment—much more never to pay though there be no want of power, is returning evil for good, injury for kindness. Would that this vexatious frailty of character were rare as it is common! In order to a radical reform in this important particular, much attention must be paid to it in the early season of education. It is a great deal easier to form the young mind to correct habits, than to cure it of bad ones once contracted. For which reason, children should be carefully taught to mind their promises, and to restore whatever they borrow, in good condition, and by the set time. Nor is it enough merely to give them precepts upon this subject; it must be worked into their practice, even from their earliest years.

In conclusion, there is one description of borrowers, who may fitly be termed *leeches* or *sponges*. These are persons who, out of pure stinginess, are in the habit of borrowing of their neighbors the necessary implements of their daily business. They think it cheaper to borrow than to buy, but generally, in the long run, they are losers by it themselves; and meanwhile, in this way, they are giving a deal of trouble to those about them, whose smothered resentments are neither few nor small.

NUMBER LXII.

OF THE PRINCIPLE OF SHAME.

No point is more clear, than that moral worth is superior to every thing else which bears the name of worth; that virtue in rags is more respectable than vice in brocade.

"In the drama of life it is not to be considered who among actors is prince or who is beggar, but who acts prince or beggar best." So taught Epictetus, a celebrated philosopher of ancient Greece; and Pope has versified him in the following couplet.

> "Honor and shame from no condition rise:
> Act well your part; 'tis there true honor lies."

All this is well said. That the point of honor lies, not so much in having a grand or a conspicuous part to act, as in acting well the part that Providence allots us, is a position that admits of no dispute. But although it contradicts the theory of almost nobody, it is contrary to the practice of almost every body.

He that acts upon the stage of life a high part, will be courted, and he that acts a low part will be slighted; though the latter should very far excel the former in all that relates to the qualities of the heart. The man that comes in with the gold ring, and in goodly apparel, is respectfully invited to sit here, in a good place; while the child of poverty, whose raiment is vile, is ordered to sit there, at the foot-stool; and that without any regard to real merit or demerit. This is the fashion of the world; a fashion which all do more or less follow.

It would in nowise be difficult to carry this train of thoughts to any reasonable length; since the subject is no less prolific, than evincive of the distempered condition of the world we live in. But all that I further intend, is to remark, in few words, on *shame*—understood not in the sense here given it by the poet, as synonymous with dishonor or disgrace; but as denoting a certain kind of bosom sensation, utterly indescribable, and yet most clearly distinguishable from every other feeling of the heart.

Shame then, meaning the *sense* of shame, is one of the powerful principles of our fallen nature; and, like our other natural principles, it does good or mischief according to the direction it takes. It operates most powerfully in the seasons of childhood and youth, and effects on the whole much more good than ill; for it is a preventive of indecency, and an incentive to laudable emulation. An over-diffident youth, if properly encouraged, will exert himself to arrive at such attainments as shall give him confidence; but an over-confident one, being full of himself, thinks he has attained enough already, and of course bcomes remiss. I believe it would be found, upon a close inspection of mankind in past ages as well as the present, that of truly great and excellent characters, a very large proportion had felt the pains of diffidence, and displayed upon their cheeks the blush of shame in their juvenile days.

The most virtuous do nothing to be ashamed of before men, and the most vicious are without shame. But between the utmost limits of human virtuousness on the one side, and viciousness on the other, there is a vast interval which is filled up with mixed characters of both sorts; and upon *them* well directed shame has a great and powerful influence.—"Many who have not resolution enough to avoid a bad action, have yet feeling enough to be ashamed of it." And that feeling of shame may prevent their repeating the misdeed; whereas, of an offender who is utterly shameless, there is no hope.

Shame has a prodigious influence in enforcing the laws of decency. Multitudes of people would not act as well as they do, if they were not ashamed to act worse. And it is better at least for society, that they have the grace of shame than no grace at all.

Vice loves the company of its like. And why? It is that it may keep itself in countenance, or escape the confusion of shame. Vice is conscious deformity; and vicious persons are enabled to hold up their heads in society, chiefly from the knowledge or supposal that numbers about them are deformed like themselves. Whereas, if one stood quite alone in the practice of vice, and at the same time had the eyes of the good upon him, he would, unless desperately hardened, be ashamed of himself. Hence, a notoriously vicious person, living in a place where all the rest were virtuous, would be impelled, as it were, of very shame, either to amend his ways, or to remove to a more congenial society. In short, the benefits of shame are alike great in number and in magnitude; so far forth, that it is questionable whether, in the society of civilized man, there be not more persons who act decently from the sense or fear of shame, than from the impulse of a sound moral principle.

This matter was well understood by the sophists of the last age, who in the war they waged against *Prejudice*,—or rather in their nefarious efforts to banish from society not only pure morals but even the common decencies of life,—artfully directed their efforts particularly at the total extinction of the feeling of shame. And for some time their success corresponded to their zeal. It is a recorded fact, that, during the short-lived popularity of the writings of Mary Wolstoncraft, a *blush* incurred a *penalty* at several of the boarding schools for young ladies in England.

Here two things are to be observed very carefully in the training of children.

1st. Their natural sense of shame should not be put to trial too frequently, or too severely. "Shame," says Mr. Locke, "is in children a delicate principle, which a bad management of them presently extinguishes. If you shame them for every trespass, and especially if you do it before company, you will make them shameless. Moreover, if you expose them to excessive shame for their greater faults, they will be very likely to lose all shame, and if once lost it is gone irrecoverably. By tampering with this feeling too often or with a rough hand, children the most susceptible of shame, may be made quite callous to its influence."

2d. Children should be guarded betimes against *false* shame, which, in all its multifarious ramifications, and, oftentimes, in the name and under the disguise of *honor*, has done frightful mischiefs to our misjudging and deluded race.

NUMBER LXIII.

OF VIRTUOUS POVERTY.

"Man needs but little here below,
Nor needs that little long."

And yet to possess but little, though it be full enough for the real wants of nature, is deemed wretchedness. Poverty is to many a delicate ear one of the most frightful words in the whole vocabulary of our language; but it should be remembered that the word has several degrees of signification, and is really frightful in the extreme degree only.

True enough, the rags and filth, and the corresponding ignorance and depravity, so common in the abodes of squalid poverty, are objects of disgust and horror; as they exhibit human nature in its utmost deformity, without aught to shade the picture. The lazy poor, the vicious and profligate poor, compose a mass of wretchedness that is frightful indeed, and not only frightful, but loathsome; and but little pity can be felt for the suffering which they bring upon themselves by their idle and vicious habits.

This is not, however, simple poverty, but poverty and the grossness of vice in alliance; and it is the latter that gives the former its hideous coloring. Virtuous poverty, on the other hand, however disrespected by a scornful world, is, in sober truth, respectable. It has a moral gracefulness that is peculiarly its own.

It is not in the splendor of wealth, or on the lap of ease, that man, considered as a moral being, usually exhibits the finest features of character. For the highest order of virtues can be developed only in a condition of considerable hardships or suffering;—namely, the virtues of fortitude, self-denial, patience, humility, and quiet resignation. A family, that once had seen better days, struggling with misfortune, suffering "the rich man's contumely," and the neglect and scorn of former familiars, but suffering with fortitude and with pious resignation; a family always poor and accustomed to endure hardships, but of pure morals, industrious, honest, unrepining, contented, daily offering up thanks to God for that little which it enjoys; a father, a mother, oppressed with poverty, yet striving with all the little means in their power to send their children to school, and at the same time, both by precept and example, training them up at home, in the way they should go;—these, to the moral ken, are among the most lovely spectacles that are ever exhibited in this fallen world. True, these humble virtues are like the flowers that "blush unseen." They are scarcely noticed, and much less admired; while thousands greet with admiration and applause, whatever of shining virtue the eye can descry in the ranks of wealth and grandeur.

The Rev. G. Crabbe, "the poet of reality, and of reality in

low life," has portrayed with masterly powers of description both vicious and virtuous poverty—not from fancy, but from what he saw, and knew. If the images of depravity in his poem, *The Borough*, be too coarse, too naked, and too hideous, to excite other emotions than those of disgust,—the images of virtue, which, also, were taken from the deepest shades of poverty, possess almost unrivalled charms. The tale, for instance, of the *Sad Girl*, a poor maid of the Borough, who, after waiting a long time in anxious expectation of the return of the young sailor who had promised to marry her, at length received him emaciated and mortally sick, and nursed him day and night with the utmost tenderness, till he breathed his last;—this tale, in point of heart-moving interest, perhaps has scarcely a rival in the history even of romance and fiction.

The following few lines of it show how venerable, how sacred, how lovely is the cottage of the poor when adorned with virtue and pure religion.

> "Still long she nurs'd him; tender thoughts meantime
> Were interchang'd, and hopes and views sublime;
> To her he came to die, and every day
> She took some portion of the dread away;
> With him she pray'd, to him his Bible read,
> Sooth'd the faint heart, and held the aching head:
> She came with smiles the hour of pain to cheer;
> Apart she sigh'd; alone, she shed the tear;
> Then, as if breaking from a cloud, she gave
> Fresh light, and gilt the prospect of the grave."

Blessed indeed are such poor! and of such the number is, in all probability, far greater than is generally imagined; the virtuous deeds and heavenly dispositions of the obscure children of poverty being very little known or noticed, save by the Omniscient eye.

NUMBER LXIV.

OF FRIVOLITY OF CHARACTER.

There are of both sexes a number of volatile persons, who bear a near resemblance to the little playsome birds that skip perpetually from bush to bush. Their attention is never fixed; their thoughts run upon every thing by turns, and stay upon nothing long. In conversation they are unsettled and flighty; when they read, " they gallop through a book like a child looking for pictures."

Characters of this sort abound in the upper regions of life, among those who have been badly educated, and have nothing to do; and by a celebrated writer they are admirably hit off in the following pictorial sketch of *Vetusta.*

" She is to be again dressed fine, and keep her visiting day; again to change the color of her clothes, again to have a new head, and again to put patches on her face. She is again to see who acts best at the playhouse, and who sings finest at the opera. She is again to make ten visits in a day, and be ten times in a day trying to talk artfully, easily, and politely about nothing.

She is again to be delighted with some new fashion, and again angry at the change of some old one. She is again to be at cards and gaming at midnight, and again in bed at noon. She is to be again pleased with hypocritical compliments, and again disturbed at imaginary affronts. She is to be again pleased at her good luck at gaming, and again tormented with the loss of her money. She is again to prepare herself for a birthnight, and again to see the town full of company. She is again to hear the cabals and intrigues of the town; again to have secret intelligence of private amours, and early notices of marriages, quarrels, and partings."

Such is the description of an elderly fashionable lady, of the London stamp; a description which, under the fictitious name of a single individual, was meant to embrace a large class.

Nor is it only in the regions of fashion and high life, that frivolity of character is seen; though *there* it has the strongest stimulants, and the most ample means of displaying itself. Fortunate are they, on whom is imposed the salutary necessity of doing something valuable with their existence; whose daily occupations, as well as worldly circumstances, withhold them from an imitation of those called the great, but who by their frivolous pursuits, render themselves least among the little.

A flighty, frivolous turn of mind, is owing partly to nature, partly to education, and partly to habit.

Every body that is observant, must have seen that some children are more sedate, and others more volatile; and that the latter, during their infantile years, are peculiarly pleasing for their pert vivacity. They perform childish things in the most engaging manner. And not in childhood only do they gratify and please; in the following stage of early youth there is a charm in the vivaciousness of their temper, which we are apt to mistake for the germ of genius. But the expectation is often disappointed at the period of mature age. There is then found a gay surface, but no depth; a high-fed fancy, but a lank understanding and feeble judgment. The man, even the *aged* man, is still as volatile, still as fond of little sports and of little things, still as boyish, as when he was a boy.

The fruit of age is generally corresponding to the education of childhood. Education goes far, very far, in determining and fixing characters; and of none more than of young minds remarkably vivacious. Though a more than ordinary degree of vivacity, in the early years of life, affords no sure promise of superior strength of understanding, neither is it to be interpreted, on the other hand, as a sign that the understanding will be weak; for it sometimes is an accompaniment of great and shining parts. But in either case, the management of children of this description is a matter of peculiar delicacy. If prudent care be taken to curb and regulate, without extinguishing, the vivacity of their tempers; if their attention be directed betimes to things most important and serious; if the solid parts of education be well wrought into their minds;—in such cases, although, at last, they should turn out to be but merely of moderate abilities, yet they would stand a fair chance of being not only useful, but peculiarly agreeable members of society. Contrariwise, if their education be conducted, as too often it happens, in a manner calculated to nourish and confirm the volatile bias of their nature, there will be very little hope of their future respectability or usefulness. For should they have talents never so bright, the chances are ten to one that they will misemploy them. Or, on the other hand, if their understandings prove but slender, they will be always children in manners and behavior;—pert, lively, frolicksome children, with hoary heads, and spectacles on the nose.

"Habit is second nature." Especially when habit is superadded to the strong bias of nature, it is the hardest thing in the world to overcome it. And thus it happens that children of more than common liveliness of temper, so seldom learn to "put away childish things," when they come to be full grown men and women. Permitted to spend their early days in little else than trifles, the habit of trifling becomes firmly rooted, and triflers they continue to be throughout the whole of their lives. The same volatileness, which made them so pleasing in their childhood, renders them shiftless, worthless, and of small repute, ever after.

NUMBER LXV.

OF THE NATURAL AND THE MORAL HEART.

"Thy own things, and such as are grown up with thee, thou canst not know."

To obtain conviction of the truth of this observation of Esdras, the Jewish sage, we need look only to that part of our own system, called the heart. Both the *material* and the *moral* heart of man are of mysterious and wonderful construction; too deep to be fathomed by the line of philosophy, and too intricate to be explored by human ken.

In regard to the *material* heart, as stated in Keil's Anatomy, "each ventricle of the heart will at least contain one ounce of blood. The heart contracts four thousand times in one hour; from which it follows, that there passes through the heart, every hour, four thousand ounces, or three hundred and fifty pounds of blood. Now the whole mass of blood (in a common-sized human body) is said to be about twenty-five pounds; so that a quantity of blood equal to the whole mass of blood passes through the heart fourteen times in one hour; which is about once in every four minutes."

Dr. Paley upon this stupendous subject, says, " The heart is so complex in its mechanism, so delicate in many of its parts, as seemingly to be little durable, and always liable to derangement; yet shall this wonderful machine go, night and day, for eighty years together; at the rate of a hundred thousand strokes every twenty-four hours, having, at every stroke, a great resistance to overcome; and shall continue this action this length of time, without disorder, and without weariness.

It is a fact worthy of notice, that in this wonderful piece of mechanism, there is, as it were, the power of repelling the meddlesome eye of curiosity; since, whilst we are in sound health, the mighty labor that is perpetually going on in the little laboratory within, gives us no sort of disquietude, so long as we pay no close attention to the process; but no sooner does one contemplate it with close and undivided attention, than unpleasant and almost insupportable sensations check his impertinent inquisitiveness. Perhaps no one living would be able to fix his whole mind, for the space of a single minute, upon the pulsations of his own heart, without experiencing sensations of indescribable uneasiness.

All this is wonderful.—" A mighty maze, *but not without a plan.*" Who, that takes a sober view of the mechanism of his own heart, can say in that very heart, *There is no God !*

Nor is the *moral* heart of man less wonderful than the *material.* It is remarkable that this too, as well as the natural heart, is repulsive to careful and strict scrutiny. It is one of the most difficult of performances, for one to scrutinize the moral frame and operations of one's own heart with a steadfast and impartial eye; the difficulty principally consisting in a violent aversion to that kind of scrutiny, and the irksomeness of the process. And hence it is, that a great many persons know less of their own hearts, considered in a moral point of view, than of any thing else with which they are in a considerable degree conversant. Partial as we always are to our own understandings, and to our intellectual powers in general, we judge of them with a great deal more uprightness and truth than we do of our hearts. The defects of the former we perceive, and own; but those of the latter we conceal as much as possible, not only from others, but from ourselves; and are mightily offended when the finger even of a friend points them out to us.

As the heart is the source of the affections and the volitions, so it is the seat of all real beauty and of all real deformity belonging to man or woman. By its qualities, and by no standard else, is the worth or the vileness of every human character to be determined. No splendor of talent, no brilliancy of action, even on virtue's side, can countervail the want of rightness of heart. Hence, while we are bound to judge others to be virtuous, in so far as they appear so from the tenor of their overt acts; we must look deeper, far deeper, in forming a judgment upon ourselves.

In choosing a wife, a husband, or any familiar and bosom friend, the first consideration is to be had to the qualities of the heart; for if those be vile, no intellectual excellence can give promise of good. A man or a woman, either bad-hearted or *heartless*, however gifted with intellect, or furnished with accomplishments, is not one that will brighten the chain of friendship, or smooth the path of life.

The heart that gravitates the wrong way, draws the understanding along with it; blinding, perverting, and duping that noble faculty; so that it judges of a thing, not according to what it really is, but according to the feeling and inclination of its treacherous adviser. This makes it so difficult for one to determine right in one's own cause.

It is no less melancholy than true, that, in general, we take infinitely less pains to improve our hearts, than to improve our understandings. Yet no point is clearer than that the improvement of the intellectual faculties can turn to no good account, without a corresponding improvement of the moral faculties.

Again, in educating children, the least degree of pains is usually taken with their hearts. It is not their *moral* education that is so much attended to; the body and the mind are too generally made the chief subjects of tuition, and not the heart, the temper, the moral frame. The vast superiority of the Christian morality over the best part of the morality of the wisest pagans, consists very materially in this, that the former embraces the views, motives and feelings of the heart, whereas the latter regards the outward act only. Socrates taught some things excellent in themselves, but his system reached only the surface of morality. It was for the Divine Teacher, alone, to inculcate moral duties upon true principles, by prescribing the cleansing of the fountain, as not only the best and the shortest, but as the only way to purify the streams.

A word on *sensibility*. No quality, especially in female character, is so much praised, admired, and loved; and for that reason, no quality is so often counterfeited. And what is it? Not the susceptible temperament, which feels only for self or for one's own.—Not that sickly sensibility, which so enervates the mind, that it yields to even the lightest wind of adversity.

—Not that mock-sensibility, which weeps over a fictitious tale of woe, but has no sympathy for the real woes of life. No. These, and various others that might be named, are of the spurious brood. Genuine sensibility—that sensibility which is indeed so estimable and lovely—is a *moral* quality; of which it would be difficult to find a better definition, than is given in the following admirable lines of the poet, Gray.

> "Teach me to love and to forgive;
> Exact my own defects to scan;
> What others are to feel; and know myself a man."

Extraordinary sensibility, under the guidance of sound discretion, is the source of noble virtues; but if discretion is wanting, it may be the source of lamentable errors and faults. We are rational, as well as sentient beings, and our sensibilities, however genuine and generous, will lead us astray, if they are at variance with the sober dictates of the understanding.

NUMBER LXVI.

OF MORAL EDUCATION.

FEW subjects have employed a greater number of tongues and pens than that of education, and yet few subjects are so generally misunderstood. Most admit the importance of education, and are forward to laud it, though, perhaps, scarcely one in twenty is sensible of the full meaning of the term.

Education, in the common or popular acceptation, is made to mean mere learning. So that, when people talk of education, they generally understand by it little or nothing else than teaching children reading, writing, orthography, grammar, arithmetic, and so on ; and when they have got these, and whatever else of learning is taught in the schools, they are accounted *well* educated, and it is thought to be altogether their own fault if they fail to act well their part upon the stage of life. Often it is said that such and such youths have an excellent education, when nothing farther is intended by it than that they have been accurately taught in the rudiments of what is called learning.

But that learning is not the whole of education, or even the most essential part of it, is a truth evinced by the divine testimony concerning Abraham, which here follows: "I know him, that he will command his children and his household after him to do justice and judgment."

Abraham, one of the greatest and best of the race of Adam, was, perhaps, of all men the most careful to train up his children in the way they should go; and his unequalled care in that respect, was the means of entailing distinguishing blessings upon his posterity. Yet, till several ages and centuries after Abraham's day, nothing that we call learning, had existence in the world. There were no writers or readers: not even the letters of the alphabet were known by anybody living.

What has been said above, is by no means meant to depreciate learning, which is to be regarded as one of the choicest of human blessings; far more to be valued than treasures of gold and silver. Indeed, we can hardly be sufficiently thankful that we live in an age, so far exceeding all former times in the facility of the means of imparting learning to the rising generation, and for zealous co-operations to diffuse it among all classes of society. A happy prospect will this open, provided the means be directed to the right end. Otherwise, giving children learning makes them wise but to do evil; for the increase of faculty effected by learning, will be turned to good or ill, to benefit or mischief, according to the direction it receives in the early years of life.

Now, as learning only supplies ability, the great thing is to turn that ability to good account; to prevent its running into mischief, and to incline it toward things that are excellent.

For what though one had all the learning of the schools? So much the worse would it be for himself and for society, if his inclination led him to make a vile use of it. Though a man have all knowledge, if he have not sound moral principle with it, he is the more dangerous and pestilent in proportion to his superior advantages and faculties.

Every day's experience gives proof of this. The fraternity of forgers, swindlers, and cheats, so numerous and formidable at the present instant, consists, for the most part, of men of good education, as far as mere learning is regarded. Of *that* they have more than an equal share. But their early moral education having been neglected, their learning is a curse to themselves and to all about them. Who would not choose that his son should rather never learn to write, than be tempted and led by means of his adroitness in penmanship, to the commission of felonious deeds, that would fix him in "durance vile" for years or for life? And who can reasonably expect that the learning given his children, will not be abused to their own shame, and to the shame of their kindred, unless he takes at least as much pains to shape aright their moral frame, as in their intellectual training?

Moral education, without which there is nothing of literature or of science that is not liable to be perverted to the worst purposes, is to be begun from the cradle. The first step is to teach the infantile subject implicit obedience to parental authority; and then to rule with such moderation and sweetness, that it shall entirely trust and love the hand that guides it. In this way, the good impressions made upon the young mind are likely to be indelible, and there is ground to hope that the moral and religious instructions you instil, will sink deep in the heart. Nor is it precept alone that will suffice. Though "precept upon precept" be given children, and their memories be stored with moral and religious lore of the purest kind, it will be of little avail, except a corresponding example be daily presented before their eyes.

"It is well known to the students in ornithology, that the younglings of singing birds listen to the old ones, and carefully learn their notes." And this propensity to imitation is no less obvious in children. Like those little birds, they are prone to mimic whatever is done or said in their presence, and especially the ways and manners of their parents and instructors. So that the example set before them by those who have the care of their education, together with that of their young companions, has, of all human means, perhaps, the greatest influence in forming and fixing their characters for life.

In closing this subject, I will venture to throw out a few hints on a particular, to which has been paid far less attention than it obviously deserves.

The education of our youth should be adapted to the nature of our government. A free people, whose rulers by election proceed from themselves, have virtues to maintain as well as rights to defend ; and unless they pay assiduous attention to the former, they must inevitably lose the latter: the only sure foundation of their liberty being an enlightened morality pervading the general mass. Nor is this all. In educating the rising generation, which will soon succeed to the present busy occupants of the stage, besides teaching them useful learning in such measures as their various conditions and occupations may require, and besides the careful inculcation of religion and morality, which is the elixir of life to a community; there should be woven into their principles and habits, the republican virtues of industry, economy, and frugality, together with *practical patriotism;* the patriotism, which consists in the assiduous discharge of all the social duties; which venerates our republican institutions, and makes the public good its paramount object;—a patriotism which the female part of the community are capable of cherishing and promoting in a superlative degree by their united influences and examples.

Though human nature is radically the same every where, the varying modes and customs of different nations give it a diversified appearance: pomp and grandeur are the natural appendages of monarchy, while simplicity or plainness is a natural characteristic of a free republic, which ever assimilates to monarchy in proportion as it apes its manners, and arrays itself in its trappings. It is, therefore, of no small importance that our customs, manners, and habits, be congruous with the genius of our political institutions, or that there be a distinct *nationalness* in the American character; and this can be effected only by a general system of education, possessing, in certain respects, *republican peculiarities.*

Such was the manner of Athens and Sparta; whose youth, however, in one most important respect, were incomparably less privileged than ours, who, not left to nature's light alone, have an unerring guide in the *Star of Bethlehem*—who are blest with a system of religion and morals, which, wrought into the hearts and practice of the general community, would contribute, more than all other means, to exalt its condition and secure its freedom.

It may be laid down as a maxim, which should be engraven in the minds both of the rulers and the people, that the strongest bulwark of liberty is *moral force*, consisting in the united influences of knowledge and virtue.

NUMBER LXVII.

OF THE POWER OF THE IMAGINATION OVER YOUNG MINDS—INSTANCED IN GEORGE HOPEWELL.

"The man that once did sell the lion's skin
While the beast liv'd, was kill'd with hunting him."
SHAKESPEARE.

In the season of youth especially, the imagination often runs away with the judgment. A young man gifted with a warm imagination, but whose judgment is immature for want of experience, views things through a deceptious perspective. His throbbing head teems with flattering visions. Every thing that *may* turn to his own favor he takes for granted, and every untoward incident, on the contrary, that may chance to thwart and disappoint him, he leaves out of his calculations. A bold adventurer in the lottery of life, he feels quite sure of drawing a prize; and his too great confidence is the very means of turning him up a blank. For as, on the one hand, it prevents that care and circumspection in business which is necessary to success; so, on the other hand, it leads him to square his expenses, not to his real circumstances, but to his visionary prospects.

George Hopewell, a goodly youth, took in a decent cargo of ideas for the voyage of life, but forgot to take with him a single idea of meeting with adverse winds and with misadventures. He was neither a simpleton nor an ignoramus. An honest heart had he, and a brain rather fertile than barren. He was weak in one particular only :—he was inclined to believe every thing that he found written *in the chronicles of the imagination.* In short, none was more skilful in building aerial castles; an art which, though it always gives pleasure to the artist, very seldom brings him any profit.

Thus equipped with mental stores, and furnished also with some cash, Hopewell begins business. He begins on a large scale, and naturally enough; for who, with a warm and pregnant imagination, could bear to be occupied with small things? His great stock in trade, the most of which, by far, he had taken on credit, he now views with rapture.—"All this is worth ——, and its profits from the first turn will increase to the sum of ——. Well, I can turn it seven times in seven years, and shall then be worth full thirty thousand dollars clear to myself." Hopewell, so rich in prospective funds, feels as if he had this wealth all in hand, and comes quite up to the reasonable expenses of a man already worth thirty thousand dollars.

A worm may penetrate and sink a ship as effectually as the ball of a cannon. Hopewell met with no uncommon gust of adversity. Nothing did he lose by fire or water, and not much by bad debts; yet his circumstances grew more and more narrow year by year, till, in less than seven years, he became insolvent to a considerable amount. All this was owing, or principally owing to one single circumstance,—living upon prospects, his outgoes constantly exceeded his incomes. If, instead of being led away by the sorceress *Imagination*, he had all along conformed his management and the expenses of his living to his real circumstances, he might have had, if not wealth, at least competence. Many a promising and fine young man has been upset, by carrying more sail than his bark and his ballast could bear.

And here permit me to offer a serious caution against running rashly and deeply in debt,—a ruinous imprudence, to which all the numerous, and in some respects respectable, family of the *Hopewells*, are exceedingly prone.

It is no new remark, and yet not the worse for wear, that multitudes are undone as to their worldly affairs, by viewing things at a distance.

It is thus the inconsiderate and sanguine deceive themselves, when they contract heavy debts. Viewing the thing at a distance—at a distance of time—they view it in a false mirror.

In the days of our youth, and as to many of us even up to the days of our old age, we are apt to feel as if we should be abundantly able to pay a debt six months or a twelvemonth hence. Imagination furnishes us with ways and means in abundance in aftertimes, though we have none for the present. Only give us a long pay-day, and we can do this, or we can do that. But the wheel of time presently brings round the six months, or the twelvemonth, or the yet longer period. It vanishes like a dream: and the debtor, failing in his calculations, if he calculated at all, is quite as unable to pay as he was at the instant the contract was made. He is now in the hands of his creditor, who can spare him or ruin him, as he pleases.

Running in debt is a serious business, which, if proper caution be wanting, jeopards not only property, but character also. Of those who have been adventurous and rash in this respect, how many have been utterly ruined in estate? How many have forfeited the character for truth and integrity, to which they were once fairly entitled? How many, prompted by the violent temptations arising out of their embarrassed circumstances, have acted in a manner astonishing to all who knew them in their better days?

Credit, so invaluable to all who are in any reputable kind of business, and especially to those who have little else to depend upon, is of a delicate and frail nature: it must be used with moderation, or it languishes and dies. A man disposed at all times to extend his credit as far as he possibly can, or to take up all the credit he can get, has many chances to one of being a bankrupt in credit as well as in circumstances.

A word to spirited young men;—a word that will apply fully as well to a great many who are *not* young.

If credit, long credit be offered you—pause awhile ere you swallow the bait. Consider the thing on all sides, and in all its bearings—its *mischances* as well as its *chances*.—Credit, long credit, with interest. *With interest!* "There's the rub." This same interest is a devourer: it eats like a canker.

NUMBER LXVIII.

OF THE FOUL NATURE AND DIREFUL EFFECTS OF CUSTOMARY GAMING.

THE Play at Cards, which at the first was used for mere amusement, no sooner was adopted by avarice than it turned to be *gaming*;—and through this transmutation of its nature as well as name, it has proved one of the greatest scourges of the community, every where, in all the four quarters of the world.

Avarice is a mother-sin, of whose numerous brood *Gaming* is the most haggard and wretched; for however abundant be its prey, it never thrives. It devours innumerable fatlings, and yet remains ever lean itself. There is a curse upon its basket and store; a curse that blights its gains, and turns its enjoyments to wormwood and gall. Neither is this to be wondered at, when we consider the objects of gaming; the principles of the art; and the certain and necessary consequences of the practice or habit.

The main object of the gamester, is to acquire wealth by plunder, without regard to the age, or sex, or circumstances of any who fall into his toils. For it makes no difference whether the victim be a stranger or a familiar acquaintance, a man of age and experience or a stripling, an alien from his blood or his own mother's son.

Gamesters by profession, are a migratory tribe, as strongly marked with peculiarities as the gypsies. They have a jargon that is all their own; a jargon which, interlarded with oaths and blasphemies, is in common use at their board. Also, they have a kind of police belonging exclusively to themselves. Other men form themselves into distinct bodies, for valuable and noble purposes; some for the improvement of the individual members; some for the furtherance of the arts and sciences; and some for the promotion of the holy cause of religion and morality, and particularly of charity: and all these have by-laws and regulations corresponding to the worthiness of the ends in view. So, also, gamesters have a code of laws—the laws of the table—perfectly corresponding, in the main, to the base ends they aim at. But it may be said, and indeed it has been said that the laws of the gaming room prohibit *foul play*, under the penalty of expulsion; that a considerable portion of gamesters are men of rank, and of a delicate sense of honor—men who would sooner lose their heart's blood than trespass upon the rules of the game. Be it so. The question then arises, *What is foul play?* Its meaning, I believe, is pretty much confined to direct fraud, or downright cheating in the management of the cards. *This* touches the honor, and the *moral sense*, forsooth, of gamesters; so that the delinquent, if his fraud be manifest, falls under the general reprobation, and is no longer considered fit for the company of gentlemen. On the other hand, what is *fair play?*

Assuredly it has a marvellous latitude of meaning. For according to the casuistry of even the most upright and honorable gamesters, "Every advantage may be legitimately taken of the young, the unwary, and the inebriated, which superior coolness, skill, address, and activity can supply." Yes, the gamester may inveigle the unwary youth to the table, and artfully lead him on, step by step, till he has stripped him of his whole patrimony; or he may secretly help to intoxicate a fellow player, and, taking advantage of his inebriation, instantly plunge him into a condition of wretchedness and ruin—he may do all this, and much more, and yet be considered as a fair gamester, a gentleman of honor!

The dreadful consequences of gaming are too numerous to be told in a short essay, and some of them are too obvious to need it. I touch not upon the most awful part of the subject—the hopeless death of the unrepenting gamester, and the peculiar terribleness of his audit. Nor will the narrow limits I have prescribed to myself, permit me to detail the deplorable consequences that this practice brings after it upon society at large. I will only mention, therefore, some instances of the harm which gamesters inevitably bring upon themselves in the present life: meaning this for the special benefit of those, who are but on the threshold of the practice.

"Every amiable propensity in the heart of man, every endearing tie, every sacred pledge, every honorable feeling, are set aside and forgotten when gaming takes possession of the human mind." This is not said at random; it is the voice of truth and experience, and has been exemplified in innumerable instances. And yet the danger is neither seen nor apprehended by the young beginner. Many a youth of fair promise enters upon the career of gaming more out of thoughtlessness than viciousness. Not aware of the fraud with which the system is implicated, nor of the train of bad propensities that necessarily enter into the composition of a gamester, he steps into the fatal path without intention of pursuing it far, and without fear of being lost in its labyrinths. But presently the leprosy seizes him, and the plague of it overspreads his whole mind and heart. His love of gaming increases alike, whether he gains or loses. It fixes, and as it were fascinates his whole attention; so that every thing else is neglected. The company he keeps, the language he hears, the scenes of depredation he daily witnesses, poison within him the source of moral feeling. The jealousy, the rage, the revenge, incidental to the employ in which he is engaged, generate a ferocity of temper. He is lost to all that is good, and prepared for every evil. He who, by habits of industry, might have been of competent wealth; he who might have been the source of joy and felicity to an amiable wife, and the father of children that would have blessed his memory; he who might have been an ornament to society, and an honor to the family of man, is at last a vagabond—as destitute of property as of principle—the grief and shame of his kindred—despised of the world, and a burden to himself.

NUMBER LXIX.

OF THE ALMOST INSUPERABLE POWER OF HABIT.

The Brazilians had been so long and so generally inured to the abominable practice of eating human flesh, that the Christian missionaries found it less difficult to reform them of any other of their evil practices than of this. The chief joy of these savages was in their cannibal feasts; the women and the children, as well as the men, partaking of them with delight; insomuch that nothing was harder of cure than this unnatural appetite.

Mr. Southey, in his history of Brazil, relates a story of the following tenor. No very long time after the Portuguese had obtained possession of Brazil, a Jesuit undertook to Christianize a Brazilian woman of great age. He catechized her, he instructed her, as he conceived, in the nature of Christianity. Finding her at the point of death, he began to inquire whether there was any kind of food which she could take.—"Grandam," said he (that being the word of courtesy by which it was usual to address old women), "if I were to get you a little sugar now, or a mouthful of some of our nice things which we get from beyond the sea, do you think you could eat it?"—"Ah, my grandson," replied the old woman, "my stomach goes against every thing. There is but one thing which I think I could touch. *If I had the little hand of a little tapua boy, I think I could pick the little bones; —but woe is me, there is no one to go out and shoot one for me!*"

As this extraordinary morsel of history corroborates an observation not unfrequently made, that with some of the pagans, among whom Christian missionaries have labored, cannibalism had been found the most incurable of any of their vices; at the same time, it strikingly exemplifies generally the almost incurable nature of inveterate, vicious habits. It is a counterpart to that portion of inspiration, which represents it as extremely difficult, and next to impossible, for one that is accustomed to do evil to learn to do well.

It is a proverbial saying, that habit is second nature; meaning, I conceive, that whatever of taste, appetite, inclination, or affection, we acquire by habit, becomes as natural to us as if it were born with us. This is a thing obvious to general experience and observation. But there is one other thing near akin to it, which though not quite so obvious, is perhaps equally true. It is this: the *second* nature, that has grown out of evil habits, cleaves to us, in some degree, as long as we live, and that, notwithstanding principles of real piety at heart.

It is freely admitted that the grandam, whose strange story has just been rehearsed, was merely a nominal Christian, and but very imperfectly instructed in even the doctrinal knowledge of our holy religion. But suppose the reverse of this; suppose she had become a Christian indeed. What then? No doubt she would have abhorred the idea of shooting a tapua boy, that she might pick the little bones of his little hand. No doubt she would have abhorred cannibalism as a monstrous crime. But it is not quite so certain that her *appetite* would at all times have been entirely free from hankerings after the unnatural food to which she had been so long accustomed, and which, of all things, was the most delicious to her taste.

The truth is, any one who contracts bad habits, admits into his garrison inveterate and restless foes, whom he can never entirely expel. Sometimes he may seem to get a complete mastery of them, when, of a sudden, they muster anew their rebellious forces, and quite overpower him. Or even though, by the force of moral and religious principle, along with ever-wakeful vigilance, he keep under these foes, yet they give him incessant alarm, inquietude and vexation. They are the torment of his life, and embitter his last moments. In many a virtuous bosom there is a hard struggle between principle and propensity; between a deep sense of duty, morality, and religion, and the violence of appetites and passions that had been nourished by habit till they were grown up to gigantic strength. A struggle, in which though virtue gain the victory, it is gained at the expense of pains which are neither few nor small—of pains comparable to those occasioned by cutting off a hand, or plucking out an eye. So true is it that vicious habits are either our ruin and destruction, or, at the best, will be a plague to us, however much we may wish and strive to uproot them utterly from our minds and hearts.

It was with reference to the almost invincible force of habit, that the wise man penned the aphorisms so worthy to be put in letters of gold, and hung up in the mansion of every rising family:

—"Train up a child in the way he should go; and when he is old he will not depart from it." Upon the same principle of the power of habit, if, reversing the aphorism, you train up your child in the way he should *not* go; if you countenance his faults; if you encourage rather than check his vice; there are many chances to one, that shame and ruin will be his portion. But though this is clearly the voice of truth and experience, yet many infatuated parents lull themselves in the expectation that the faults of their children will be cured by time: a notion no less fatal than it is false. Indeed, time may, perchance, correct the errors of inexperience, or the mere follies of childhood and immature youth; but not immoralities—not real viciousness of disposition and action—not falsehood, fraud, profaneness, profligacy, or any real *vice* that can be named. Diseases of the mind, like those of the body, usually become the more inveterate by time. Time ripens the inceptive evil into habit; and time again strengthens and confirms the incipient habit. Every day adds somewhat to its strength: every new indulgence gives it a firmer root; and it incorporates itself at last with the very fibres of the heart.

See the knurly oak, which no arm of flesh can bend; which nothing but the bolt of heaven can rive:—this same oak was once a pliant twig.

Guard, then, with utmost care—let parents guard their children, and let all those of the young, who have come to years of discretion, guard themselves—against the inceptive ingress of any and every vicious habit: for—

"———When the fox has once got in his nose,
He soon finds means to make his body enter."

NUMBER LXX.

OF THE WORLD.

Two English poets, of eminent but very unequal genius, are diametrically in opposition to one another in their descriptions of the same great object—*The World.* The following lines of Milton, give only the bright side of the picture.

> " Wherefore did nature pour her bounties forth
> With such a full and unwithdrawing hand ;
> Covering the earth with odors, fruits, and flocks,
> Thronging the seas with spawn innumerable,
> But all to please and sate the curious taste,
> And give unbounded pleasure unto man ? "

On the contrary, the disappointed Dr. Young, contemplating the world through the spleen and gloom of his own humor, describes it as an abode altogether dismal.

> " A part, how small, of this terraqueous globe
> Is tenanted by man ! The rest a waste,
> Rocks, deserts, frozen seas, and burning sands,
> Wild haunts of monsters, poisons, stings and death!
> Such is earth's melancholy map ! "

A melancholy map, indeed; but, thank God, not the true one.

There are some who seem to make it a point of conscience to speak disparagingly of the world they live in, as if they thought it was honoring the Maker to despise his workmanship. True enough, it is an *evil* world; and why? It is not so of itself, but by reason of the evilness of the race of moral beings that inhabit it. It is the *moral*, rather than the natural map of the world, that is unamiable and hideous.

The original frame of the world was good: a commodious, beautiful and superb mansion, altogether fit for the abode of an order of sinless creatures, compounded of the rational and the animal natures. And notwithstanding the frightful change it underwent by means of the apostacy, it is still in itself a good world; that is to say, it is a building well adapted to the condition of the guilty tenants—"prisoners of hope"—who are destined to pass a short residence in it. What though the "thorn and the thistle," the noxious weed and the prickly brier, grow up spontaneously, whilst plants and trees that are good for food, must be cultivated with great care and toil? And what though man is impelled to eat his bread in the sweat of his face, and to be daily mustering up the resources of his mind and body in order to reduce stubborn matter to his use and convenience? All this is entirely befitting his present condition,—to wit, the depravation of his affections, appetites and passions, and his state of trial: it precludes the possibility of general idleness, which would render him more vicious by many degrees than he is now. What though crosses and disappointments, sickness and sorrow, are common to the lot of man, and there is such an emptiness or deficiency in even the best of his enjoyments, that not a single individual of the whole race is in all respects happy? These very evils are preventives of moral evil. Through the divine influence, in a thousand instances they curb our passions, humanize our dispositions, and bring our minds to a right state of recollection, and to new and better purposes of action. And finally, what though, while worldly enjoyments are ever mixed with alloy and are ever unsatisfactory, life itself is frail and fleeting? What though death is daily mowing down his thousands and tens of thousands without distinction of age or degree? Awful as is this law of mortality, and clearly evincive as it is of original transgression, it is a dispensation of which there is a moral necessity. If men were in this world immortal, or held their lives upon a secure lease for hundreds of years, in all probability a great proportion of them would extend their transgressions far beyond the present bounds of human depravity. The consciousness of the shortness and brittleness of life, bridles in avarice and ambition. The fear of death is a strong curb upon appetite and passion. Death breaks in pieces gigantic schemes of oppression, delivers the world from unfeeling oppressors, scatters abroad the unrighteous hoards of avaricious worldlings, and is the great humbler of upstart pride and arrogance.

It is, I repeat, the *moral* condition and conduct of the tenant, that mars the beauty and poisons the comforts of the tenement. The promised "new earth wherein dwelleth righteousness," would be no unhappy world, even with the physical form and properties of the one we inhabit.

Were the heavens above as black as sackcloth, or glaring with light of a frightful hue, and were the earth beneath us presenting to our senses nothing but objects of disgust and horror; then, indeed, the world would correspond with the rueful descriptions which querulous genius has given of it. Then, indeed, the following lines of poetry would possess no less truth than beauty.

> "For ah! what is there of inferior birth,
> That breathes, or creeps upon the dust of earth,
> What wretched creature, of what wretched kind,
> Than man more weak, calamitous and blind?"

But the truth is, though fallen man is weak, and blind, and sinful, yet his earthly condition, so far from being *calamitous* beyond that of all other creatures, is attended with a great many circumstances of comfort and delight.

The earth, even in its present state, is filled with the goodness of the beneficent Creator; and *Man* is the object of his especial care and bounty. Is it nothing that, above and around us, light and colors, with their corresponding shades, are infinitely diversified, to soothe and gratify the eye? That we are furnished with such sweet and melodious sounds to charm the ear? That the earth affords such a variety to delight the palate? That it is decked with the enamel of innumerable flowers of varied colors and delicious fragrance? That by a nice admixture of its different elements, the atmosphere is so exactly fitted for respiration? That the silk-worm spins to adorn, the sheep bears a fleece to warm, and the ground itself yields the rudiments of fine linen to array our frail bodies? That, in all parts of the world, there is furnished a supply of medicaments for the particular diseases of the climates? That fire, air, and water, along with a great variety of minerals, are made, in so many ways, to minister to the convenience and adornment, as well as to the subsistence of our race? Is all this aggregate of earthly benefits and blessings to be accounted as nothing? Shall man, loaded as he is with so many unmerited temporal blessings, complain and fret because they are mixed with natural evil? Especially shall he do it, when a full moiety of the calamities he suffers, are brought upon him, not by the direct hand of Providence, but by his own follies and crimes?

To love the world more than Him who made it, and life more than Him who gave it, is that worldly mindedness which is base and criminal. But a moderate or subordinate love of the world, of life, and of all its innocent enjoyments, along with lively gratitude to their donor, is what becomes our rational and moral nature. Whereas, on the other hand, to think or speak contemptuously of the common gifts of Providence, betokens as little of humility as of thankfulness.

NUMBER LXXI.

OF THE INQUISITIVENESS OF CHILDREN.

One of the distinctive qualities of our nature is the principle of curiosity; whereby we are distinguishable even more clearly than by the principle of reason from the brute animals, of which several kinds seem possessed of some small degree of rational faculty, but very seldom, or never, manifest an inquisitive curiosity after any kind of information. Whereas, in our own species, the disposition to pry into the *How*, and the *Why*, is sometimes seen from the very cradle, and is always to be regarded as an auspicious token; it being, in fact, the germin of all future improvement—the genuine bud of intellectual fruit. Nor scarcely is it conceivable, how great advantage might be taken of such a toward disposition, were it under the constant management of superior skill united with patient industry. But in the nurture and training up of children, this important particular is, for the most part, overlooked, and their early curiosity either damped or misdirected. And, in this way, many are made dullards or frivolous, who might ave been shaped to intellectual excellence.

"Curiosity in children," observes the admirable Locke, "is but an appetite after knowledge, and therefore ought to be encouraged in them, not only as a good sign, but as the great instrument nature has provided to remove that ignorance they are born with; and which, without this busy inquisitiveness, will make them dull and useless creatures."

The passage here quoted, is a *text*, which might furnish matter enough for a long practical discourse on education. But my design is only to throw out hints, to be improved and enlarged upon by the intelligent reader.

Were we ourselves cast upon a strange country, where every thing was unknown to us, and were we destined to spend our lives there, our only way of acquiring the knowledge of it, would be by questioning the experienced inhabitants. Accordingly, if not downright dolts, we should feel disposed to ask them a multitude of questions, of which the most part would seem frivolous, impertinent, and even ridiculous, to those who knew the country well. Now should they all, with one accord, refuse to answer our questions, or turn us off with false or improper answers, or laugh us to scorn for our ignorance and impertinence, and even proceed to chide us, with contumelious expressions, for the interruption and trouble given them by our inquisitiveness; such treatment would naturally damp and discourage us, and involve us at last in the hopeless condition of contented ignorance.

But should we find there only a few to heed our inquiries; to give patient and correct answers to our questions; to encourage our curiosity by the gentleness of their manners and the readiness of their replies; how deeply should we feel ourselves indebted to those precious few, and how happily facilitated would be our progress!

And such as this, but yet more eminently so, is the condition of little children. Not merely are they strangers in a strange land; they are come into a world, where to them every thing is new and strange; a world, of which, and of all therein, they are utterly ignorant. And how do these newly-born citizens of the world act? Why, just as persons come to years would act under the like circumstances. God hath given them an appetite for knowledge, and they seek after it with ardency. *What is this? What is that made for? How is it done, and why is it so?* These, and scores of similar questions are asked in early childhood; and though they would be impertinent and ridiculous if coming from the lips of adult age, yet from the mouths of these little prattlers they are strictly proper. To *them* the information they inquire after is material, though their questions may seem trifling in the eyes of those to whom the things were long since known.

A great deal might be made out of the inquisitiveness or curiosity so natural to children. If rightly managed, it would be the mainspring to intellectual improvement. Were their inquiries properly encouraged, it would lead them to think for themselves; it would put them upon the exercise of their reason, as well as of their memory; and would settle in them the habit of inquiry. At the same time, whenever there was observable in them a forward pertness, or any real impertinence, it might easily be checked, without dampening their curiosity, by parents or teachers possessing any considerable degree of prudence and skill.

But all this requires a considerable degree of toil. It is by much the easier way, barely to give the child a lesson to learn by heart, and whip him if his memory fail, than to aid in enlightening and enlarging the infantile faculties of his understanding. And so, we generally take this easier way. We stop their little mouths, when they presume to interrupt, or *puzzle* us, with their questions, and instead of encouraging them to start subjects of themselves, we confine them to our own prescriptions. We pinion the young mind, and then bid it soar.

Some parents, observing carefully the old proverb, to "nip in the bud," indignantly rebuke the inquisitiveness of their children, as insufferable impertinence. And sure enough, such children are effectually *nipt in the bud*; for it is ten to one that they will never become men and women of inquiring minds. Others, again, turn off the questions of their children with false answers, and thereby directly lead them to the practice of lying. I have seen fathers so stately and stern, that their children scarcely durst speak to them, and much less familiarly question them. And I have seen schoolmasters, who would requite the familiar questions of a little pupil with a frightening frown, if not with a hard blow.

NUMBER LXXII.

OF THE INFLUENCE OF EARLY IMPRESSIONS UPON ALL THE FOLLOWING PERIODS OF LIFE.

Mr. Locke, in his invaluable treatise concerning Education, relates the story which here follows.

"There was in a town in the West, a man of disturbed brain, whom the boys used to teaze, when he came in their way. This fellow, one day seeing in the streets one of those lads that used to vex him, stepped into a cutler's shop he was near, and there seizing on a naked sword, made after the boy, who, seeing him coming so armed, betook himself to his feet, and ran for his life, and, by good luck, had strength and heels enough to reach his father's house before the madman could get up to him. The door was only latched; and when he had the latch in his hand, he turned about his head to see how near his pursuer was, who was in the entrance of the porch, with his sword up, ready to strike, and he had just time to get in and clap to the door, to avoid the blow, which, though his body escaped, his mind did not. This frightening idea made so deep an impression there, that it lasted many years, if not all his life after; for, telling this story when he was a man, he said, that after that time till then, he never went in at that door (that he could remember) at any time, without looking back, whatever business he had in his head, or how little soever, before he came thither, he thought of this madman."

This instance, though a most extraordinary one, is rather so in degree than in kind; for thousands have been haunted, all their lifetime, with frightening ideas received in childhood.

I will venture to lay it down as a position at least probable, that the children of Adam's race are born into the world very much alike, excepting the rare instances of idiotism. Their faculties and inclinations are nearly the same, and the differences which appear in after-times, are owing, in a great measure, to the instruction they receive, the company they keep, and the manner in which they are managed. This assumption is, I humbly conceive, fully defensible on the broad ground of reason and experience, and too obvious to escape general observation. But it is far less obvious, though equally true, that *early impressions* contribute very materially to make the difference in human characters —relative to their tastes, their dispositions, and the bent of their faculties.

Whilst the infant is yet cradled in the mother's arms, long ere it can articulate words, it is beginning to receive impressions, which will influence, more or less, the future periods of life. And though we know not in what precise degrees such early impressions operate; how far their opposites render some irascible, revengeful, or sullen, and others mild, well-tempered, and social; how far they contribute to the firmness of the future character on the one hand, and to a cowardly timidity on the other; yet it is beyond all reasonable doubt, that their influence is great and durable. The Arabs of the Great Desert, have all a sameness of character among themselves, together with striking points of difference from every other class of mankind ; and their character has been all along the same, from the time of the patriarch Jacob to the present day. Nor is it altogether unaccountable, though truly wonderful. For they have all, always, been used to the same scenery, and derived their earliest, as well as their later impressions from the same objects and sources. Now, were it possible to reverse the conditions of two newly born infants—the one an Arab, and the other of good Christian parentage—by placing each in the family of the other ; it is full likely that the latter, when come to years, would be altogether an Ishmaelite in feeling and manners, and the former considerably assimilated to the family that adopted him. Nay, there will be no great hazard in saying farther—It is full likely that this assimilation would begin to be visible in each, antecedently to any direct and positive education ; that the one would take the stamp of the fierce and furious-looking mother, while at her breast ; and that the other, at the same early period, would begin to be oppositely moulded from impressions occasioned by the mildness and sweetness of maternal care.

A simple metrical verse learnt in infancy, is clearly remembered for scores of years. And much more ; early incidents occasioning horror, terror, distressing shame, or violent indignation, leave such deep and distinct impressions upon the memory as are seldom, or never, effaced entirely. I am told by a respectable, pious woman, advanced very far in age, that even now, as all along heretofore, she seldom shuts her eyes for sleep but she is haunted with the horrible spectres, as it were, of the savage Indians, who murdered her father and mother before her face when she was a little child. How great must have been the whole amount of her sufferings from that circumstance, during the long space of upwards of sixty years!

And neither few nor small, throughout the whole course of their lives, must have been *their* sufferings, whose infantile minds had been accustomed to the frightening bugbears of superstition. For even though, in riper years, their reason should convince them never so clearly of the absurdity of such fears, yet the impress upon the imagination is indelible. Times have been, when stories of witchcraft, of spectres in the dark, and especially about the sepulchres of the dead, were commonly reported and fully believed; when a candle burning blue was the sign of a spirit in the house; when the tallow rising up against the wick of the candle, was styled a winding-sheet, and reckoned an omen of death in the family; and when a coal in the shape of a coffin, flying out of the fire toward any particular person, betokened that the death of that person was near.—With what labor and pains did they weave for themselves, and for their children, the web of misery! In those ages of gloomy superstition, which even now are but recently past away, the real ills of life were far exceeded by the imaginary ones.

But to return from this digression: children possessed of a more than common susceptibility of shame, may be injured for life by putting that distressful feeling to a too severe trial; and others may be made shameless by shaming them too often; while a temper naturally stiff and unyielding, may be made revengeful, and desperately malignant, by impressions of injustice and cruelty experienced in the season of childhood.

In families, and in schools, where almost the popish inquisition is practised upon the children; where they are compelled to confess unproved and unprovable faults, and sometimes made, by the torture of the whip or ferule, to confess faults of which they are not guilty;—how pernicious are the impressions left upon their minds, which ever after will rankle in their memories! And so again, when children, by bad management at first, are made disgusted with their learning, seldom, and not without great difficulty, can they be brought to love it heartily thereafter.

NUMBER LXXIII.

OF CALAMITOUS REVERSES IN RESPECT TO WORLDLY CIRCUMSTANCES.

"Think how frail
And full of danger is the life of man,
Now prosperous, now adverse; who feels no ills
Should therefore fear them; and when fortune smiles
Be doubly cautious, lest destruction come
Remorseless on him."———

SOPHOCLES.

In this free, commercial, speculating and money-loving country, the wheel of fortune is turning up blanks and prizes alternately; some families decaying and sinking, and others rising to wealth; the griefs of the former greatly overbalancing the *real* joys of the latter.

One of the bitterest calamities of life, is the sudden fall from affluence, or competence, to poverty. Not that what *we* call poverty, is so very distressing of itself. In some countries, it implies a privation of the indispensable necessaries of life, or the sufferance of hunger and nakedness: but *here*, few are so poor that, with prudent care and assiduous industry, they may not provide themselves with wholesome food and comfortable raiment. Multitudes, in this country, of the poorest classes, are neither the least contented, nor the least happy. Unaccustomed to the elegancies and luxuries of life, they feel no hankering after them; and accustomed to earn their bread by their toil, they regard labor as no hardship. It procures them two very essential enjoyments—keen appetite and sound sleep; and with respect to real and heartfelt jovialness, they very often have more than an equal share.

That degree of poverty, which includes not in it the pinching want of real necessaries wounds the *mind* alone: and it often deeply wounds the minds of those who have fallen from easy and plentiful circumstances. To *them* it is an evil indeed. A comparison of the past with the present, renders the present irksome to them, if not intolerable. The real or imaginary neglects they experience in society, and from even their former familiars, plant, as it were, thorns in their hearts. Time wears away, however, the pungency of first impressions. There is (and the goodness of the Creator is clearly manifested in it), as it were, a principle of elasticity in the minds of human beings, which enables them to recover themselves when crushed down by the shocks of adversity, and to accommodate, after a while, their feelings to their circumstances with marvellous facility. But far above and beyond this, the balm that Religion furnishes has the never-failing virtue of removing the corrosions of the heart, occasioned by worldly misfortunes.

No human prudence can always secure its subject from disastrous reverses in worldly circumstances. In times of old, "there came a great wind from the wilderness, and smote the four corners of the house," in which the sons and daughters of the man of the East—as distinguished for benevolence and charity as for wealth—"were eating, and drinking wine." In a single hour, his vast substance, and the natural heirs to it, were all swept from him. And recent experience teaches that, in America as well as in Asia, *a great wind* may destroy in a single hour, what many years of painful industry had accumulated. The most flattering condition of worldly prosperity is sometimes found to be like the smoothness of the surface of the waters, in their approximation to a cataract.

But though it is not in the power of prudence to secure earthly possessions in all cases, yet often, and for the most part, they are lost by imprudence. It ought to be held in general remembrance, "that nothing will supply the want of prudence; that negligence and irregularity, long continued," will sink both fortune and character, and that if there be but little *moral* good in worldly prudence, there is a great deal of moral evil in imprudence, or in such wastefulness and improvidence as not only lead to want and wretchedness, but often to the ruin or deep injury of creditors.

If we take a careful survey of American society, I believe we shall find, that the greater part of the families who have experienced a distressing reverse in their circumstances, owe it to one or other of the three following causes: the inheritance of wealth—the greediness of wealth—or the affectation of wealth.

"Riches certainly make themselves wings; they fly away." Now these wings, as of an eagle, that bear away riches from the places of their wonted residence, it is worthy of particular notice, are such as naturally grow out of riches; they are wings which *riches make themselves*;—they are idleness, wastefulness, improvidence, and prodigality; all of which a very large proportion of the children of wealth inherit, along with their estates.

A great many fall into poverty, not for lack of industry, but from inordinate greediness of wealth. "They make haste to be rich." Scorning the secure competence they already possess, or which is fairly within their reach, they put it to risk upon the precarious contingency of suddenly attaining the condition of opulence. Impatient of slow gains, the fruits of regular industry, they dash into hazardous enterprises. If unsuccessful—and they have more than an even chance to be so—they are presently ruined: or if brilliant success attend their steps for awhile, so that they heap up riches in sudden abundance; this run of good luck expands their hopes and desires, and they plunge anew into still deeper speculations, till, unexpectedly, the fallacious ground on which they stand cleaves from under them, and their fortunes are all swallowed up.

If the two great destroyers, which I have just mentioned, have devoured their thousands, the one that is yet to be mentioned has devoured its ten thousands. The heritors of overgrown wealth are but few: and though there are very many greedy and rash adventurers, yet their numbers bear no proportion to the numbers of those who are ruining their circumstances by an absurd, and a pitiful affectation of wealth. This last is in economics, what consumption is among bodily distempers, the most common and fatal disease of all. The affectation of wealth, or the vanity of making a show beyond our condition, in apparel, in the elegancies of the table, in furniture, and in every thing else that is thought likely to attract attention and admiration, is the consuming *Plague* that has already destroyed, and which is even now destroying, the earthly substance and comforts of innumerable families who, but for this disease, might rank with the happiest of mankind.

NUMBER LXXIV.

OF THE ATTENTION DUE BOTH TO MIND AND BODY.

"To hold the Golden mean—
To keep the end in view, and follow nature."

THE union of an eminent degree of moral, intellectual, and litirary endowments, with such bodily activity as is common among the savage tribes, would form a singular but a very desirable character. The wild man of the woods can run as fast as the four-footed animals with which he associates; and sometimes, it is said, runs them down, and seizes them as his prey. A savage who depends upon his bow, has not the swiftness of the wild man, yet he can walk, or amble along, seventy or eighty miles a day, and thirty or forty miles upon a stretch. One cannot help observing a peculiar dignity and gracefulness in the gait of our American Indians, particularly in that of the chiefs of their tribes. They go forward with a firm step, their body kept in a straight line, their head erect, and seem to move with as much ease as a boat in a fair wind. Strength, agility, and hardiness of body, together with courage, being with them the highest point of perfection, the whole course of their education has a bearing towards this end. They live in the open air, and exercise and repose themselves alternately, and so as to give suppleness to their joints, and ease and nimbleness to their motions.

Mr. Bartram, in his account of the Lower Creeks, a tribe of Indians inhabiting East and West Florida, says:—"On one hand you see among them troops of boys; some shooting with the bow, some enjoying one kind of diversion, and some another: on the other hand are seen bevies of girls, wandering through orange groves, and over fields and meadows, gathering flowers and berries in their baskets, or lolling under the shades of flowery trees, or chasing one another in sport, and striving to paint each other's faces with the juice of their berries."

These Creeks, I would venture to presume, resemble considerably the ancient Greeks, about the time they instituted their celebrated games, consisting of running, wrestling, boxing, &c.; which are often alluded to in the writings of St. Paul. In the Heroic, or rather in the Barbarous ages of Greece, that people was little, if any, better informed or more civilized than our American Creeks. Their first object, in the education of their children, was to inspire them with courage, and give them strength, agility, swiftness, and all the other bodily perfections; so that they might be able to defend their liberties, and the independence of their respective tribes. After a while they were smit with the love of learning, and Greece became finally the fountain of literature, and even spread the arts and sciences over Italy; whence at last they were diffused throughout Europe. But the Greeks still kept up their games, and all their customary exercises of body: and they are the only people upon history, who have taken much care and pains to make the improvements of body and mind keep an even pace together. Their circumstances were peculiarly favorable to this; since, as to labor, it was all done by their slaves.

Amongst modern civilized nations, the great masses of the people follow daily labor for a livelihood; and among these again, the tillers of the ground stand in the foremost rank. They, living in the open air, and using exercises which expand the chest and brace the nerves and muscles, acquire an uncommon degree of hardiness and vigor of body; yet, by reason of the intensity of their toils, they soon lose that jauntiness of limbs, that ease of motion, that nimbleness of gait, which the savage retains even to old age. Laborers in the mechanical arts have more or less bodily activity, generally, according to the nature of their occupations. Those trades which require a sedentary life, a seclusion from the air, and a curved posture of body which compresses the lungs, as well as those that expose the artificers to poisonous effluvia, tend to bring on weakness and disease, and oftentimes hasten death.

The wealthy part of mankind, whose circumstances free them from the necessity of constant, drudging toil, might, one would think, rise superior to others in proportion to their superior advantages. But how rarely is it so in fact. Their luxury and debauchery poison both mind and body; insomuch, that where vast possessions are vested unalienably in certain families, as in some parts of Europe, most of those enormously wealthy families, in the course of ages, dwindle down to a race of pigmies, in comparison with whom the savage holds an enviable rank. The savage state, and the state of luxurious refinement, are the two extremes; between which, *somewhere*, there lies a point that is most favorable to the happiness of man, and to the general development of his faculties.

The learned might have the best chance to unite in themselves bodily and mental excellencies, if prudent care were early begun and constantly continued. If there were used frequent exercise in the open air, both at the commencement and throughout the whole course of a life of study; if study and exercise were alternate, at short intervals, the body would retain its vigorous tone, the mind would be relieved, and the progress of learning would be promoted rather than retarded. But this is often reversed in practice. Observe a scholar that has just left the occupations of agriculture; observe his ruddy countenance and florid health. Observe the same scholar two or three years after; see his dim eye, his faded cheek, his emaciated body, the debility of his whole frame! And what has wrought this melancholy change?—Continued mental exercises, without corresponding exercises of the body. He has been a hard student, and has treasured up Greek, and Latin, and Algebra, and Logic; but for want of frequent intervals of exercise in the open air, the juices of his body have corrupted, like the water in a standing pool.

We are compound beings, consisting of physical and of mental parts and faculties. It is a most desirable thing to have "a sound mind in a sound body;" and, therefore, whilst the principal attention is to be paid to intellectual, moral, and religious improvements, there is no small attention due also to the health, soundness, and agility of the corporeal part of our nature.

NUMBER LXXV.

OF THE GENERAL PRONENESS TO PETTY SCANDAL.

As if there were not prattle enough from human tongues, a great deal of care is taken to teach birds to talk. Some families of opulence and rank are said to have devoted a considerable portion of their time to the advancement of this species of education: nor would it be altogether time lost, if they would mind to teach their birds a few sound and pithy maxims for domestic use, and the benefit of their visitors.

The following anecdote I will cite as an example, for the purpose of showing to what good account the lingo of speaking birds might be turned, if their education were conducted either on moral principles, or upon principles of domestic economy. In the city of London, as Goldsmith informs us, two men, living directly opposite to one another, in the same street, had a quarrel together, on account of the one having informed against the other for not paying the duties on his liquors; and the aggrieved party, after teaching his parrot to repeat the ninth commandment, placed the cage at the front of his house; so that, whenever the informer on the opposite side of the street stepped out of his own door, he heard from the parrot this admonition, *Thou shalt not bear false witness against thy neighbor.*

This sacred precept is to be understood as possessing a very wide latitude of meaning; comprehending not only perjury and gross calumny, which are both punishable by civil law, but also evil speaking, in all its multifarious shapes and degrees. It is obvious to remark, that although the prohibitory precepts in the eighth article and the ninth of the holy decalogue, are both levelled against evils that are alike prejudicial and pernicious to society, yet the laws of society take much more concern in the one than in the other. Every well-regulated civil society arms itself against theft, and metes out punishments as well to petty pil ferers as to the highway robber; and yet the violations of the next succeeding article of divine prohibition pass, for the most part, without punishment, and almost without notice. Not but that money is *trash*, in comparison with character; so that he who steals the one, does far less injury than he who wounds the other. But the fact is, civil law is quite incompetent to the task of taking cognizance of the violations of the ninth commandment, save in a few instances of flagrant enormity.

The trespasses of the tongue, in this way, are so innumerable, so diverse, and ofttimes so artful, that no legislator could classify them, and much less enact laws that would reach them wholly, without destroying the liberty of speech altogether. And, besides, there is in society a great deal less averseness to evil speaking than to theft. If one have his money or his goods stolen, he no sooner makes it known, than his neighbors join with him in searching for the thief, who, if found and convicted, is sure to be punished; because common zeal, as well as common consent, takes side against the culprit. But the pilferers from character fare less hard; or rather, they are tolerated, provided they manage with art and address, and mingle some wit with their malice or their levity.

And as petty violations of this part of the decalogue meet with impunity, so also they meet with encouragement. Few are altogether without envy, which ever takes delight in a back-biting or detracting tongue. Few are without some conscious and visible faults; and the faulty are naturally prone to take pleasure in the noticeable faults of others, as they tend to quiet them about their own. From these causes, and still oftener, perhaps, from thoughtless levity, encouragement is given almost every where to the small dealers in detraction, who, altogether, compose a pretty numerous body.

It requires no great stretch of charity to believe, that there are many persons who never have been guilty of any dishonest action, and much less of downright theft. But it is to be apprehended that there are very few indeed, who have never, in all their lives, *borne false witness against a neighbor*, in some degree or manner, either by unwarrantably spreading ill reports, or else by giving too willing an ear to slander and defamation. It is the evil that most easily besets us, of which we are least apt to be aware; and which many men and women practise without compunction, and almost without thought, although apparently of estimable characters in other respects.

Sempronia is such a very fury in the cause of virtue and decorum, that, first or last, nearly the whole sisterhood of her acquaintance has been lampooned by her tongue. So far from showing partiality to her own sex, nothing heats her temper, and throws her into a fit of boiling rage, like the faults of *women.* Not to mention the abhorrence with which she ever speaks of the wretched victims of seduction, she is of purer eyes than to be hold, in a female especially, even the least aberration from the path of propriety, without emotions of indignation and expressions of reproach. Frugal of praise, and liberal of censure, she speaks but little of those whose characters furnish no topics for scandal; whilst all her eloquence is employed in expatiating on faults, frailties, and follies. The truth of it is, there are very few whose garments are so white that she can discover on them no spots; and it is on the spots, rather than the fair parts, that she fixes her attention and bestows her remarks.

Yet, after all, Sempronia is remarkably perpendicular in much of her conduct. Not for the world would she tell a downright, wilful lie. She means to speak the truth, and nothing else; but the truth she spices with a vengeance. Sour in nature, elated with an extravagant opinion of herself, jealous of qualities that threaten to eclipse her, and thinking her own excellencies will show to the best advantage by displaying them in contrast with the foibles of other women, she no sooner finds that a female acquaintance has spoken or acted a little awry, than her passions are let loose, and she talks herself into a sore throat. In the meanwhile, she mistakes her fastidiousness of humor for delicacy of taste, and her censorious, irritable temper, for extreme sensibility.

Were one to admit the old absurd notion of our being born under some particular planet or constellation, one could hardly help exclaiming: "What a pity that the birth of Sempronia, a woman of some very respectable qualities, instead of the constellation of the *Crab*, had not been under *the sweet influences of Pleiades!*"

In an old Asiatic tradition it is storied, that while Adam and Eve were in the blissful bowers of Eden, there were sent down to them twelve baskets of *chit chat*, which was scattered about the garden: that Adam, being in a thoughtful mood, and neglecting to exert himself in season, gathered up the contents of only three, while his fair partner nimbly collected, and carefully laid away for her use, the whole of the other nine; and that, by natural consequence, the stock of *small talk* belonging to women is, in proportion to that of men, as three to one.

This tradition, though apocryphal, is not unapt; women have naturally a greater volubility of tongue than men; whether that their organs of speech are more flexible, or that their animal spirits are more volatile, they begin to speak at an earlier age, and are more generally fluent in conversation. They have, besides, a more ample fund of *small talk*, which, so far from being any defect or blemish, is a real boon, bequeathed to them for several valuable and obvious purposes. But, though good in its kind, it has an aptness to the evil of petty scandal; an evil, that cannot be too carefully guarded against in female education.

It would be passing no imposition upon a young miss at school, to tell her, along with more solemn dehortations, that the feelings and dispositions from which spring calumny and backbiting, would deform her face. For what is that beauty in the female face which pleases all beholders? It consists chiefly in the aspect that indicates good affections. Every indication of candor, gentleness, and benignity, is a beauty; on the contrary, every feature, or aspect of countenance, that indicates pride, envy, or malignity, is a deformity. Nor does it need proof that in frequent instances, the face becomes at length the index of the passions which one habitually harbors, whether they be of the benevolent or the malignant kind.

One remark more, and no trifling one; there scarcely can be a more attractive feature in the character of a woman, than her veiling, or treating with a sisterly candor, those petty blemishes in her female acquaintance, from which she is happily exempt herself.

NUMBER LXXVI

OF ENJOYING INDEPENDENCE AS TO WORLDLY CIRCUMSTANCES WITHOUT POSSESSING WEALTH.

INDEPENDENCE in regard to worldly condition, is an object of rational desire and laudable pursuit. But the word, *Independence*, must here be understood in a qualified and very limited sense. Strictly speaking, no man living is independent. For not to mention, that all depend alike on Him in whom we live and have our being; there is amongst mankind a mutual dependence, from the lowest even up to the highest point in the scale of society: so that the rich man needs his poor but industrious neighbors well nigh as much as they need him. Should they refuse to sell him their labor, he would be fain to drudge for himself, notwithstanding the vastness of his wealth. This mutual dependence is a salutary restraint both upon the rich and the poor; it curbs the pride of the one, and the envy of the other; and even tends to link them together in mutual amity.

Moreover, that independence of circumstances, which should be made the object of general desire and pursuit, does in no wise imply large possessions. So far otherwise, one possessed of but barely competent means of support, provided he lives within his means, is hardly less independent than if he were in the enjoyment of a fortune. Does the possessor of an ample fortune enjoy personal independence? So also does the possessor of a small farm, which furnishes him with only the necessaries of life: and so also does the useful laborer, whose labor affords a supply to his real wants. But if the small farmer must needs be a man of fashion or pleasure, he loses his farm, and withal his independence. Or if the laborer neglects his calling, or spends faster than he earns, his independence is quickly gone. Nay, even though the laborer should support himself independently throughout all the days of his health and vigor, yet, assuredly, he must fall into a condition of dependence at last, unless he have the foresight and prudence to lay up some part of his earnings against the seasons of sickness and old age.

"Our views in life," says the celebrated British Junius, "should be directed to a solid, however moderate independence; for without it no man can be happy, nor even honest."

This sentiment has in it, however, as I humbly conceive, some mixture of error. Virtuousness of disposition depends not upon exterior circumstances. In the deepest shades of poverty, and even in situations of abject dependence, there are persons not only very honest but very pious, and who are happy in the daily enjoyment of the banquet of contentment. There are those, and not a few, in almost every part of the Christianized world, of whom the following lines, in a Scotch ballad, are no less descriptive, than of the happy old couple, in whose mouths they are put.

"We have lived all our lifetime contented,
Since the day we became first acquainted;
True, we've been but poor,
And we are so to this hour,
Yet we never repin'd nor lamented."

Nevertheless, *our views in life should be d rected to a solid, however moderate independence.* It is as much our duty as our interest, to employ diligent and prudent endeavors to escape poverty and want; to provide "things honest" for ourselves and our families; to lay up against seasons of sickness and the decay of age; and even to strive hard to put ourselves in a condition, in which we can be rather the dispensers than the receivers of charity. Utter negligence in these matters, so far from evincing nobleness of spirit, is, for the most part, dishonorable and mean, and commonly terminates in abjectness both of circumstances and of mind. The loss or destitution of personal independence or the condition of beggarly want, has no little aptness and likelihood to occasion the loss of integrity and of all moral principle. It was when Esau came from the field, at the point to die of famishment, that he sold his birthright.

It would be impossible to tell what precise quantity of worldly estate is just sufficient, and no more than sufficient; since it would depend upon a variety of circumstances growing out of the particular state of society, and on a number of other items which could not be calculated with precision. The best rule is, to rest satisfied with the appointment which Providence makes, and, having food and raiment, therewith to be content.

The middle state of life has been thought, by the wise, to afford the best means both for the enjoyment of comfort and for the practice of virtue. Under this impression, a pious sage of old made the following petition to heaven: "Give me neither poverty nor riches." I know of none among the moderns, however much they may differ in points of religion or of politics, who have any objection to the first clause of this prayer of Agur; but in this money-loving age, it is questionable whether many can be found, either male or female, who pray heartily that riches may not fall to their lot, or who would run with all their might to escape from a shower of gold that should threaten to fall into their laps. It is however certain, that riches and poverty are two extremes, each encompassed with peculiar evils; and without saying what none will believe, that extreme riches are as much to be dreaded as extreme poverty, I would wish to impress this useful truth, that people in middling circumstances, if they would only think so themselves, have enough; and have reason to be thankful for their lot, rather than to repine at it.

Sir William Jones, alike eminent for genius, learning, and Christian philosophy, wrote his own epitaph, which begins with these expressions:—"Here was deposited the mortal part of a man who feared God, but not death, and maintained independence but sought not riches."

If any worldly happiness is enviable, it is that of such a mind. They only are truly rich, who are sensible they have enough, and have no disquieting desires after more; a happy condition, which does not necessarily imply large possessions, nor is often the consequence of them.

NUMBER LXXVII.

OF THE EARLY AND ARDENT DESIRE FOR POWER.

The love of power is as natural as to breathe. It shows itself in the first dawn of reason. How soon the infant begins to struggle to have his will and way! Ere he can speak, or walk, in the tone of his cry, and in his visage and motions, you may plainly read the stout words, *I will and I wont.* With impotent violence he squirms in his mother's arms, in order to command the utmost of her attentions. The oftener he gains his point, with the more resolute boisterousness does he proceed to assert his claims to her submission, and to the devotion of all her time and faculties to the service of his single self.

Having brought under him his nursing mother, no sooner is he able to run about upon his legs, than he strives to extend his dominion. He exacts of the other children, and of all about him, an implicit compliance with his will. When opposed or thwarted, he regards it as downright rebellion against his rightful authority; and accordingly swells with rage, which he deals out by blows, or vents in harsh and grating music.

Moreover, among the earliest of his covetings is that of property. Scarcely any thing is more common than for little children to ask, with peculiar earnestness, *May we have this for our own?* Nor are they willing to take up with any thing short of such a covenant. And why is it, that, not content with the mere use of the thing, they are so fain to have it as their own? It is because property is power. One has exclusive power over that which is exclusively one's own. Of this matter of fact, the child of four seems almost as sensible as the man of forty; and hence it is, I conceive, that our appetence for property—which is but another name for power—begins even in infancy, and enlarges as our years increase. So true is it, that the passion for power is the ruling passion in human nature.

A question then arises here, as to the bearing that early education and discipline should have on the predominant passion or principle under consideration:—a question of vast importance, which, however, I could but barely touch now, even were I better able to do it justice.

In weeding a garden we take great care lest, with the weeds, we root up also some precious plant. In like manner should we endeavor to weed, as it were, the faults out of the minds of our children; looking diligently that we neither spoil nor mar what the Eternal Wisdom has planted in them, or any part of the natural constitution of their frame. If, then, the love of power be a part of the radical constitution of man, the proper method of education is not to eradicate, but to temper and curb it.

This species of discipline should be begun at a very early age, and managed with a firm but prudent hand. It is a task, which, for the most part, devolves chiefly upon the mother. As soon as her infant offspring evidently appears to set up a resolution for the mastery, she has no alternative but either to conquer or submit; for there is no such thing as balancing or dividing the power betwixt them. If she submit for the first time, it prepares the way for a second defeat, and indeed for an endless series of submissions; as the child, in such a case, constantly becomes more refractory and usurping, and she more tame, yielding, and slavish. Thus she nurses up, not so much a son, as an imperious master. But provided the mother begins betimes, and manages the matter with discretion, she may subdue the infant to her authority, and that without overmuch correction, even though she should have to encounter a more than ordinary obstinacy of temper; which, so far from being an ill symptom in children, might, by proper curbing and culture, be made to issue in manly firmness of character.

The strife for mastery, as I said before, begins in the cradle; and if not properly decided and settled there, it will be full likely, as years increase, to appear in frightful shapes. For the contentions of little children, first with their mothers, and afterwards with one another, are the germen, as it were, of the contentions of grown men, which fill the earth with violence and blood.

Wherefore, nothing of human means would, perhaps, so much conduce to the future peace and happiness of mankind, as to break children betimes of a domineering spirit, and to weave, as it were, into their tender minds, sentiments and habits of mutual deference, civility, and benevolence. If it were generally made a main part of education (as assuredly it ought to be of *Christian* education), to teach children to curb their wills and to respect the rights and feelings of one another, an auspicious revolution in the affairs of the human kind might be reasonably looked for. A new and happy era might be expected, when fighting and killing would not, as always hitherto, be the main subject of the history of man; when the fame and renown of men would no longer be built on the destruction of their fellow-men.

NUMBER LXXVIII.

OF GIVING IN MARRIAGE.

MARRIAGE, which is the first and most important of social institutions, is, in civilized countries, generally regulated by law; but *giving* in marriage is a matter of custom. And upon this last point, custom is very diverse in different parts of the world.

In the simple patriarchal ages, a father was, as it were, a sovereign and independent ruler over his own household. His daughters, especially, were quite at his disposal. Yet, in *giving* a daughter in marriage, it was the custom to consult her own inclination, as appears in the twenty-fourth chapter of the book of Genesis, with respect to the case of Rebekah. In process of time, however, it seems to have become customary in Asia, for fathers to betroth their daughters with little or no apparent regard for their preferences or wishes. In that enslaved country, where women are held in a condition of extreme debasement, a irl is compelled to accept the husband assigned her by family authority, how much soever she may detest him in her heart.

Not that it is quite so all over the vast continent of Asia. For there are in it some nations, simple in their manners, that still retain the primitive custom of allowing females the privilege of a *negative* upon such of their suitors as are not fortunate enough to find favor with them.

In Dr. Clark's description of the manners of the Calmuck Tartars, resident in Asiatic Russia, is an instance in point respecting their conjugal rites. "Calmuck women," he says, "ride better than the men. A male Calmuck on horseback looks as if he was intoxicated, and likely to fall off every instant, though he never loses his seat; but the women sit with more ease, and ride with extraordinary skill. The ceremony of marriage among the Calmucks is performed on horseback. A girl is first mounted, who rides off in full speed. Her lover pursues; and if he overtakes her, she becomes his wife, and the marriage is consummated on the spot; after which, she returns with him to his tent. But it sometimes happens that the woman does not wish to marry the person by whom she is pursued, in which case she will not suffer him to overtake her; and we were assured that *no instance occurs of a Calmuck girl being thus caught, unless she had a partiality for the pursuer.*"

Somewhat similar to this account of the Calmucks, is the following fabulous story of ancient date: "Atalanta had many admirers, but the only condition of obtaining her hand, was to beat her in running a race. At last Hippomenes ran with her, and dropping some *golden apples*, which she stopped to pick up, he won the race and married her." How much or how little this old fable, so obvious in its meaning, is illustrative of the female heart in the present age, is a delicate question, that I shall not take upon me to decide.

Western Europe, from which we ourselves have borrowed most of our customs, allows women a rank unprecedented and unknown in the Eastern world. This is owing greatly to its superior civilization, but primarily and chiefly to the influence of Christianity, to which indeed, in no inconsiderable degree, its superior civilization is also to be attributed. But even in Western Europe, the females of the highest rank are disposable property, as respects *giving* in marriage. In a matter so deeply interesting to their comfort and happiness, there is denied them all liberty of choice. A royal maid is disposed of in marriage upon the principle of state-policy altogether, and she must accept the husband that is selected for her, or else draw down upon herself an intolerable weight of scorn and indignation. Moreover, among the several ranks of nobility, *giving* in marriage is conducted on a principle of calculation, rather than of attachment. So that, in this interesting particular, the liberty of European females is in an inverse ratio to the rank of their families. The deplorable consequences are the same that might reasonably be expected ;—such as coldness, alienation, domestic feuds, and conjugal infidelity, so common and notorious among those high-born ladies who have been given in marriage contrary to their own wishes.

Nor does it by any means follow, on the other hand, that paternal authority has no concern in this matter. It has indeed a deep concern, but it is rather negative than injunctive. A father has an undoubted right,—nay, he is in duty bound to refuse consent to an alliance, which he thinks would be deeply prejudicial to the interests of his child, and to use all proper means in his power to prevent it. So far is this from cruelty, that it is a mark of affection, and an act of kindness. But if he overleaps this boundary; if he assumes the right of selection; if he attempts to give his daughter in marriage against her own inclination; if he would sacrifice her peace to the Mammon of avarice, or to the Moloch of ambition;—it is then that he acts the part of a tyrant, and is deserving of severity of censure.

Such instances, however, do seldom happen in common life; in which there is a much greater number of children who rush into the state of marriage with a criminal disregard of parental authority and feeling, than of parents who abuse their authority in the manner above mentioned. Nor does this species of undutifulness often fail of resulting in matrimonial infelicity.

NUMBER LXXIX.

OF USEFUL INDUSTRY, CONSIDERED AS A MORAL DUTY

THE fourth commandment in the sacred decalogue lays upon us two distinct obligations; it imposes labor no less expressly than it enjoins a holy rest. "*Six days shalt thou labor, and do all thy work.*"

Hence it is a just and fair inference, that a life of voluntary idleness is a life of disobedience to the law and will of heaven. If of your own choice you spend the six working days idly, you are as verily a transgressor of the moral law, as you would be in disregarding the day that is consecrated. And besides, we are the better fitted for the duties of the Sabbath, by means of our industry in "providing things honest" during the rest of the week; whilst, on the other hand, he that idles away the six days of labor, is very ill prepared for the sacred day of rest. The idle body, who, nevertheless, appears occasionally devout, separates what God hath joined together; for he that said, "Remember the Sabbath day to keep it holy," hath also said, "Six days shalt thou labor."

Well-directed industry is a moral and Christian duty; a *scriptural* duty, which none that are capable of it can dispense with, and be guiltless. Neither wealth, nor rank, nor sex, can excuse a person in good health, and of competent faculties, from all and every kind of useful labor, either of body or mind, or of both. Mere amusement is for little children. Employment, useful employment is for men and women. And, indeed, as little is there granted us the liberty of doing no good at all with our faculties, as of employing them in doing evil and mischief.

Labor is either mental, or bodily, or mixed. There are none whose labor is a greater "weariness of the flesh," as well as of the nobler part of humanity, than men of close and unremitting study; and there are none whose industry is more useful to mankind. The man of talents, who in solitude, and perhaps in neglected poverty, employs discreetly the faculties of his mind, to enlighten and instruct his fellow-beings in their immortal, or even their mortal interests, is a benefactor to the community, rather than a burden.

Nevertheless, he, even *he*, errs wofully, if he neglects to exercise his body. It is lamentable to see how many men of study, how many promising youths, waste away their strength, impair their constitutions, and bring upon themselves incurable diseases and premature death, solely for the want of a proper mixture of bodily exercise with the strenuous labors of their minds.

In the proud and fastidious times in which we live, manual labor of the *useful* kind is accounted a thing too vulgar for those of the better sort. Many a young gentleman would feel himself dishonored by doing any thing called *work;* and many a young lady would blush to be found employed in an occupation really useful; even though both were in circumstances imperatively demanding their industry.

In this respect the manners of society have suffered a deplorable change. The time was, when labor was held in honor among even the rich and noble; when even ladies of the highest fortune and rank, thought it not beneath them to work occasionally with their hands. Near the conclusion of the last century but one, Queen Mary, of England, who was joint sovereign with her husband, the heroic William the Third, "used frequently," as history informs us, "to employ some part of her time in needle-work; appointing one or other of her maids of honor to read something lively, as well as instructive, to her, and to the rest, whilst they were busy with their needles."

The age next preceding that of Mary, furnishes at least one example in high life, that is still more remarkable. Sir Walter Raleigh, lodging at the house of a noble Duke, early in the morning overheard the Duchess inquiring of her servants if the pigs had been fed, and, with a significant smile, asked her, as he was going to the table, if her pigs had had their breakfast. She archly replied, "They have all been fed, except the strange pig that I am now about to feed."

The man, who, of all the American worthies, was "first in war, first in peace, and first in the hearts of his countrymen," was no less remarkable for industry than for wisdom and integrity.

One of the biographers of Washington remarks of him, "his industry was unremitted, and his method so exact, that all the complicated business of his military command, and civil administration, was managed without confusion, and without hurry. It was the assemblage of these traits of character, so early visible in him, that recommended him, when scarcely more than a boy, to an embassy of no ordinary importance, hazard, and difficulty. Happy were it if the youths of America would, in this respect, copy the example of one whose memory they so delight to honor.

Few things are impossible to industry, skilfully directed. By it, men of but moderate talents rise sometimes to deserved eminence; by it, the man of "small things" expands himself by little and little, till he comes at last to occupy a respectable space in society; and by it the face of the living world is illumined and gladdened.

What difficulties have been overcome, what wonders have been wrought, and what immense benefits have been procured by the industrious application of the mental and corporeal powers of man!

On the other hand, no gifts of nature, or of fortune, can supersede the necessity for industry. Sloth is a rust, that eats up the finest ingredients of genius, and mars and consumes the greatest of fortunes. He that is slothful of mind, loseth his mind; instead of enlarging it, it contracts and diminishes as he increases in years. He that is slothful in business, will at last have neither business to do, nor any thing to sustain his declining age. In short, a downright slug, whether in high life or low, *vegetates* rather than *lives.* Habitual indolence is one of the worst symptoms in youth; a fever is less hopeless than a lethargy.

NUMBER LXXX.

OF THE MORAL USE OF THE PILLOW—WITH REFLECTIONS ON SLEEP.

"Consult thy pillow." This short counsel contains "more than meets the eye." The pillow is the close friend of meditation, of serious thoughtfulness, and of freedom of conscience, in so far as it gives that faithful monitor the best of opportunities for administering wholesome reproof.

"*The day is thine; the night also is thine:*"—and with the like graciousness are they both given, the one for labor, and the other for rest—nor yet for rest alone, but also for a sober survey of past life, and more particularly of the day that has fleeted last. The mantle of darkness, which hides exterior objects, turns the busy mind upon itself, willingly or unwillingly, according to its moral frame and habits.

Human greatness, that lords it by day, is not at all exempt from stern admonishment on the pillow. *There*, no longer able to show off splendor and prowess, its pride is not flattered, nor are its feelings spared. Ahasuerus, for example, the richest, the most splendid, and the most puissant of all the monarchs of the East—reigning from India even unto Ethiopia, over a hundred and seven and twenty provinces;—this Ahasuerus laid him down upon his bed of gold, in a spacious room supported by pillars of marble, and adorned with white, green, and blue hangings, fastened with cords of fine linen and purple to silver rings. Thus he laid him down, amid an unrivalled profusion of Eastern magnificence—but on that night, could not the king sleep. The world else was asleep. The man-servant and the maid-servant, the meanest of slaves, the veriest wretches in the whole realm, were fast asleep. And could not the lord and master of them all, the monarch in the palace of Shushan—could not *he* woo slumber to his eyelids? Alas, no! It turned, however, to good. Of necessity, rather than of choice, the luxurious and effeminate despot, to relieve him from sore restlessness, bethought himself of improving the wearisome vigils of the night in looking into the affairs of his government. He called for the reading of the book of records of the chronicles; and finding that an upright and excellent servant, to whom he owed his life, had been utterly neglected, he ordered him a bounteous reward.—A righteous deed, which never, in any probability, would he have done, had he not *consulted his pillow.*

It is upon the pillow that *the book of records of the chronicles* is most frequently set before the eyes of those mortals, who sadly misspend their time, and abuse the high privileges of their nature. Conscience presents the *handwriting*, and there is no such thing as turning their eyes away from it. In vain they turn, and toss themselves on this side, and on that, longing for sleep; *the records of the chronicles* are still full in their view—

and they are fain to make vows and solemn promises, too often unheeded on the morrow.

Projects of too great hazard—plans of questionable nature and doubtful issue—resolutions taken up of a sudden, and without being duly weighed :—these, engendered by the fever of the day, are abandoned, or rectified, upon coolly consulting the pillow. So that many a one has risen up in the morning, with more reasonable sentiments and views respecting his personal affairs, than those with which he had lain down. And many a one, also, by consulting the pillow, has cooled hot resentments, and abandoned purposes of revenge.

In consulting the pillow, one thing especially is to be ever kept in practical remembrance ; and that is, to offer up the silent adorations of the heart, both at the instant of falling asleep, and at the moment of waking. "*I will both lay me down in peace, and sleep: for thou Lord only makest me to dwell in safety.—I laid me down and slept; I awaked; for the Lord sustained me.*"

And what art thou, *Sleep?* Of what stuff art thou made? Whence comest thou when thou visitest our pillows, and whither goest thou when, ceasing to press gently our eyelids, thou art borne away upon the wings of the morning? Thou incomprehensible *Something*—thou invisible solace of heavy-laden man—should one gain the whole world in exchange for thee, how pre-eminently miserable would be that one!

"The great cordial of nature is sleep. He that can sleep soundly, takes the cordial; and it matters not, whether it be on a soft bed, or on the hard boards. It is sleep only that is the thing necessary." This sovereign cordial, so often denied to worldly prosperity and grandeur, is, for the most part, bountifully furnished to those in circumstances most deplorable and forlorn.

Behold the wretchedest of the wretched—a captive and slave to the wild Arabs. Day after day he suffers with hunger, with thirst, with fatigue, with terror,—the very utmost that human nature is capable of enduring:—night after night he reposes in sound sleep, nor is he ever disturbed with even *a single unpleasant dream*, though stretched upon the bare ground, and in the bleak and open air, or lodged amidst the noisomeness of dungeon filth.

Perhaps, of all the immense percipient beings, above as well as below us, there is only ONE, who neither slumbers nor sleeps —from that ONE, cometh the inestimable gift of quiet sleep.

Next to the goadings of a guilty conscience, the principal banishers, or rather *murderers* of sleep, are these:—Luxury, Dissipation, Ambition, Avarice, Envy, Malice, together with whatever other of the family of the malignant passions. "O miserable of happy"—more especially upon their pillows—are many, very many, of those whom the world deems the happiest of men and women!

On the contrary, next to pureness of conscience and soundness of health, the most successful wooers of sweet sleep are Temperance, Useful Labor, Benevolence, Resignation, Gratitude for the good that Providence bestows.

It is obvious to remark, that Intemperance in sleeping is to be guarded against, as well as Intemperance in eating and drinking. This *cordial of nature* should be used as a cordial. The habit of over-sleeping weakens the frame both of body and mind; and besides this, is a clear loss of precious and invaluable time.

Only the space of two hours in the twenty-four, if redeemed from unnecessary sleep, to what vast account might it not be turned in the course of twenty years.

Once more: Sleep has, in several respects, so near a resemblance to Death, that the relation, in "Paradise Lost," of the conceptions of Adam when falling into his first slumber, has no less of nature than of beauty.

"On a green shady bank, profuse of flowers,
Pensive I sat me down: there gentle sleep
First found me, and with soft oppression seiz'd
My drowsed sense, untroubled, though I thought
I then was passing to my former state
Insensible, and forthwith to dissolve."

As a counterpart to which, I will quote another Christian poet—the admirable Montgomery.

"There is a calm for those who weep,
A rest for weary pilgrims found;
And while the mouldering ashes sleep
Low in the ground;

"The soul, of origin divine,
God's glorious image, freed from clay,
In heaven's eternal sphere shall shine,
A star of day!"

NUMBER LXXXI.

OF THE TWO OPPOSITE ERRORS—THE EXTREME OF SUSPICION AND THE EXTREME OF CONFIDENCE.

Mankind are alike betrayed by the excess of suspicion and of confidence. The maxim, that in suspicion is safety, is true only in a qualified sense; for overmuch suspicion errs as often as overmuch confidence. As to believe nothing would be quite as wrong as to believe every thing, so to trust nobody is no less an error than to trust every body. Indeed it is the worse error of the two, because there is more evil in causelessly thinking ill, than in causelessly thinking well of our fellow-beings.

Bad men, who look chiefly into themselves for information concerning the human kind, are ready to believe the worst of others. Conscious of their own insincerity, they can hardly think that any speak friendly to them or act kindly toward them, with intentions that are really sincere. They suspect religion to be hypocrisy, and that apparent virtue is but a mask to conceal the naughtiness of the heart. Piety, self-government, munificence, and all the charities of life, they impute to corrupt or interested motives. Hence thy repose firm confidence scarcely in any one. Now as to persons of this cast, they are not only the dupes of their own jealousy, but its victims. A suspicion of every body they have to do with, as it keeps them in perpetual fear and disquietude, and prevents their enjoying the common comforts and benefits of society, so it precludes all likelihood, and almost all possibility of self-amendment. For their minds are too intent upon the faults of others, to attend to their own; and besides, their mistrusting ill of all about them, furnishes a powerful opiate to their own consciences.

It has been boasted by some men of business that they never, in all their lifetime, suffered by imposition or imposture; that they had always accustomed themselves to keep so sharp an eye upon mankind, that nobody could cheat or deceive them. This is not, however, any great matter of boasting; for it is scarcely possible that they should have been so constantly on their guard against deception, if they had not had a vigilant monitor and prompter in their own hearts. Upon the same ground, it is an ill mark in any one to decry apparent virtue in others, and to assign bad motives to their good deeds; since it argues that the only motives that can fall within the ken of his own mental eye, are generally faulty, if not totally corrupt. In short, it is better now and then to be deceived, and even duped, than never to confide.

On the contrary, persons of honest, benevolent views, are apt, from that very circumstance, to run into the opposite extreme. Conscious of their own uprightness and probity, they are hard to suspect that any, who wear the semblance of these virtues, should have it in their hearts to beguile them; and, of course, for want of prudent caution, are peculiarly liable, through an amiable weakness, to be ensnared, and sometimes desperately injured. It is especially in youth that we find this error, which is commonly cured by time and experience. An unsuspecting youth, soured by bitter experience, may become too suspicious in old age; whilst a youth of an excessive jealousy of temper, commonly grows more jealous or suspicious, as he advances in years.

There are two classes of men who are often betrayed by an excess of confidence: these are creditors and debtors. As it respects the former, the remark is too obvious to need proof or illustration. The error of giving indiscriminate credit, is too visible in its deplorable consequences to be generally seen. But the opposite error—that is, the error of *taking* too large credit, is not quite so manifest, though equally fatal.

As the creditor trusts the debtor, so, on the other hand, does the debtor trust the creditor, except in instances in which he is morally certain of making punctual payment. If one runs in debt beyond his ability to pay in good season, he has to trust to the mercy of his creditor, not merely as to his house and lands, goods and chattels, but sometimes even for the liberty of going at large. The creditor has a power over his property, and in some places over his personal liberty. If he exact the last farthing of the debt the very instant it becomes due, and that notwithstanding the plea of inability to pay, he may, perhaps, be called hard and unfeeling, but not unjust. The promise in the note or bond entitles him to be thus rigorous, and the law is on his side. Neither is any debtor entitled, ordinarily, to expect any thing short of this rigor from his creditor, except on principles of compassion: and surely it evinces too much of confidence, as well as too little of spirit, when one places himself, unnecessarily, in circumstances to need the *compassion* of a fellow-man as his only earthly resource.

NUMBER LXXXII.

ON SUNSHINE FRIENDS.

An ancient naturalist tells us, that the rats will leave a house which is about to fall.

But whether it be so or not, there is in some human animals a sort of instinct very nearly like it .—they are your sunshine friends, who stick to you closely in prosperity; but no sooner do they perceive a bleak storm of adversity hovering over you, than they estrange themselves and stand aloof.

Nor is this an upstart race of modern origin. Contrariwise, we find it distinctly noted and described in writings of early antiquity; but in none more admirably than in the following passages of the Son of Sirach:—"For," says that skilful remarker on mankind, "some man is a friend for his own occasion, and will not abide in the day of thy trouble. And there is a friend, who, being turned to enmity and strife, will discover thy reproach. Again, some friend is a companion at the table, and will not continue in the day of thy affliction. But in thy prosperity he will be as thyself, and will be bold over thy servants. If thou be brought low, he will be against thee, and will hide himself from thy face." So also, in another part of his admirable book, the same writer further describes this sort of gentry :—" If thou be for his profit, he will use thee : but if thou have nothing, he will forsake thee. If thou have any thing, he will live with thee : yea, he will make thee bare, and will not be sorry for it. If he have need of thee, he will deceive thee, and smile upon thee, and put thee in hope ; he will speak fair, and say, What wantest thou ? He will shame thee by his meats, until he have drawn thee dry twice or thrice, and at the last he will laugh thee to scorn : afterward when he seeth thee, he will forsake thee, and shake his head at thee."

The common saying, *Prosperity makes friends*, is admissible only in a qualified sense. Most of the friends of prosperity's making scarcely deserve the name ; for no sooner do they perceive your fortune falling, than they make off with themselves, like the rats from a falling house.

To exemplify this truth, instances almost without number might be drawn from history, ancient and modern, sacred and profane. But narrowing the subject to a single point, my object will be the rectification of a very prevalent error ; namely, the idle notion of attracting regard by a style of living too expensive for our condition.

Nothing more distinctly marks the age and the country we live in, than this species of folly. If the former days were not better than these in other respects, yet in this one respect they were a great deal better : they were times of sober, prudent economy. Poverty was not arrayed in costly attire ; mediocrity did not ape the splendor and expense of wealth ; industry was coupled with frugality; the great bulk of the yeomanry were plain in their living, and accustomed their children to plainness of food and raiment; the trader made it a point to win gold ere he wore it; it was fashionable for families to live within their income; it was creditable to be provident and economical.

Marvellous is the change, which the short term of a single age has brought forth. Now, the general language of practice is, "Away with the old-fashioned maxims of frugal economy, and up with the expenses of high life." The distinctions of wealth are lost in the general blaze; all being alike fine, all alike accustomed to sumptuous fare. The two extremes in society, to wit, Wealth and Pauperism, as it were, meet together; the middle class, of such magnitude and might in other times, having lost its distinctive marks of genealogy.

This ruinous course is entered upon, and obstinately persisted in, not unfrequently in the full view of some of its baleful consequences. It needs very little of arithmetic to calculate how it will end. The youth must know that if, in his days of health and vigor, he spends all as he goes, he will, in the seasons of sickness and decrepit age, be a forlorn dependant upon charity. All must needs know the inevitable effects produced by the outgoes exceeding the incomes.

But as an offset to the disadvantages of embarrassment, poverty, and debt, a great many, peradventure, are soothed with the idea that they are obtaining notice and regard, or, in other words, are making to themselves friends. In the estimate of their own imaginations, they do not *waste* their substance; they only *barter* it for honorable connections, for distinguished rank in society, for a close alliance with wealth and fashion, for claims upon the hearts of a large circle of respectable ladies and gentlemen. These, they are confident, will never abjure their friendship, nor forsake them, come what will.

Alas! too late are they undeceived. Too late are they taught by rueful experience, that *the companions at the table abide not when they are brought low*—that they are sooner forsaken by none, than by those who had *lived upon them, and drawn them dry*—that these flesh-pot friends are among the first to *laugh them to scorn, and to shake the head at them.*

Harmanicus—I have known him well—Harmanicus, of proverbial hospitality, had made to himself an endless train of friends. His house was for all the world like a public inn, except that the customers had not a farthing to pay;—a precious circumstance which gave it the decided preference. Far and near was Harmanicus known, and for his profuse liberality far and near was he admired. Fashion, and Wealth, and Rank, did him the honor to eat of his "savory meats," and to drink of his delicious wines. The *itinerant* gentry neglected not to spend one night at least, both going out and coming in, with the liberal-hearted Harmanicus. Even travellers and sojourners on business, found time, nevertheless, to breakfast, and dine, and sup, and lodge, with Harmanicus, who provided withal "both straw and provender." The worshipful Bencher, for many years his close table-friend, never failed to *live with him* in term-time. They served themselves of him to the last. They eked out their friendly visits till they had milked all his resources dry; till poorly, poor man! was he barely able to shift for himself;—and then—What *then?*—Read the Son of Sirach for an answer.

NUMBER LXXXIII.

OF THE MISUSE OF THE FACULTY OF MEMORY.

In the little citadel of the mind, the *Memory* acts as a sort of subaltern; and hence it is often blamed, and sometimes wrongfully, by the commander-in-chief. We seldom find men dissatisfied with their understandings, or their judgments, or with the character of their hearts. Very few are disposed to own that any of these are radically defective, or greatly in fault. But nothing is more common than to hear them berating their memories, as not only weak, but treacherous. The aged I have often heard complain of their memories, but seldom of their judgments.

> "'Tis with our judgments as our watches—none
> Go just alike, yet each believes his own."

I said just now, that the memory sometimes is blamed wrongfully; and truth would bear me out were I to add, that nothing is more common than to tax the memory with faults of which it is in no wise guilty. In very many of the cases, in which forgetfulness is pleaded for excuse or apology, if the memory were al lowed to speak for herself, she would let it be known that the imputations cast upon her are slanderous falsehoods, and that, in those particular cases, she had performed her part in full measure.

Artificial methods of assisting the memory have been suggested by writers, and at least one invention for that purpose has been made, and put in practice by those who could not write. It is worthy of notice as a curiosity, if not for its use.

According to Smith's history of the colony of New York—in 1689, commissioners from Boston, Plymouth, and Connecticut, had a conference with the Five Indian nations, at Albany; when a Mohawk sachem, in a speech of great length, answered the message of the commissioners, and repeated all that had been said the preceding day. The art they had for assisting their memories was this. The sachem, who presided, had a bundle of sticks prepared for the purpose, and at the close of each principal article of the message delivered to them, he gave a stick to another sachem, charging him with the remembrance of that particular article. By this means the orator, after a previous conference with the sachems who severally had the sticks, was prepared to repeat every part of the message, and to give to it its proper reply. This custom, as the historian remarks, was invariably pursued in all their public treaties.

The gift of memory, like the other gifts of nature, is distributed to some individuals more, and to others less. Wh le all are blest with such a measure of memory as might suffice them, if well improved, some few possess it in an extraordinary measure; and, what is truly wonderful, a very strong memory is sometimes found yoked with a very feeble intellect. There are some persons that can repeat, word for word, a long discourse, upon hearing or reading it only once or twice, and yet are possessed of minds too weak and slender to reason upon matters with any considerable degree of ability, or to judge of them accurately. A man of this sort, ever makes himself tiresome, if not ridiculous, by dealing out wares from the vast stores of his memory, without regard to time, place, or fitness. But whenever, on the other hand, an excellent memory is united with a sound and vigorous understanding, nothing but indolence can hinder such a one from becoming great—nothing but the want of good principle at heart, can prevent his acting, with superior excellence, some part or other upon the theatre of life.

In general we forget, for want of attention, more than for want of memory. Persons of very indifferent memories find no difficulty in remembering certain things that have excited their attention in a very high degree; while a thousand other things of far greater moment have been utterly forgotten by them. Once on a time, an Indian preacher said to an assembly of white people, who were gathered together to hear him—" Though you will forget what I say, you will remember as long as you live, that you have heard an Indian preach." It was even so. None of the assembly did, probably, forget this striking circumstance; though few retained in memory either sermon or text.

The good we do is registered faithfully in our memories, but our reprovable deeds we consign to oblivion, by concealing them as much as possible from our own sight, as well as from the sight of others.

" Creditors," generally speaking, " have better memories than their debtors." The former are never known to forget the *bond*;

while the latter are very prone to forget it, or at least, to forget its *date*, or the day of promised payment.

The doer of a favor or benefit, is apt to remember it a great deal longer than the receiver.

It is one of the worst and most treacherous memories, that forgets friends, and even benefactors, in their adversity, when they stand in need of aid. " *Yet did not the chief butler remember Joseph, but forgat him.*"

All of us inherit from nature better memories for injuries than for kindnesses. This lamentable error of memory, it deeply concerns us to remedy by all the means in our power.

A man of a truly great mind, who had been both obliged and disobliged by the same persons, magnanimously resolved to forget all that might diminish his gratitude, and to remember only what might increase it.

NUMBER LXXXIV.

OF ATTAINING A FACILITY OF UTTERANCE, OR VOCAL EXPRESSION.

A MAN well versed in the knowledge of the world, made this pithy remark: "*Words are things.*" Not like inarticulate sounds, devoid of meaning, they are the instruments of an intercommunity of minds, and so are real *things*, highly necessary to be well understood; the knowledge of them being the first step toward almost all other knowledge.

Language is twofold, *written* and *spoken*. About the former, the generality of scholars employ much more labor and pains than about the latter, notwithstanding that this, or *colloquial* language, is requisite for use almost every wakeful hour of our lives.

Dr. King, a first-rate scholar of the last age, who had long been familiar with the most distinguished literary characters in England, observes, in his Memoirs, that he had been acquainted with three persons only, who spoke English with that eloquence and propriety that if all they said had been immediately committed to writing, any judge of the English language would have pronounced it an elegant and a very beautiful style :—and one of these was Dr. Johnson. Further he states, that, among the

French and Italians, few learned men are met with, who, are not able to express themselves with ease and eloquence in their own language. This defect on the part of the English, he attributes to the neglect of the study of their mother-tongue; whereas the nations just named sedulously study theirs.

To which it may, perhaps, be fairly added, that the partakers of the English blood, are inclined to be constitutionally phlegmatic and humdrum; and conversing together much less than do some other portions of mankind, their colloquial faculties are much less improved by use and exercise.

Be that, however, as it may, it is clear that English scholars fall far short of perfectness in the language, though ever so learned and accurate in its theory, unless they are able to speak it, on every occasion, with promptness, propriety and ease. To arrive at this rare attainment, or even to approximate to it, would be well worth no small degree of labor.

The faculty of communicating thoughts with facility, is one of the most precious faculties belonging to the human kind:—a faculty, which all who aspire to shine as *lights* in the world should strive to acquire. Though a man have all knowledge, if unable to express what he knows, it can be of little more use than a lamp that is hid; while, on the other hand, the complete power of expression gives the utmost advantage to the powers of the intellect. As a wrestler who can put forth his whole strength in a moment, and at the nick of time, is able to lay upon his back a slow-moulded man stronger than himself, so a speaker or a talker who has words at will on all occasions, has it in his power to baffle one possessing more extent and depth of understanding, but embarrassed and faltering for want of words. Hence, one human understanding is often compelled to yield the palm of victory to another that is inferior to it, even when truth and right are on the side of the former.

How shall difficulties be obviated, and the thing in question be attained ?

The aforementioned Doctor King proposes to youth, the method of committing to memory some of the finest passages of the English classics, for colloquial use. But with great deference to so high an authority, I must needs think that this method is very exceptionable.

The practice of echoing in conversation the express sentences and phrases of celebrated authors, besides being pedantic and fulsome, tends to enfeeble the understanding, how much soever it may strengthen the memory. It is like leaning on a staff in walking; the staff, however substantial and beauteous, either *finds* the body inert and clumsy, that leans much upon it, or *makes* it so.

Speech is the vehicle of thought, and approximates toward perfection in proportion to the ease and celerity with which it conveys thought. This depends very much on judicious practice ; as a theoretical knowledge of the rules of any of the arts is insufficient without practice, so it is with respect to language. Though one had a critical knowledge of all the rules of English grammar, and could give the meaning of all the words in this language, still he would be awkward both in speaking and writing the language, till practice had made him ready and expert. It is by practice that one gets the aptitude of conforming to the rules of grammar without effort, or even so much as thinking of them, and it is by practice that we learn so to connect and arrange words, that each shall be in its proper place, and the fittest for the place which it is put in.

To combine, and express with readiness the thoughts represented by language, requires not only a sufficient knowledge of the meaning of words, but also the faculty of having them always at hand; in which case, one can always express distinctly whatever he conceives distinctly—otherwise, he hesitates, however clear are his ideas. In this last respect lies the principal difficulty with many: though ideas or thoughts are clear in their minds, and they have a good knowledge of words, their speech is rather faltering than fluent, because the proper words do not spontaneously occur at the moment they are wanted.

There is, perhaps, a method to remove this great difficulty, in part, if not altogether. A thoroughly practised artisan, whose trade requires a variety and frequent change of tools, spends not a moment in studying which tool he shall take up next; the proper one presents itself without any effort at selection. Now words are the tools of intellect. If thoughts be only distinct in the mind, there will be no need to ponder and search for words to express them; which, on all occasions, will be on the tongue, ready to be uttered, if they are enrooted in the memory. A good speller is not puzzled for letters, nor how to place them: only make the requisite words as familiar to the mind as the letters of the alphabet, and they will come to the speaker, whenever they are wanted, as letters to the speller: both occur habitually.

To effectuate this, let one write down, alphabetically, from a dictionary, the roots of as many well-selected words, as in fine hand would cover about three sheets of paper, and with his eye run over them occasionally, till they become as familiar as the letters of the alphabet. It would take up not much time, and might be done in vacant hours; and perhaps the consequences, at length, would be a copiousness of words, ready for use, and, as it were, offering themselves whenever wanted.

None that I know of has made this experiment, except one: and he too far advanced in age to expect to receive benefit from it himself, other than that of obviating, or partly obviating the dreaded effects of an inveterate malady of an *oblivious* character. This verv imperfect experiment, I am well certified, resulted in his full belief that, had he hit upon it in his juvenile years, and tried it thoroughly, it might have helped him considerably to the faculty of ready expression, or fluency, of which he has ever felt the need.

Some few are gifted with a happy fecundity of words and a volubility of tongue, while the minds of others, though equally intelligent, are slow; and it is only these last who need the *nostrum* which I have ventured to prescribe notwithstanding its liableness to ridicule.

NUMBER LXXXV.

A COMMENT UPON THE FABLE OF THE INVISIBLE SPECTACLES.

"JOVE, once upon a time" (as an old heathen fable relates) "having ordered that Pleasure and Pain should be mixed, in equal proportions, in every dose of human life; upon a complaint that some men endeavored to separate what he had joined, and taking more than their share of the sweet, would leave all the sour for others; commanded Mercury to put a stop to this evil, by placing upon each delinquent a pair of invisible spectacles, which should change the appearance of things, making pain look like pleasure, and pleasure like pain, labor like recreation, and recreation like labor."

If by the *Invisible Spectacles* we are to understand the illusions which mislead the judgment in regard to the true comforts and interests of life, it is pretty certain that no kind of spectacles is in so general use. In the days of youth, almost every thing is seen through these false glasses, which very many wear all their lifetime, in spite of age and experience.

One of the most needful of all arts, is the art of *computing*.

It is deemed indispensably necessary in all kinds of business. And hence we send our children to school, to learn the use of figures, and how to cast up accounts, and foot them to a nicety. One who has no knowledge at all of the nine figures of arithmetic, who even knows not that two and two make four, is regarded as fit for no sort of business above that of a menial servant. But besides the knowledge of figures, there is another branch of the art of computing, which is of superior importance: I mean an accurate knowledge of the value of things, considered in relation to our own real comfort and happiness. This is a kind of knowledge not in itself so very difficult to learn, but which, nevertheless, is hidden from multitudes of men and women of good natural parts, by reason that their manner is to view things through the medium, as it were, of magic spectacles, rather than with the naked and unprejudiced eye of reason.

Apart from considering the common and fatal illusions through which immortal joys are sacrificed to transient pleasure, a great many, for want of skill in the art of computing, make wrong judgments about *Pleasure*, on the right choice of which their worldly weal depends in no inconsiderable measure. Scorning, or overlooking the simple and innocent pleasures of life, which are given in common to human beings, which no arts of refinement can considerably increase, and which excess never fails to embitter,—they lose the good they have, by their unfortunate longings after some unattainable state of earthly felicity. Pursuing pleasure with eagerness, and as an employment, they purchase pain; and that, at the expense of fortune, health, character, and peace of mind. At this dear rate they purchase the most grievous of pain,—to wit, that of satiety, which consists in loathing life and its enjoyments. He that is not man enough to govern his appetites, cannot make himself brute enough to indulge and pamper them without remorse; and, therefore, in the very circumstance, in which he places his chief good, he is far less happy than some of the irrational animals around him.

But to return to the fabulous spectacles. It may be taken for certain that, though invisible, they are actually worn by all persons belonging to any of the following classes.

They certainly wear them, who fondly hope to find happiness in a life devoted to idleness and an unrestrained indulgence of passion and appetite. With respect to their true good, as relates even to this life alone, they are under a deplorable mistake. For it is an axiom built upon irrefragable experience, that if mere corporeal gratification were intended to be the main object of our pursuits, yet even then, with regard to real enjoyment, industry would be preferable to sloth, and temperance to excess.

They wear them, who incessantly moil and toil, are hard dealers, illiberal, uncharitable, incompassionate to the poor;—and all for the sake of hoarding up treasure for their children. Blind infatuation! Often, very often, it happens that such hoards are squandered in a much shorter time than it took to gather them.

They wear them, who, though possessing a competence, fret their hearts and imbitter their lives with covetings after riches. Were they to view things in a true light, they would be thankful, rather than discontented and querulous; since their condition is precisely that which is best calculated to furnish the greatest amount of genuine earthly comfort.

They wear them, who sacrifice realities to appearances, substantial comforts to airy notions, who would rather *feel* misery than not *seem* happy, who impoverish and beggar themselves for the sake of appearing more prosperous and felicitous than those of the common sort. The folly of such people's calculations is seen by everybody but themselves.

They wear them, who lay the scenes of their happiness abroad rather than at home. It is a certain trnth, that one who lives on uneasy terms with himself, can find very little enjoyment in extrinsic objects. So that the very first step in the road to solid happiness, is the acquirement of a contented mind ; because without a disposition to contentment, any change of place, or of outward condition, is only the exchange of one sort of disquietude for another. And as the spring of happiness is found in our own minds, or nowhere ; so, "well ordered *Home*" is the true centre of its enjoyment. Mothers, whose chief satisfaction lies in circles of fashion and scenes of amusement, have their vision wofully distorted by means of the magic spectacles. Else they would clearly see that the occupation of nursing, rearing, and instructing their families, is what furnishes the sweetest of pleasures, at the same time that it is one of the first of duties.

NUMBER LXXXVI.

OF THE MISUSE, AND THE PROPER USE, OF READING.

"Read not to contradict or confute, nor to believe and take for granted, but to weigh and consider."

LORD BACON.

THE age we live in, has been remarkably a reading age. Books are more numerous and of more easy access, than at any former period; and the number of readers has increased astonishingly since the middle of the last century. In a general view this is of good omen, for reading is one of the principal keys of knowledge; it unlocks, as it were, a mine of intellectual wealth, and contributes to its general diffusion. There is much reason to think, however, that the progress of real, sound knowledge has not kept pace with the progress of reading: for the slow pace of the former in comparison to that of the latter, there being the several causes which here follow.

By reason of the abundance and superabundance of books, the best are commonly read superficially, and by many not read at all; the attentions of the reading public being distracted with such a boundless variety. If there were only one book in the world, and its copies so multiplied that it were in every one's hands, almost every body would have it by heart. Or, if there were only a few books, and they accessible to all, those few would be pondered and studied till a considerable part of their contents were treasured up in the minds and memories of the generality of readers. But now that books are so numerous, the readers skip from one to another, without settling their attention upon any; so that many who are fairly entitled to the credit of great reading, are very little improved in their intellectual faculties. They eagerly devour books, but properly digest and appropriate scarcely any thing therein, and their minds are plethoric, but destitute of vigor.

Besides this, with the bulk of the bookish tribe, reading has become an idle amusement rather than a serious and laborious occupation. They read for pleasure more than for profit. The acquirement of a fund of really useful knowledge scarcely comes within the scope of their object, which is chiefly to beguile the tedious hours by furnishing food for the imagination. And hence it is, that no books are so palatable, or so generally read, and with so much eagerness, as the lighter compositions which are fraught with amusement, but are barren of sound instruction. A novel even of the lowest cast, finds more readers than a serious work of great merit.

Moreover, the perpetual influx of new books has occasioned a raging appetite for novelty of some kind or other, no matter what; so that the attention of most readers is directed rather to what is new, than to what is valuable and excellent. This kind of curiosity is insatiable; for the more it is fed, the more it craves. Old authors are neglected because they are old, and new ones engross the attention because they are new. The standard compositions of former ages are cast aside as lumber; while a new pretender, with less than a fourth part of their abilities, is sure to find a momentary welcome at least.

From these causes it happens, that a great deal of reading does by no means imply a great stock of valuable knowledge. On the contrary, it often leaves the mind empty of almost every thing but vanity; none being more vain, or more intolerable, than those who, having learned by rote a multitude of maxims and facts, deal them out by the gross, on all occasions, and in all companies. The food which they have derived from reading lies in their minds undigested, and while it occasions a preternatural tumor there, it gives neither growth nor strength. Their reading has scarcely brought into exercise any one of the intellectual faculties besides the memory, which has been loaded and kept in perpetual action, whilst their understandings and judgments remain dormant. They are proud that they have read so much, but have reason rather to be ashamed that they know so little.

One who would really profit by reading must take heed *what* he reads, and *how*.

The use of reading is to render one more wise and virtuous, rather than more learned; and that point is to be gained, not so much from the quantity, as the quality of the books which we peruse. No single individual has leisure enough, nor is any life long enough, for a thorough perusal of even the tenth part of the books now extant in the English language. A selection is, therefore, necessary, and much depends upon making it judiciously. An inconsiderable number of well chosen and well studied books, will enable one to make far greater advances in real knowledge, than lightly skimming over hundreds of volumes taken up indiscriminately.

In reading, attention is to be paid also to the *How*, as well as to the *What*. The proper object of reading is not merely to inform us of what others think, but also to furnish us with materials for thinking ourselves, or for the employment and exercise of our judgments and understandings, and of all our intellectual and moral faculties. It is not enough that it supplies us with a multitude of facts; for the knowledge of facts is valuable to us chiefly for the inferences that we ourselves may draw from them, or because they furnish us with the means of exercising and exerting our own powers in the way of comparing, reasoning, and judging, and of drawing sound conclusions of the future from the past.

Knowledge cannot be bequeathed as a patrimony, or purchased with money; there is no other way to obtain it but by close attention and labor of the mind. Whoever would get knowledge in any uncommon degree, must seek for it as for silver. If it be a toil, it is one that is sweetened with pleasures peculiarly its own. Indeed it is questionable whether it would be so well for us if we could get learning without labor; for one of the essential benefits of education is, that it inures the mind to apply itself steadily to any thing that requires its particular attention in a word, it tends to form the precious habit of calling home our wandering thoughts at pleasure, and bringing them to a point.

After all, book learning alone is insufficient for human concerns. To use a quotation from Dr. Johnson: "Books, says Bacon, *can never teach the use of books.* The student must learn by commerce with mankind to reduce his speculations to practice, and accommodate his knowledge to the purposes of life."

One observation more I will make, and hope it may be carefully heeded. We err no less in not turning to good account what we know, than in neglecting to increase our stock of knowledge. What doth it profit though a man have much knowledge, if he is not better, more wise and virtuous in his conduct, and more useful to the community? If it makes him but the worse, he turns the blessing to a curse.

NUMBER LXXXVII.

OF EXCESSIVE AND INDISCRIMINATE NOVEL READING.

The age we live in, may justly be called the age of Novels and of Novelists. This brotherhood and sisterhood of writers are of modern origin. If we except the romances of the middle ages—who, by the by, however wild and extravagant they appear, are thought to exhibit pretty correct delineations of the coarseness, ferociousness, and brutality of the manners of their times—if we except those old romances, there were few novelists of any note prior to about the middle of the last century.

It was then that Fielding, and Richardson, and Smollett appeared before the public: an astonishing trio, whose brilliance of genius, command of language, and distinct insight into the feelings and passions of the human heart, enabled them to adorn their pages with fascinating charms. To the works of these geniuses there succeeded swarms of imitators of each sex, and of every grade, as well in Germany as in Britain: so that the reading world, for the last thirty years, has been inundated, as it were, with novels, of which every one finds readers.

It is an obvious fact, that books of no other kind are read with so much eagerness by the American youth of both sexes, as novels, or narratives of feigned incidents, characters and scenery; for though they seldom tempt to a second reading, they as seldom fail of being read once. In this respect, it makes very little difference whether a novel be the fruit of genius, or of hair-brained folly; whether it has the stamp of learning, or proceeds from the pen of conceited ignorance; whether it sketches real life, or outstrips the extravagance of Bedlam;—if the thing be but new, it is earnestly inquired for, and eagerly perused.

And where lies the harm? Not in the nature of this species of writing, for it is not censurable in itself. We have the highest of all authorities for the use of parables: they have been made the vehicle for conveying moral truth in the most cogent and captivating, and, at the same time, the most inoffensive manner. Apologues and fables are worthy of praise rather than blame, if framed with ingenuity, and made of manifest tendency to promote good morals. And the like may be said of the species of writing that goes under the denomination of novels: it is not censurable as a species of composition, but as a species of composition that has been generally and deplorably perverted by misuse. It is not to be denied that a novel may be so fashioned by well-directed talent, as to blend amusement with instruction, entertainment with the moral improvement of the mind; nor is it to be affirmed that there are no instances of this happy combination; some there are, though comparatively few. But the harm of novel reading, carried to the excess of extravagance to which the present age has carried it, lies partly at least in the following particulars, which my limits will allow me barely to mention.

1. Passing over the baser sort of novels, or such as have a direct tendency to deprave the mind and the heart, it may be confidently affirmed that the greater part of the rest, though they profess to have a moral purpose, do in no measure inculcate pure *Christian* morals, but those of a spurious kind; the standard of their morality being very little higher, if any, than that of the highest order of the pagan school.

2. There is always danger, especially as regards youth, of cultivating the imagination too much, and the more solid faculties of our nature too little; and it is of the nature of most novels to produce this effect: they expand and bloat the imagination without informing the understanding, or maturing the judgment.

3. The pictures of life given in novels, are not usually those of common, but of high life; and they can be, therefore, of no practical use at all to persons who are not destined to move in the highest circles. On the other hand, they tend to sophisticate their manners as well as their morals; the manners of dukes and duchesses being widely remote from what should be the manners of plain men and women.

4. Novel-readers, unless gifted with a more than ordinary fund of sound sense, are prone to slide into a romantic habit of thinking, and to cherish extravagant expectations. Finding in the books they are most accustomed to, a series of preternatural events; astonishing effects produced without even a shadow of cause; persons suddenly raised, as by magic, from humble circumstances to boundless opulence and loftiness of rank;—finding in the books which they ponder by day and through the vigils of

the night, a perpetual recurrence of such unearthly scenery described in glowing language; it is no wonder that they cherish preposterous hopes; nor is it a wonder if they become disgusted with the homely scenes and occupations of ordinary life, and look with contempt upon every situation, enjoyment, or connection, that is actually attainable by them.

5. If novels have the good effect of beguiling the young into a passion for reading, they have, also, not unfrequently, the bad effect of so enervating their minds that there is left them neither industry, nor relish for sober history, or for any thing else that requires the labor of their understandings and judgments.

6. This kind of reading has a tendency to vitiate the taste, as well in regard to style as to sentiment. The readers of novels—they who read them indiscriminately or without selection—are accustomed to a style nauseously sweet, or vapidly towering; consisting of spangled heaps of words and images, which smother the sense, where sense there is. Thus accustomed, their feelings are no less repugnant to plain sober language than to plain sober sense.

It does by no means follow from what has been said, that parents and instructors should lay their children under an absolute interdiction with respect to the reading of novels. For, not to mention that such is the texture of our general nature that prohibition has a stimulating power, so that if a book never so worthless were prohibited by law, almost every body would wish to read it;—there are, no doubt, some novels, which might be put into the hands of the young, with safety, and to their real advantage. The danger lies in reading them indiscriminately or without selection, and in making them a principal part of reading.—

"Those novels which paint the manners and character of the body of mankind, and affect the reader with the relation of misfortunes that may befall himself," may be perused, now and then, not only as an amusement, but as a profitable study;—yet, after all, it is *real* life, with which we must chiefly have to do.

NUMBER LXXXVIII.

OF THE IMPASSABLE AND UNALTERABLE LIMITS TO THE PLEASURES OF SENSE.

THE pleasures of sense, common to all animal natures, can admit of very little increase by the refinements of art, and, at the same time, are bounded and limited by impassable barriers. I say *impassable* barriers, for you no sooner have overleaped them than the pleasure is gone, and satiety, disgust, or some kind or other of painful dissatisfaction, succeeds to its place.

Sweet as is the light, too much of it would instantly destroy the organ of vision. Pleasant as it is to see the sun, yet to look steadfastly upon him in his meridian glory, would cause pain, and even blindness. The light of that luminary, by which alone we see the innumerable objects that are visible to us, is *colored;* else our feeble organ of sight could endure it scarcely for a moment. For what if the whole sky, the whole earth, and every object above and around us, shone with the unmingled brightness of *uncolored* light? In that case, the light itself would become darkness, since every eye must instantly be blinded by it.

And as with sight, so with hearing. A sound that is too

strong and forcible, deafens the ear. Nay, even the most sweet and harmonious sounds, when long continued, or very often repeated, become indifferent to the ear, if not tiresome.

In like manner, the smell is sickened with perpetual fragrance, and the palate surfeited by overmuch sweetness.

Even the joy of mere animal nature, when it exceeds the just bounds, becomes a disturber. Overmuch joy of this sort, is inquietude; it banishes quiet sleep as effectually as pungent grief.

Hence it falls out, agreeably to the established constitution of our nature, that scarcely any persons lead more unpleasant lives than those who pursue pleasure with the most eagerness. And so it must needs be, because their over eagerness of desire, by spurring them on to perpetual excess, turns their pleasures to pains, and their very recreations to scenes of wearisome drudgery.

If Solomon had not told us from his own experience, that such a course of life is not only vanity, but vexation of spirit; yet the world abounds with instances to prove and illustrate it.—Of these I will now cite two eminent ones of the last age.

Richard Nash, Esq.,—commonly called Beau Nash—who died, 1781, aged eighty-seven, was Master of the Ceremonies, or King of Bath, for the space of nearly half a century. His body was athletic, his constitution strong and healthy, and his ruling passions were vanity, and keenness of desire for fashionable dissipation. To his darling wishes the means of indulgence exactly and altogether corresponded. Presiding over the amusements of the courtiers, and nobility, and gentry of England, he gratified his vanity with the finery and costliness of his apparel, and with the implicit obedience paid to his orders; and whilst employed in providing banquets of pleasure for his voluptuous guests, he seldom neglected his opportunities of carving plenteously for himself.—Beau Nash, enjoyed what is called *pleasure*, for a greater length of time, and refined upon it more exquisitely, than perhaps any other man that is now among the living or the dead. Yet, setting aside all the awful considerations of futurity, no one that reads the story of his life with any degree of sound reflection, will be led to think that he had more real enjoyment of it, than falls to the ordinary lot of mankind, or even near so much. A biographer of Nash, in speaking of the latter stages of his life, observes: "He was now past the period of giving or receiving pleasure, for he was poor, old and peevish; yet still he was incapable of turning from his former manner of life to pursue happiness. The old man endeavored to practise the follies of the boy; and he seemed willing to find lost appetite among the scenes where he once was young."

A remarkable counterpart to the life of Mr. Nash, is that of Mademoiselle de L'Espinasse; which clearly shows that the most unhappy of women are those who have no taste for simple domestic comforts.

It is related of this most accomplished French lady, who had been the unrivalled leader of fashion in France, during a part of the last century, "That she not only lived, but almost died, in public; that while she was tortured with disease, and her heart so torn with agonizing passions as frequently to turn her thoughts on suicide, she dined out and made visits every day; and that, when she was visibly within a few weeks of her end, and was wasted with coughs and with spasms, she still had her saloon filled twice a day with company, and dragged herself out to supper with all the countesses of her acquaintance."

To be *temperate in all things*, is as really a matter of interest as of duty. If there were even no unlawfulness in excess, nor any punishment following it in the coming world, yet it ever brings with it a punishment here; a punishment that more than countervails the enjoyment. And, on the other hand, if there were neither virtue nor duty in moderation of enjoying the pleasures of sense, yet it carries along with it its own reward, as it is the only way of deriving from those pleasures all the satisfaction which it is of their nature to give. So that to enjoy innocently, and in strict conformity to the rules of reason and of our holy religion, results ordinarily in a greater amount of real pleasure, than is to be found by the epicure or the voluptuary. It is excellently observed by Doctor Reid, on the Mind—"If one could by a soft and luxurious life, acquire a more delicate sensibility to pleasure, it must be at the expense of a like sensibility to pain, from which he can never promise himself exemption; and at the expense of cherishing many diseases which produce pain."

Beware of *Pleasure!* The envenomed serpent couches under the gay and fragrant flower.

NUMBER LXXXIX.

OF THE DIFFERENCE BETWEEN IGNORANCE AND A NATURAL WEAKNESS OF UNDERSTANDING.

ATLHOUGH ignorance and foolishness are near akin, there is, nevertheless, a material difference between them; the former consisting in the destitution of what is called learning, and the latter in narrowness or weakness of the understanding.

Some ignorant men, or, in other words, some men of little or no learning, manifest strength of memory, clearness of conception, and soundness of judgment; and, within the narrow compass of their own observation, their remarks are just, and sometimes profound. Though not capable of reasoning exactly according to the rules of logic, yet they do reason conclusively, and not unfrequently, by a native plainness and directness of understanding, they reach the point by the shortest way. In defiance of bad grammar and uncouth phraseology, there is discoverable in them a mine of intellectual lore which, had it been properly worked and refined, might have enriched and adorned society.

On the other hand, some learned men are foolish after all.

When a strong memory is coupled with a weak understanding, (which is a union neither impossible, nor quite uncommon)—in such a case, though a great deal of learning is attainable, the possessor is not much the wiser for it; and as to the unfortunate wights who are constrained to keep him company, they are rather plagued than profited by his learning. He is incessantly throwing it in their faces, and gorging them with it even to surfeiting. The garner of his memory is ample, and it is full; every thing is there, but nothing in its right place; and having no faculty of discrimination, he more often brings out of his treasury, for use or for show, the wrong thing than the right. If you want of him only a string of *tape*, he measures you off whole yards of *brocade*. He must needs pour forth a flood of learning upon every thing, and to every body; and he lectures upon literature and science, and quotes scrap after scrap from the ancients, without any regard to time, or place, or company.

In the course of the last age, one of this sort, namely, Dr. George, of London, a most eminent Greek scholar, who knew little else but Greek, expressed his wonder at the fame of Frederick of Prussia. "For my part," quoth the Doctor, "I cannot regard Frederick as a truly great man, for I doubt his being able so much as to conjugate one of the Greek verbs;"—and the learned Grecian proceeded to name to the company a particular verb, which he thought would be more than a match for his Majesty's head.

This species of pedantry, which was more prevalent, by many degrees, at some former times than at the present, is keenly satirized in the following lines of Winne's translation of Boileau.

"Brimful of learning see that pedant stride,
Bristling with horrid Greek, and puff'd with pride!
A thousand authors he in vain has read,
And with their maxims stuff'd his empty head;
And thinks that, without Aristotle's rule,
Reason is blind, and common sense a fool."

Learned foolishness, is more egregiously foolish than the folly of ignorance. It is wayward, positive, and imperious; too conceited and indocile to be informed, and too obstinate to forsake error. Men, distempered with this kind of foolishness, imagine themselves wise overmuch, because they have read a great many books, and can repeat, in more than one language, perhaps, what others have said and written: whereas, they are like a gourmand, whose digestive faculties bear no proportion to the largeness of his swallow. They task and load the memory, without exercising the judgment. They lay up in the memory, facts heaped upon facts, without order and without distinction;—and these are in the memory *only*—the noble powers of the understanding being not at all, or very little, occupied about them.

Learning, in itself, is not wisdom. "We may be learned from the thoughts of others;—wise we cannot be but from our own."

The foregoing observations are, in no wise, disparaging to the legitimate honors of learning. For what though in some it produces the pedantry of conceited weakness, and what though as to others it is perverted to vile purposes? Learning itself is not to blame; nor is it the less excellent for these disfiguring excrescences, which no more belong to it than doth a wen to the proper form of the human body.

Literature, conjoined with science, and resulting in a high

degree of civilization, is the procurer of all the embellishments and delights, and of most of the conveniences and comforts of our present condition; the civilized world being raised now almost as much above the condition it stood in, when classical learning was first rising on Europe, in the fifteenth century, as it then was above that of the hordes of roaming savages. Add to this, that the pleasure of learning, like that of religion, is not confined to time or place, nor dependent upon the smiles of fortune. It may be enjoyed in solitude, in penury, and in old age; which last does sometimes, if not often, increase rather than diminish it.

In conclusion; having observed above, that learning furnishes food or materials for thought, I will venture to recommend to readers an excellent rule, taken from the practice of a very eminent man of the last age. It is this:—In reading, observe the course of your thoughts rather than of your books. Sometimes your reading will give occasion to a thought, not connected with the subject which your book treats of; and in such a case, drop the course of your reading, and follow the course of the thought that has been started.

NUMBER XC.

OF EVIL THINKING.

"He that would seriously set upon the search of truth," says the great Locke, "ought in the first place to prepare his mind with a love of it; for he that loves it not, will not take much pains to get it, nor be much concerned when he misses it. There is nobody in the commonwealth of learning who does not profess himself a lover of truth: and there is not a rational creature that would not take it amiss to be thought otherwise of. And yet, for all this, one may truly say, there are very few lovers of truth for truth's sake, even amongst those who persuade themselves that they are so. How a man may know whether he be so in earnest, is worth inquiry, and I think there is one unerring mark of it, viz. the not entertaining any proposition with greater assurance, than the proofs it is built upon will warrant."

These weighty sentiments, so worthy to be carried with us in all our secular, and in all our moral and religious concerns, are particularly applicable to the subject of *evil-thinking.* Downright, wilful slander is considered on all hands as a detestable vice; and a person, habitually guilty of it in its grossness, is marked as a foe to society. A man, a woman, or a family that is notoriously infected with this foul malady, is watched as carefully as is a pickpocket, or a common cheat. But it unhappily falls out that, although gross, wilful slander commonly meets with the reprobation it merits, yet what is nearly related to it, passes with very little censure or remorse.—I mean the *taking up* a reproach against one's neighbor, or *believing* an ill report of another upon slight grounds, or without sufficient evidence.

The commonness of this fault seems to evince a strong predisposition to it in our very nature. It is a remark of the great British moralist, Dr. Johnson, that "there are two causes of belief; Evidence and Inclination." When we are in no manner inclined to believe a thing, we naturally require full evidence of it before we yield our credence: and, on the other hand, when we are powerfully inclined to believe, we can do so, not only without evidence, but against it. Hence it would seem, that we naturally have a strong inclination to believe or think ill of others, since we so often do it on no real proof, or on what is next to none.

How happens it that, even in well-ordered society, scandal flies as upon the wings of the wind? That it so quickly spreads over a whole neighborhood, parish or town? That it continues to widen its circle from day to day, till every body knows it save one, to wit, the very person scandalized?—Does not this argue a general love of scandal?—Perhaps you will say No; and will hold, that two or three tale-bearers or busy-bodies may have done the whole mischief. But how could they have done it, if they had not found a multitude of ears to listen to their tale, and a multitude of tongues to aid them in its circulation? As there would be no thieves of one kind, if there were no receivers of stolen goods, so there would be no tale-bearers, if there were no eager listeners to their buzz; and as the receiver is as bad as the thief, so the eager listener to groundless scandal, is well-nigh as bad as its author, or at least possesses some portion of the same depravity of feeling and temper.

No one has travelled very far upon the journey of life, and been an observant traveller, who has not noticed the manner, in which, for a while, this "pestilence walketh in darkness," and then bursts forth into open day. The foul report is for some time communicated in whispers, accompanied with solemn injunctions of secrecy. Every one professes to hope it is not true, and yet every one whispers it to every one's acquaintance. At length it becomes a common report; a matter of public notoriety. It is in every body's mouth, and every body *must* believe it; because, according to one orthodox old saying, "What every body says, must be true;" and according to another of equally sacred authority, "Where there is much smoke, there must be some fire." It is a settled point. In the public opinion, the case is decided, and the defamed party is cast off. All are of one mind, that there must be something in it; though, here and there, one charitable body or another, expresses a faint hope that the affair may not turn out to be quite so scandalous as it is represented.

Last of all, after the lapse of months, it reaches the astonished ears of the person most immediately concerned. It is sifted, and turns out a sheer fabrication, invented and first put in circulation by *Nobody*. Search is made in vain for the author, who lies snugly concealed amidst the multitude.

Well, then the matter is cleared up, and all the slur is wiped away at last from the character of the defamed. Not exactly so, nor indeed can it be. Some are no less loath to disbelieve, than they were forward to believe. Some who pretend to be very glad at the result, secretly wish it had been a little otherwise. Some have their doubts still; and some, again, have no inclination to examine the disproof of the calumny, though they had swallowed it with a voracious appetite.

NUMBER XCI.

OF TREATING CHILDREN WITH EXCESSIVE SEVERITY.

In the excellent little tract of Dr. Cotton Mather's, entitled, "Essays to do Good," the venerable author lays down for himself the following rule, in regard to his treatment of children: "*will never use corporeal punishment except it be for an atrocious crime, or for a smaller fault obstinately persisted in.*" A maxim which deserves to be written in golden characters, or rather, and far better, to be engraven upon the hearts of parents, and instructors of schools. Nor is it at all inconsistent with the maxim in Holy Writ, "*He that spareth the rod hateth his son.*" For, by no fair interpretation, can this last be made to mean, that the discipline of the rod is necessary in any cases other than the aforementioned.

Obedience is the first lesson to be inculcated upon childhood. Ere it can discern between good and evil, the child should be taught to obey. Then it is that the task is comparatively easy, and may be effected by a small measure of prudent enforcement. No restraint, however, should be imposed upon childhood, but such as is salutary, and of obvious necessity. All and every needless restraint is tyrannous in its nature, and hurtful in its consequences. The child should be habituated to *passive* obedience, and, at the same time, be permitted to enjoy freedom of action in things indifferent;—to speak as a child, to act as a child,—to be lively and playsome as a child. One, whose childhood is closely held in trammels, whose merely childish things incur rebukes and frowns, is full likely to make a licentious use of freedom when it arrives, or else to be a mopus all his days.

Children should be carefully guarded against every species of useless vexation.

"Provoke not your children to anger, lest they be discouraged." Lay upon them none but necessary and wholesome restrictions. Never cross them for the mere sake of showing your authority. Reclaim with a lenient hand their involuntary errors. Mark not against them with a severe eye their trivial aberrations. Be no less ready to commend their well-doing than to blame them for doing ill. Otherwise, the obedience paid you will be uncheerful, constrained, and slavish. If you are of a fault-finding temper, you will occasion the very faults you seek after. Your children, out of despair of pleasing you, will become regardless both of your pleasure and displeasure, except in so far as they are influenced by slavish fear.

As to stubbornness, or obstinate disobedience, "this *kind* goeth not out" but by severe discipline. It must be mastered by blows if nothing else will do, and the earlier the better. But for the rest, mild and persuasive methods are far preferable.

Over young minds, the law of love might be made to have a much more powerful influence than the penal law. Much more easily are they drawn and guided by their affections than driven by their fears; the tenor of the former being spontaneous, steady, and uniform; while the latter operate only by occasional excitement. You have the fastest hold of the child that you hold by "the cords of love." By these cords you can draw him with ease. Delighting to please, and of course dreading to offend you, it is in your power to imprint in his mind indelible characters; to weed out his wayward propensities; to awaken his emulation; to stimulate his industry; and to mould him to sentiments and habits, preparatory to excellence in after life. But fear alone is an unnatural and odious tie, which the child is ever desirous to break loose from. It stimulates indeed, but not in the manner to produce those ingenuous sentiments and feelings, which are the foundation of excellence in character.

Experience abundantly shows, that degrading punishment has rather a pernicious, than a salutary effect, upon the minds of full-grown persons. Few culprits, if any, were ever made better by means of the whipping-post and the stocks, or by cropping their ears, or in fixing a brand of infamy upon the forehead or hand. Instead of being led to amendment by these means, they generally are made the more desperate and abandoned, by reason that they view their characters as irretrievably lost. So that, after having gone through one of these ordeals of shame, they ever after are utterly shameless.

Now it should be remembered, that children are as men and women in miniature; possessed of the like passions, and particularly of the like feelings of honor and disgrace. Moreover, in children the most promising, these feelings are the most acute. They have a keen sensibility to shame, whereof a good use may be made by prudent management ; but if this sensibility be put to hard proof, and that frequently, it becomes blunted, and their minds grow callous. And a child that is lost to shame, and to all self-respect, is in peculiar danger of being a lost child.

And besides, none are more unpitiful and cruel than those who have been brought up under the cruellest discipline, which seldom fails to blunt their feelings, and produce hardness of heart and ferociousness of temper. The cruellest of slave-drivers are those that had been bred slaves, and had daily felt the smart of the lash. And by parity of reason, children that are trained up under parents or governors, who carry punishment beyond the bounds of kind correction into those of vengeance, and who delight to inflict such punishment as attaches infamy, must needs possess more than a common measure of native amiability, if in the end they turn out sweet-tempered, humane, and of a nice sense of honor.

I will conclude with the words of the great Locke.—" To break the spirits of children by too severe usage, is to them a greater injury than the opposite extreme of indulgence, for there is more hope, that a wild undisciplined spirit will become orderly, than of raising up one made abject and heartless by severity of discipline."

NUMBER XCII.

OF DRAWING AND FIXING THE ATTENTION OF CHILDREN.

The great Locke, a man of almost unrivalled depth and acuteness of understanding, in his excellent treatise on Education, expresses himself as here follows:—"He that has found a way how to keep up a child's spirit easy, active, and free, and yet, at the same time, to restrain him from many things he has a mind to, and to draw him to things that are uneasy to him; he, I say, that knows how to reconcile these seeming contradictions, has, in my opinion, got the true secret of education."

This is a sentiment of no ordinary importance. No less just than profound, it is entitled to the strict regard of parents, of preceptors, and of all who have the management of children.

The true power over children, is that of swaying their inclinations; the power of withdrawing their inclinations from one direction, and settling them down in another. It is not hard words, nor hard blows, that can gain this point. The *will* is wrought upon by other methods. Of many examples that might go to illustrate this matter, I will adduce one, and a notable one.

Horatio Nelson, so famous in naval history, had at first an utter aversion to the sea ; of which, in no long time, he came to be extravagantly fond. And what miracle, or magic, wrought this change in him ? It was wrought neither by miracle nor by magic, but by a very natural process. The captain, who was his uncle, caressed the boy, treated him with familiarity and confidence, and not unfrequently consulted him as if he were a man, and his equal. This management enkindled in him the dormant sparks of genius and emulation, and changed, as it were, his inward frame. He was quite another boy. From being diffident and sheepish, he at once became most active and enterprising; and from loathing the service, his whole inclination was bent upon excelling in it. Had his boyhood fallen into different hands, he might probably have turned out a very different character. Nor would it, perhaps, be too much to assert, that the victory of the Nile, was an event in connection with the impressions made on the tender years of Nelson by Captain Suckling.

In whatever you would teach your children, the main thing is to bring their minds to it in good earnest; after which, the rest is easy. In their play they are all alike active, because they all love it; and so it would be as to their learning, if they could be once brought to love *that* as well as they love play. For it is generally for want of attention, rather than of sufficient faculties, that children are dull to learn; and in exciting and fixing their attention, the great art of the teacher lies.

Now the habit of attention, that is, attention of the genuine sort, is seldom, or never, wrought in them by operating merely upon their fears. The dread of pain might indeed force them on to the performance of their task, but still they would perform it *as* a task, and with any other feelings than those of delight: whereas the proper attention springs from a real delight in the thing they are about. This is wrought in them by awakening the more generous feelings of their nature—the love of esteem, and the desire of excelling. It is what requires skill, patient industry, and able management; while, on the other hand, to make children attentive, after a sort, to their learning, by means of menaces and stripes, is a short, easy, and lazy method, requiring as little of trouble, as of talent; but always falling wofully short of the true mark.

And as in learning, so in whatever reputable and useful employment else, the young mind, by skilful management, might be made to prefer it, and to take more pleasure in it than in doing nothing. The busiest age is that of childhood. It is then they are most inclined to be ever about something, and make it their chief delight to keep moving. This seems to furnish clear proof that industry is natural to our species; in which case, education has little else to do than to give it a proper direction. Children, who of their own accord *play* with unweariable industry, might always, perhaps, be induced to apply themselves, at the proper age, with the like spontaneous industry, to things of importance. But then, in order to it, their inclinations must be led, rather than forced. Play itself would presently become irksome and disgustful to children, if they were driven to it, and kept at it, by main force. And much less can you expect that they will be diligent and active in business, unless you so prevail over their inclinations, as that they choose it of their own free will: a thing of no great difficulty, for the most part, if it be set about in season, and conducted with prudence.

There is a great difference between lumpish laziness, and frisky idleness. One who is too lazy to move himself about, is diseased in the very core, and there is no help for him. Of such however the number is small. Whereas the numerous tribe of idlers, or of such as spend their time without profit to themselves or others, are generally, nevertheless, frivolously busy, and quite active in their own way; and had they been tutored aright in their early years, their natural activity might have turned to excellent account.

NUMBER XCIII.

OF BALANCING THE PRINCIPLES OF HOPE AND FEAR IN THE GOVERNANCE OF CHILDREN.

Hopes and Fears are the great springs of human actions; and though seemingly standing in opposition to one another, they jointly contribute to the accomplishment of the same ends. Hope that is altogether fearless, acts with rashness, or sinks into torpitude; but accompanied with fear, it is vigilant as well as diligent. On the other hand, fear unaccompanied with hope, is despair: and despair furnishes no stimulation at all to enterprise. It is by the due balancing of these two grand principles, Hope and Fear, that the human species is governed, and stimulated to actions tending to the preservation of the individuals, and to the general weal.

Our holy Religion, itself, addresses alike our hopes and our fears. Every well-principled and well-poised civil government, is calculated to operate upon each of these masterly principles of our nature. And it is with a nice regard to these universal and powerful principles, that children are to be governed and managed in families and schools.

It requires no inconsiderable skill in parents, as well as faithfulness, to qualify them for the all-important task of governing their children. Tacitus, the Roman historian, remarked of Agricola, that "he governed his family; which many find a harder task than to govern a province." And why is this task so hard? Not because it is altogether difficult of itself, but mainly because parental affection runs into error, one way or the other. On the one hand, we are blind to the faults of our children, and spoil them by indulgence; or, on the other, from the desire of rearing our children to an ideal perfection, and of exalting them above the condition of childhood and of human nature itself, we mark in them even the pettiest of trespasses, with a keenness of severity that chills their hopes, and either breaks their spirits, or renders them restless and refractory. The Golden Mean between the extreme of indulgence and the extreme of rigor, is what few parents clearly discern and steadfastly pursue.

Preceptors, or instructors of schools, are, for the time being, the foster parents of the children committed to their tutorage. And though they lack that yearning of affection that is felt by the real parent, they are, for this very reason, the less apt to swerve from the *golden mean* I just now mentioned; provided they possess all the requisite qualifications for their business. These requisite qualifications are generally thought of easy attainment, and so indeed would they be, if they consisted only in a competent measure of learning, along with rectitude of moral character: but all this, though absolutely needful, is quite insufficient of itself. Superadded to a competent ability to teach, there must be considerable skill in governing and managing a school; otherwise, time and labor will be in a great measure lost.

An eminent degree of this kind of skill, is no less precious than rare. One who, besides possessing in full measure all the other requisites, is an adept in the science of managing a school; who knows the avenues to the minds and hearts of his pupils; who can seize alike upon their hopes, their fears, their emulation, and combine these jarring affections, and, as by mechanical force, can make them all minister together for improvement; who has the faculty of encouraging the timid, of giving hope to the despondent, of repressing exuberant vanity, of quickening the dull, and of teaching "the young idea how to shoot," even in minds backward to learn:—an instructor thus gifted, and possessed withal of excellence of moral character, together with a sincere affection for his pupils, and a fondness for his calling, is one of the most useful, and ought to be regarded as one of the most estimable of human beings.

Whether in families, or in schools, there must needs be government, else the means of instruction will be employed in vain. In these little communities, the government should be impartial and unwavering; firm, but mild; energetic, but not tyrannous.

There are some, whose manner towards their children varies in exact proportion to the variations of their own fickle tempers. When in a pleasant humor themselves, they indulge them in every thing; when moody, and especially when downright angry, they will punish for almost nothing. This sort of government, if government it may be called, is nearly as bad as none: it tends alike to discourage, and to breed contempt.

Some seem to think that the sure way of gaining and keeping

the affections of their children, is never to thwart their inclinations; but experience sooner or latter discovers to them their mistake. Children that have been treated with unlimited indulgence, often, very often, not only despise the counsels of their parents, but unfeelingly neglect their persons when destitute and needy; the overweening indulgence given them, having soured their tempers, and corrupted their hearts.

Others, running into the opposite error, apply their discipline altogether to the fears of their children, whom they unfortunately treat with stern and inflexible severity. They are feared indeed, but it is with a hopeless, joyless, an unaffectionate fear; and by thus treating their children as if they were entirely base, they take the ready way to make them so.

NUMBER XCIV

OF BREVITY IN RELATION TO SUNDRY PARTICULARS.

Dr. Cotton Mather, of venerated memory, in order to escape the calamity of tedious visits, wrote over the door of his study, in large letters, Be short. A pithy sentence, in truth, it is, and well worthy of remembrance in a great many more cases than I can now enumerate.

The interchange of friendly visits is one of the most precious sweets of life. But then, it must not be overdone; else it becomes irksome and disgusting. Hence, in the book of the Wise Man, we meet with the following wholesome counsel; "Withdraw thy foot from thy neighbor's house, lest he be weary of thee." Now the necessary discipline of the *foot*, which is here inculcated, is, if I may presume to comment, of the following import:—Beware of spinning out your friendly visits beyond due length. Retire, if you perceive any necessary business which your stay might interrupt; retire, ere the family, after an hour's yawning, begin to steal off one by one, to bed; retire, ere plain symptoms of weariness appear in the countenances of the little circle you are visiting; retire, ere, in some indescribable manner or other, it be manifested that your room would be more welcome than your company. When you have made your friends glad by your coming, stay not so long as to make them still more glad by your going away.

In time long past, the lord of a manor upon one of the banks of the Hudson, is said to have had a way of his own to clear his house of visitors. When his tenants, to whom he was affable and courteous, seemed disposed to prolong the visits which they now and then made him, he dropped the Dutch tongue, and began to speak to them in English: whereupon, the honest Dutchmen, understanding the signal, hied away.

But the sage counsel, BE SHORT, applies not to visitors alone. It might be made of like precious use to authors and public speakers, who too often lack one valuable kind of knowledge, namely, "that of discerning when to have done."

"Tediousness," as a writer of eminent abilities observes, "is the fault that most generally displeases: since it is a fault that is felt by all, and by all equally. You may offend your reader or hearer in one respect, and please him in another; but if you tire him out with your tediousness you give him unmingled disgust."

A book can do but little good if it be but little read: a destiny that befalls almost every book that is found to be unnecessarily prolix and bulky. This was the error of a former age. The massy folios of the last century but one, folios written by men of great talents and astonishing learning, have lain as lumber and been confined to the shelves of the curious, for no other reason than because every thread has been spun out to the greatest possible length. Whereas, had the highly respectable authors learned to *be short*, or given heed to the art of compressing their thoughts, they never would have wanted readers.

Writers, sometimes, eke out their subject far beyond what need requires, from a mistaken ambition of making a great book. But readers of the present age generally lean to the sentiment in the old Greek proverb, "*A great book is a great evil.*" It frightens them: they will scarcely open it, and much less set themselves to the task of reading it throughout.

Thus, in this respect, it is with books as with money. As small change in quick and constant circulation, does more good than ingots of gold and silver hoarded up, so a small book that has a great many readers, is, if truly a good one, of much more benefit than a volume of enormous bulk, which for that single reason is scarcely read at all. Nay, I will even venture to affirm, that the Bible itself would be much less read, and read with much less delight, were it one and indivisible. But the Bible, though bound together in one volume, is not a single book, but a collection of sixty-eight different books, all penned with brevity, as well as with inimitable simplicity; and arresting the attention, alike by the weight of their matter and their engagingness of manner.

Speak, young man, if there be need of thee, but be short—is a monitory saying of the son of Sirach, which, together with the two following short sayings of that eminent sage—*Learn before thou speak*—*We may speak much and yet come short*—composes a very good recipe for young men to carry about, and make use of as occasion may require.

Speeches in the forum, pleas at the bar, and even sermons,

when they are of immoderate length, seldom fail to be tiresome. So that public speakers consult their own credit as little as they do the feelings of their hearers, when they are more solicitous to say much, than that every thing they do say should be to the purpose.

Whether in visits, in public speaking, or in common conversation, all can discern and reprobate the fault of tediousness as respects others; and yet very few are fully aware of it as respects themselves. Their own company is, forsooth, so delightful, that their visits can never tire; they, themselves, speak so well, that nobody can wish them to have done; they talk so charmingly that their own loquaciousness always gives entertainment rather than disgust.

Thus it is that some men, otherwise of good sense, unconsciously give pain by their prolixity, though, in regard to the prolixity of any body but themselves, their taste is delicate even to squeamishness.

NUMBER XCV.

OF SOME PARTICULARS CONDUCIVE TO CONJUGAL PEACE AND HAPPINESS.

"While yet we live, scarce one short hour perhaps,
Between us two let there be peace.——"

THESE are the words which Milton puts into the mouth of Eve, to pacify and soothe her incensed husband, at the moment he found himself involved, along with her, in a condition of guilt and misery occasioned primarily by her fault; nor is there, perhaps, any thing more exquisitely pathetic in the immortal work of that poet. Indeed, throughout the whole speech of Eve, in the latter part of the tenth book of the Paradise Lost, the affectionate and pathetical tone in which she pleads, and her general manner, are such as must touch with commiseration any heart but one of stone.

In the lines selected for the present motto, there is a *moral*, which comes home to the bosom of every intelligent man and woman in the married state. Next in importance to the serenity of a good conscience, is the enjoyment of domestic peace. With it, adversity is soothed by the repose of home; without it, prosperity is but a gilded misery. Connubial harmony sweetens as well as enhances the common blessings of life, while its opposite imbitters whatever of enjoyment the smiles of fortune can bestow; so that the "dinner of herbs" is far better in the one case, than the "stalled ox" in the other.

It is not to my present purpose, however, to describe at large either the blissful fruits of connubial harmony, or the baneful consequences of domestic discord, but rather to suggest ways and means for securing the one and avoiding the other; by which course, while shunning the beaten track of declamation, I am led into by-paths, or to observations very little connected. But if only one of these unconnected observations shall be found really useful, it is hoped that the reader will excuse all the rest for the sake of that one.

Although marriages, to be happy, must be founded in mutual affection, yet even that essentially necessary basis is not sufficient to build hopes upon, without one's possessing, in addition, a reasonable prospect of competence,—the real amount of which, as respects the fashionable class, is not definable by any fixed metes and bounds, being diverse according to the diversity of tastes and habits. It is but little that man absolutely needs; and were his desires in any measure proportionate to his real needs, a competence would, in most instances, be of very easy attainment. But in the highly artificial state of society now existing, it unfortunately happens, that the despotic court of Fashion dooms very many to a life of celibacy, not for their want of ability to support the mere necessary expenses of a married state, but for want of ability to support its expenses in that sphere of life to which they have been accustomed, and from which it is their settled resolution never to descend; choosing rather to forego the first and sweetest of social comforts, than to sink only a few degrees in Fashion's scale. Again, from the same cause, it happens still more unfortunately, that very many in the married state turn their weal into woe, and sometimes their amity to discord, by beginning with, and persisting in a style of living, utterly incompatible with their fortunes or their incomes. Of all the sources of domestic infelicity, this is at present one of the most prolific.

But to come more closely to the point in hand;—in choosing a wife, examine carefully whether her domestic character be estimable. If her temper, her moral qualities, her deportment toward her parents, and the general tenor of her conduct in the domestic circle, speak highly in her favor, good earnest is then given that she will act her part well in a family of her own.

Expect not too much from *Woman*. It is neither an angelical, nor a paradisiacal being, that you are to enter into connubial alliance with, but an inheritor of the infirmities of fallen nature, —one who, at best, has some of the ingredients of folly and perverseness in her composition. If then you must needs have a perfect wife, the better way will be to wait till you become perfect yourself.

If your heart be infected with the scrofula of contempt for female nature, marry not at all till cured of that foul disease.

Popinjay values himself greatly, as it would seem, upon his *manly* contempt of womankind, and particularly of his wife. In his estimation, almost every thing she says is foolish, and more than half she does is wrong. That manner on his part, has occasioned in her an intellectual and a moral debasement,

Treated daily with disrespect and scorn, she has lost by degrees almost all respect for herself.

There are other pairs who, in this respect, are very equally matched. For instance, *Pertinax* and his conjugal mate, dispute it together all the year round about trifles, because he is always in the right, and she never in the wrong. They are as like as "cherry to cherry," in their general qualities, which are passably good; and it wants only a little condescension on both sides, to render their union felicitous rather than otherwise.

Fix it as a maxim in your mind, that it is of more importance, generally speaking, for one to keep well with his wife, than with any other earthly friend. Acting on that maxim, and yet more on the sacred principle of moral and religious duty, ever treat your wife with heartfelt benevolence. Cast the mantle over the common frailties incidental to humanity; esteem and cherish her better qualities, and habitually maintain a tender and sympathetic consideration for her feelings.

Of the other sex, I crave the indulgence of hazarding the monition and the advice, which here follow.

Marry not the man who is known to be unkind, contemptuous and scornful to the mother that bare him:—it will be a miracle if he treat his wife any better.

Marry not a blasphemous infidel, however rich, or however accomplished. For, besides the weighty consideration of the contaminating influence of such an alliance, he that contemns the God that made him, is not one that will give due honor to the wife that is subject to him.

Marry not a profligate libertine in hopes of reforming him. Too feeble will be your cords to bind down the headlong passions of a man, alike regardless of the authority of moral principle, and of the opinions of all the respectable part of society.

Marry not a man because you think him one that will tamely submit to be ruled by you. It had been the jesting boast of *Azuba*, that she intended to make a fool of her husband. She was saved that trouble by chancing to wed a ready-made one; but she found his obstinacy and contrariety invincible. No effect at all could her reasoning have on a mind incapable of comprehending it; nor any effect could her persuasions have upon a heart ever jealous of a rival power, and the more constantly alive to suspicions for its dwelling *in the dark*. It is a fact often attested by experience, that none are more jealous of falling under the dominion of their wives, or more unyielding to their reasonable influence, than men of inferior understandings and pertinacious tempers. "Nothing is so dogmatical and inconvincible as a very shallow man, who counts himself to be wise."

Sweet is power to the human heart, and as sweet to the heart of woman as of man. It is no wonder, therefore, that there are sometimes rivalries for power in domestic government, as well as in governments of wider extent. It is a complaint of long standing, that very many women would fain read St. Paul thus: *Husbands, be obedient to your wives.* A flagrant misconstruction, which, with all the orthodox of the masculine sex, can be regarded as very little better than downright heresy. Nevertheless, wives, who deserve the name, are entitled to much influence with their husbands. Nor, with husbands possessing good understandings and a considerable share of the benevolent affections, will they often fail to obtain all the influence they can reasonably desire, provided they take, and steadily pursue, the right way for it. This nice point I will illustrate by a living example.

Susannah is a plain woman, of plain good sense, possessing neither beauty nor wit: yet her husband, a very sensible and worthy man, and not at all of a cringing spirit, is dotingly fond of her, and some even say that she governs him. And what has been her artifice? None at all. Where is her ruling hand seen? Nowhere. Susannah had adorned herself with "the ornament of a meek and quiet spirit;" and, from her bridal day, she has continued to wear it all along. Now, however marvellous it may seem to some, that same old-fashioned ornament so charms the husband, that he scarcely can find it in his heart to deny her, and much less to chide her. If he happen to be moody, as now and then he is, the irresistible influence of the "law of kindness in her tongue," presently restores him to good humor. If I have a correct notion of the trim of that man's mind and heart, no termagant of a wife, however beautiful, or artful, or accomplished, could have gained half so much influence over him.

NUMBER XCVI.

OF REGARDING ACCOMPLISHMENTS AS THE PRINCIPAL PART OF FEMALE EDUCATION.

Among all the wants of humanity, few are more deplorable than the want of discrimination between things of great and things of little importance. The absence either of the existence or of the exercise of the faculty of such discrimination, occasions a considerable part of the errors of life. For, not to speak of the fatal error of preferring the things which are temporal to the things that are eternal—often, very often, in merely our worldly concerns, we sacrifice the greater to the less. It would not be difficult to exemplify this sentiment in a variety of instances; but I will confine myself to one only—*Female Education.*

We live in an age in which few, if any, whose opinons are worth notice, will deny the necessity of educating, and of *well* educating the female part of our species. Passing over, therefore, this point upon which there is so general an agreement, I will mention, and but barely mention, the primary qualities of a good female education.

The great benefit of education, and what should ever be its ultimate design, consists in its tendency to prepare the pupils to act the parts allotted them with propriety, both as immortal and as mortal beings: and, in this view, education has an equal bearing upon both sexes.

Female education, conducted upon rational principles, regards the parts that females are ordinarily destined to act upon the theatre of social life. Female children, in common with those of the other sex, are moral and accountable beings, destined to an immortal existence, and should, therefore, be assiduously taught " the moral and religious knowledge of right and wrong,"— or their duty to God, to themselves, and to their fellow-creatures. As social beings, their understandings must be cultivated. As moral beings, their hearts must be cultivated. They *may* meet with unforeseen temptations and snares; and should be taught self-government, modesty, and delicacy of thought, of speech, and of action. They *may* meet with hard and distressing trials; and should be early taught the value of a meek and humble spirit, which, in some women under adversity, has shone with a lustre far surpassing that of the diamond. Moreover, they *may* be destined, however worthy or estimable, to lead a single and solitary life; and they should be so educated that, having resources in their own minds, they will be able not only to *endure*, but to *enjoy* their hours of retirement and solitude, and to make themselves respectable and agreeable, by the good sense of their conversation and the benevolence of their dispositions. Again, they *may* be wives; and it is the part of education to qualify and prepare them to be good wives —conversable—mild and affectionate — discreet — hospitable, and yet frugal—looking well to the ways of their households. Finally, they *may* be mothers; and it is the part of education to qualify them, as mothers, to educate their children. In this one particular, women have a most important part to act. Women, as mothers, do in a great measure form the characters of future women and of future men; since the formation of character, for the first seven or eight years of life, depends chiefly on them. If they are well-informed, discreet, and of good morals, their children are made, partly by their instruction, and partly by imitation, to assimilate to these qualities. But if they are vain and frivolous, their little ones soon catch the contagion of their vanity and frivolity.

The foregoing particulars embrace most of the primary qualities or indispensable rudiments of a good female education. And yet quite often is it remarked of females, that they have had an excellent education, merely because they have been taught the female *accomplishments*. Very little attention was ever paid to the culture of their understandings, of their minds, of their hearts, of their tempers. But with much pains, and at considerable expense, they have got a *smatter*, and a mere smatter, of what are called the *fine arts;* such as Embroidery, Drawing, Music, and so on. They have learned the discipline of the *fingers* and of the *foot;* and for this reason alone, their education is held in admiration. As if *mere* accomplishments, which usually become obsolete soon after marriage, were sufficient tc prepare women to be excellent wives, excellent mothers, and excellent housekeepers; as if a *merely* accomplished woman were fitted either to act her part respectably in society, or to take comfort in the solitude of retirement, or under the decays of age; or as if the modesty, and the refined manners of women spring from accomplishments, rather than from their being well taught in moral and religious duty. So far from all this, a married woman of mere accomplishments, and whose chief ambition is to make a figure in the eye of the public, seldom fails to render her husband unhappy, and herself too.

In the school of Fashion, female accomplishments have long had the ascendant. Nor is it to my purpose to decry or despise them. Let those have them, if they please, whose rank in life requires it, and whose ampleness of fortune can well afford the expense. Yet even by *them* be it remembered, that they are but of trifling account in comparison of the solid and useful parts of education. If accomplishments be appended to these, they may serve to adorn the whole: but hapless will be the husband and the children of the woman, and quite as hapless the woman herself, who rests her character and conduct in life upon accomplishments alone.

As to families of the common sort, possessed neither of high rank nor of ample fortunes, the plain useful education is the best for their daughters. This is all that can ordinarily do them any good; and more than this *may* do them much harm. A very ancient and a very respectable writer—whom we ought to read much oftener than we do—hath told us of a knowledge that *puffeth up*. And, perhaps, there is no kind of knowledge more *puffing*, than the one I have now been mentioning. A female of scanty information, and weak intellect, so values herself for the circumstance of her being initiated in the practice of some of the fine arts, that she loses by it the use of her hands. She will vouchsafe, indeed,to employ her pretty fingers, now and then, in fancy-work, for amusement; but in nothing that is really useful; in nothing that earns bread; in nothing that can turn to any valuable account. Perhaps she is in impoverished circumstances; perhaps her condition is such as imperiously calls for the useful labor of her hands. It makes no difference. She is not of the laboring class, but far above it. *She* do the common work of womankind,—*she*, who had gone through all the grades of a fashionable education! The idea is too monstrous.

Thus, instead of being made, by their education, the more capable of helping themselves in this world of "thorns and thistles," of labor, toil, and hardships;—there are some, and perhaps not a few, whose very education renders them but the more helpless.

NUMBER XCVII.

OF THE COMMON USE OF FALSE WEIGHTS AND MEASURES IN DEALING OUT BOTH PRAISE AND CENSURE.

—— "O, that men's ears should be
To counsel deaf, but not to flattery!"

SHAKESPEARE.

In the whole compass of human traffic, there is, perhaps, no commodity that is dealt out with less regard to weight and measure, than praise; if we except only its opposite, namely, dispraise or reproach.

In the bestowment of praise, we are very apt to be guided by our feelings, or our interests, rather than our judgments. Freely, and in more than full measure, we bestow upon our friends what costs us nothing, and what we secretly hope they will repay us in the same way. *To praise the Athenians is the way to be praised by the Athenians*—was one of the proverbs of antiquity. Neither ought it to be regarded as a peculiarity of the Athenian character, but rather as a common feature in our general nature. There is no so ready way to obtain flattery, as to bestow it plentifully. And hence men flatter, with the view of being flattered in return. Indeed it is better, of the two, to be too lavish of praise, than too prodigal of censure. But even the former is of evil tendency, because they who find it easy to obtain a greater quantity of praise than they deserve, will not only be the less careful to deserve it, but also the less likely to make a just estimate of their own characters ; self-love naturally inclining us to *think* of ourselves quite as well as we find others *speak* of us. Moreover, extravagant encomium, besides violating truth, and infusing the poison of flattery, seldom fails to injure the subject of it, by occasioning a critical investigation of faults or defects, which else might have been less noticed or sooner forgotten. Nor would it be hazarding too much to say, that undue encomium is even more likely to do us an essential injury than undue censure ; for the latter might possibly be the means of meliorating the qualities of our hearts, whereas the former directly tends to pervert and deprave them.

Whilst some praise almost nobody, others praise almost every body. These last are as nauseously sweet, as the others are crabbedly sour. Affecting the superlative of candor, they speak alike well of the generality of their species ; and so far as in them lies, they put upon one and the same level, wisdom and folly, virtue and vice, and pour the incense of their own foolishness upon the whole mass. This indiscriminate praise is the meanest of all adulation ; and it tends to destroy, among men, all sense of distinction of character. One who is accustomed to speak in nearly the same favorable terms of all, is either too weak, or too insincere, to be deserving of the esteem of any.

Next to the mischievous folly of the afore-mentioned species of indiscriminate praise, is that of bestowing unqualified applause upon characters or works, which are commendable upon the whole, but censurable in some of their parts. Men, and the works of men, are always imperfect, however excellent in a general view, and it is the part of wisdom to distinguish between their excellencies and their imperfections; noting the one sort for imitation, and the other for avoidance. But it is too much the custom to laud whatever appertains to your friend, *because he is your friend.* This is yielding to friendship more than its due, and more than good conscience can admit of; as it partakes of the dishonesty of using false weights and measures. Not that it is not allowable, and even dutiful, in many instances, to conceal the fault we know; for oftentimes circumstances require that, in speaking of others, we make it a rule, " rather to say nothing that is false, than all that is true." Nevertheless, to eulogize the *whole* of characters, which are adorned with manifest excellencies, and at the same time blemished with defects which are alike manifest, is to blend truth with falsehood, and to present to the view a fallacious, rather than a real likeness. As to speak well of every body is false candor, so to commend alike every thing in, or done by one's friend, is false praise. *De mortuis nil nisi bonum—say nothing but good of the dead*—is an old maxim, and, in a qualified sense, a very just one. But though humanity demands that we " tread lightly on the ashes of the dead," and although decency forbids all *unnecessary* exposure of the failings and blemishes in their lives; yet the sacred laws of truth peremptorily prohibit exaggerated praise even of *them.* This is an error, to which the ardor (not to say the *pride*) of friendship, is exceedingly liable. Funeral panegyrics, epitaphs, and biographical memoirs, often, very often, portray the affectionate feelings of surviving friends, rather than the real picture of character. Not to mention, that over-praising the dead is done, sometimes, for the sake of flattering the living.

Eulogy, whether of the living or the dead, which evidently overleaps the bounds of truth, defeats its own purpose, and has even the effect of satire. So that we may do our friends as real injury by excessive praise, as by defamation.

As we are prone to over-praise those we have a warm affection for; we are still more prone, on the other hand, to disparage or undervalue those we dislike; grudging to allow them such good qualities as they really possess, or to commend them for such good deeds as they have really done; and displaying all their failings in the highest colors of aggravation. This perverse propensity, wrought into the very web of our fallen nature, is exceedingly difficult to cure. How few possess enough of magnanimity, not to say of the genius and spirit of Christianity, to do full justice to the good deeds of a real or supposed foe; or even to one belonging to an adverse party in religion, or in politics!

"The true critic" (said Dean Swift, ironically,) "is a discoverer and collector of writers' faults."

But not to run foul of the critics; some men and women, like flies, feed altogether upon the sore part of the characters of those about them. These *scavengers* of reputation, are ever hunting about, with a microscopic eye, for foibles, infirmities, and blemishes; and are too busy abroad, to regulate things aright at home.

Pliny relates of Julius Cæsar, that he blamed in so artful a manner, that he seemed to praise. On the contrary, others are as artful in their praises, as Cæsar was in his reproaches; and that too, with the basest intentions. "They use envenomed praise, which, by a side-blow, exposes, in the person they commend, such faults as they dare not any other way lay open."

The tooth of calumny never wounds more deeply, nor ever infuses more poison into the wound, than by this insidious method.

NUMBER XCVIII.

OF AN OFFICIOUS MEDDLING WITH, AND A TOTAL DISREGARD OF THE AFFAIRS OF OTHERS.

Society has been infested, in all ages of the world, with persons prone to intrude themselves into the concerns of their neighbors; with tattlers, busybodies and intermeddlers, who must needs have their spoons in every body's porringer. These unwelcome and troublesome guests were distinctly marked by the sagacious eye of the king of Israel, who has given them their full due. Indeed, some of this sort are quite ingenious in their way, and so much the worse; for by how much greater is their ingenuity, by so much the more mischief they do; their minds resembling a fertile soil which, for want of proper culture, bears nothing but weeds and poisonous plants.

Not but that, now and then, an officious intermeddler, or even a tale-bearer, may mean no harm; the one being actuated by an undue opinion of his own importance, and the other by the vanity of appearing to know the characters and the concerns of all about him. But intentional sowers of discord, who from envy, malice, or the love of mischief, employ themselves in breeding dissensions in families and neighborhoods, are well nigh as pestilent as thieves and robbers; and the less they are punishable by civil law, the more should they be made to feel that species of punishment which public opinion inflicts.

Parents and preceptors can hardly do a better service for their children, than by principling their minds, and fixing their hearts against faults so pernicious to society, and so ruinous to character: faults which are curable when they first appear in the young mind, but which grow into inveterate habits by the indulgence of neglect. It is hardly conceivable what a vast amount of evil might be prevented, if the young were taught as generally and as carefully in this particular as they are in the first rudiments of learning.

By those who, from habit, or from temper, make it their business and delight to pry into and publish the failings of others, be it remembered, "*that at that day when the failings of all shall be made manifest, the attention of each individual will be fixed only on his own.*"

There is a fault, however, directly opposite to that of officiously meddling with the concerns of our neighbors: I mean the absence of all heartfelt concern for any but ourselves and our near kin. This fault, however artfully it may be covered, springs, for the most part, from sordid selfishness, or from anti-social apathy of heart.

Selfishness, which is the love of self and of every thing else for the sake of self, has the power of keeping some persons at a vast distance from intermeddling with their neighbors' affairs, for which they care not a straw any farther than such extraneous, affairs have a bearing upon their own personal interests. So, also, the cold-hearted, in whose bosoms is the perpetual calm of apathy, trouble not their neighbors, as busy-bodies in their matters; because they have not enough energy of soul either to love or to hate in good earnest. Now it often falls out, that some belonging to each of these two classes, value themselves highly upon their practical abstraction from all concerns but their own, and boast of it as a shining virtue. "*We are not meddlers, not we. It is our manner to mind our own business, and to let all other folk alone.*" Nevertheless, if they would open the folds of their own hearts, and observe fairly what is going on there, they would find that their not being meddlers is owing to any thing else, rather than to a pure principle of virtue.

And here it is not unimportant to remark, that it is no less the purpose and business of proper education to foster and encourage the social feelings of our nature, than it is to eradicate dispositions of intrusive meddling: for if one without all warmth of heart, be seldom tempted to become a busy-body in other men's matters, he as seldom is much better than a mere blank in society—doing little mischief, and as little good.

Am I my brother's keeper?—We know who said it. And so, in manifold instances, when one is ruining himself and his family by the mismanagement of his affairs, or when one betrays the symptoms of an inceptive vice, which, growing into a habit, will land him in perdition; his neighbors coolly look on, saying in their hearts, and to one another, "*It is his own affair.*" Not employing a single effort to save him, though often, betwixt themselves, they shake the head, and remark, that he is on the road to ruin. Perhaps it is a youth, that is supposed to have stepped into this fatal road; a young man of goodly promise, or a young woman of amiable dispositions, but wanting discretion. Perhaps that youth is an orphan, and errs for lack of the guiding hand of a parent. It is all the same. Every body is sorry, very sorry indeed, but nobody moves the tongue, or lifts a finger for the purpose of rescue or prevention.

It is not so that we act in other respects. We struggle hard to save a fellow-being that is drowning before our eyes. Should we see a man stand upon the brink of a frightful precipice, and unconscious of his danger, doubtless we should instantly give him warning. Hardly should we neglect to snatch either the empoisoned bowl from the lips of one that mistook the poison for a wholesome beverage, or the knife or razor from the throat of a man or woman in the act of committing suicide. Common humanity impels us to acts of this sort. And yet when we see in scarcely less jeopardy of another kind, a neighbor, an acquaintance—one whom the offices of discreet and faithful friendship might perhaps rescue and restore—we are listless—we let him alone—we'll not meddle—*'tis his own affair!*

Apathy is the *Limbo* of the mind—an intermediate state, equi-distant from the two opposites, happiness and misery. As they who have no care but *for* themselves, have, at the same time, very little comfort but *from* themselves, their lot, in a comparative view, is not to be envied.

NUMBER XCIX.

OF TURNING GOOD TO ILL BY TAMPERING WITH IT.

A GREAT part of the *ill* that we suffer, might be avoided, if we would only learn to let *well* alone. But such is the plague of our hearts, in regard to temporal as well as higher matters, that we are seldom or never quite contented with our lot, when even it is no unpleasant one, but mar and spoil what we perversely endeavor to mend. For if we dally with any good which Providence gives us, we run the risk of either impairing or losing it.

How often is comeliness of features disfigured by affectation which would make better, what God hath made well.

How often do we lose our health by tampering with it, in order to make it better. When we are well, we cannot be easy, and let *well* alone, but must needs be meddling with our corporeal mechanism while it is going exactly right. An Italian nobleman, whose fatal folly it was not to let *well* alone, ordered, as a solemn warning to others, the following line to be engraven on his tomb; "*I was well—I wanted to be better—and here I am!*" In innumerable instances, the grave has been peopled immaturely, by means of nostrums, which the *well* have used to preserve and prolong their health.

Mark the children that are fed with dainties, enticed to eat before they are hungry, and kept from the air, like chickens in an oven—mark their sallow and sickly faces,—the feebleness of their whole frames. They were *well born*, and well they might have continued, but for the tampering of false tenderness.

Almost innumerable are the instances of well-conditioned men and families, who are mourning over the ruin of their worldly circumstances—not by any direct providential stroke of adversity, nor by means of conduct of their own that was morally bad, but solely because they did not let *well* alone.

One " sells the pasture to buy the horse." He barters away his fast estate for goods. A single turn of the wheel of fortune, turns him to a bankrupt.

Another, not content with being a farmer *merely*, is eager for the distinction of a barren office. Luckily for his feelings, but unfortunately for his circumstances, he obtains it. He neglects his farm, and his farm neglects him. His expenses increase, and his income diminishes : it is needless to tell the rest.

A third, possessing a sufficiency, and but a bare sufficiency, for a plain and frugal living, is fashionable and splendid ; for he must needs let the world know that he is *Somebody*. So he goeth ; and " his poverty cometh as an armed man."

A fourth, though snug and comfortable at home, fancies he can do a great deal better abroad. He has heard of the goodly lands which yield astonishing abundance, and almost without labor. He sells all he possesses, and on he goes at random. He arrives ; when, lo ! he finds, even *there*, a full measure of the thorns and thistles of the curse, and, peradventure, finds himself cheated at last out of his all.

Not uncommon, at the present time, is that fatal defect in character, which the venerable patriarch imputes to his first-born :—" *Unstable as water, thou shalt not excel.*" Of very many it may be said, that their greatest error, and the source of most of their misfortunes, is a fickleness of temper: they are ingenious, active, industrious, and yet poor; because they pursue no single object long enough to reap benefit from it. No sooner do they begin to do well in any particular business, than they forsake it for another.

Perhaps there is no one quality that more thoroughly runs through the warp of our fallen nature, than the disposition to be restless. There is a *something more*, or a *something different*, which we are ever prone to covet; and unless our minds are well disciplined, we shall poison the cup of life by our absurd attempts to sweeten it, or lose the good within our reach, while grasping at that which is beyond it.

Of all morbid habits, that of being dissatisfied with even the comfortable conditions of life, in which Providence has placed us, is one of the most unfortunate. With persons of this cast, it makes no difference though their success in life be never so great; the same sickliness of heart cleaves to them as a garment, even after their fortunes have never so much exceeded their own expectations.

The following form of devotion, used by one of the ancients, is suitable to blind mortals of Adam's race, who know not, nor can know, precisely, either the quantities or the qualities of worldly enjoyment most conducive to their own good.—" Give me whatsoever may be good for me, though I should neglect to pray for it, and deny me whatsoever would be hurtful, though I should ignorantly make it the object of my supplications." The ways of Divine Providence are mysterious but unerring; its kindness is manifested frequently in withholding as well as in giving; as well in restraints as in indulgencies; as well in disappointments as in crowning our wishes with success. How oft, in our journey of life, has Providence thwarted our inclinations, and by this means prevented our wanderings. How often have we been walking blindly upon the edge of a precipice, prepared to take the fatal leap, when an invisible power diverted our course by disappointing us of our purpose. How oft have incidents, that seemed evil to us at first, been productive of good; and how oft might the things which our hearts desired, and of which Providence disappointed us, have been hurtful in the enjoyment. As little children cry for what would injure them, and struggle with the hand that restrains them from running into dangers; so *we*, children of a larger size, but in many instances not knowing what is good for ourselves, frequently desire, with most eagerness, what would be most for our hurt, and perversely repine even at those providential restraints and trials which are the effects of a merciful purpose.

"During the violence of a storm," says a German fable, "a traveller offered up his supplications, and besought Heaven to assuage the tempest. But the storm continued with unabating fury; and while he was drenched with the flood, fatigued with his journey, and exposed without shelter, he became peevish, and even complained aloud of the ways of Providence.

Approaching at length the borders of a forest, he said to himself, " Here I shall find protection, notwithstanding Heaven has neglected me, and turned a deaf ear to my prayers." But as he went forward, a robber sprang out suddenly from behind a bush, and the traveller, affrighted at the prospect of instant death, fled out of the forest, exposing himself again to the tempest, of which he had so grievously complained. The robber, in the mean time, fitting an arrow to his bow, took exact aim; but the bow-string being relaxed by the moisture of the weather, the arrow fell short of its mark, and the traveller escaped unhurt. As he continued his journey, a voice proceeded, awful, from the clouds: " Cease, mortal, to repine at the divine dispensations; and learn to acknowledge the goodness of God, in refusing as well as in granting your petitions. The storm, which you complained of so bitterly, has been the means of your preservation. Had not the bow-string of your enemy been rendered useless by rain, you had fallen a victim to his violence."

NUMBER C.

OF A RESTLESS DESIRE TO KNOW WHAT OTHERS SAY OF US.

"Take no heed to all words that are spoken, lest thou hear thy servant curse thee."
SOLOMON.

PERHAPS no weakness of our fallen, feeble, and erring nature, is more disquieting to ourselves, or more troublesome to our acquaintances, than an overweening curiosity to know what is said of us.

A person of this turn is never at his ease. Jealousy is, in him, an ever-waking sentinel. Even his familiars, he fears, will slander or undervalue him; and if he happens to hear that any one of them has spoken of him slightingly, he instantly regards that one as his foe, and thenceforward is the more jealous of all the rest.

In company, he views every look with a suspicious eye. He reads a plot against himself, even in a nod, or a whisper. If what he finds to have been said of him can admit of a double meaning, he gives it the worse meaning of the two. If he finds himself commended as to his general character, but censured in some particular instance, he is wounded, just as though the whole of his character had fallen under reprobation.

This restless curiosity to know what is said of him, keeps his mind perpetually upon the rack. Day by day, he is anxiously inquisitive upon this point. If he fail of the object of his inquiries, and can hear of little or nothing said about him, either one way or the other;—then he is stung at the heart with imagined neglect. And, contrariwise, if he chance to find that which he so anxiously inquires after, he finds it, perhaps, to his own cost and discomfort. He will have gained an article of intelligence which he had better have been without. His experience, peradventure, will have accorded with what we are plainly advertised of, in the above-cited pithy, admonition of the Wise Man.

The distemper of mind here spoken of, may arise fom an ardent desire of esteem, and the consequent dread of disesteem; and it may be found in persons possessed of some very estimable qualities of heart. But whatever be its origin, or in whomsoever it be found, it is the cause of a great deal of useless disquietude, and ever exposes one to wanton sport and ridicule.

Now, it being a great pity that persons of the one sex or the other, who are estimable in some respects, and yet labor under this infirmity, should not reason themselves out of it; I crave leave to lay before them the following considerations.

1. Those even, whose characters are good in the main, must needs be sensible, if they have any competent measure of self-knowledge, that they are not quite perfect. And why, then, should they be angry that others too, are sensible of it, and that their imperfections are sometimes spoken of? It is by no means certain that there is in this thing any enmity or real ill-will.

2. Persons possessed of this morbid or excessive sensibility

with regard to their own reputations, cannot but remember that themselves, one time or another, and in free conversation, have remarked on the foibles and faults of those whom they highly esteem upon the whole, and for whom they have, at the same time, a sincere friendship. And assuredly it is unreasonable for one to be angry for receiving the same measure which one metes out. If a person you thought your friend, hath spoken slightingly of you, in one single respect or other ;—what then? Have you not yourself, sometimes, and in some particulars, spoken slightingly of those whom you were inclined to rank in the number of your friends? If you have done it, you should not be angry when the same is done to you.

3. In a fit of levity, or of ill-humor, it is not uncommon for some folks to speak with partial disrespect of the self-same persons whom, at other times, they mention with expressions of high esteem and affectionate regard. So that a great part of people's ill sayings of one another, are attributable to peevishness or thoughtlessness, and not to malignity alone. Hence the author of the admirable book of Ecclesiasticus observes,—"*There is one that slippeth in his speech, but not from his heart.*"

4. Even the ill-natured remarks of an enemy might be turned to a profitable use, by carefully correcting in one's self the fault or foible that occasioned them. It is told of the Prince of Condé, who was the most eminent hero of his day, that, his domestics observing with what great attention he was reading a certain pamphlet, one of them said to him: "This must be a very fine piece, since you take so much pleasure in reading it." To which the Prince replied: "It is very true that I read this with great pleasure, because it tells me my faults, which no man dares

venture to do."—The pamphlet was in the strain of severe invective against the errors, faults, and foibles of the same Prince of Condé.

5. We seldom miss it more than in imagining that all about us take an interest in our ordinary concerns. If we think the world spends much attention about us, one way or the other, we have a mistaken notion of our own consequence. For, with a few exceptions, the individuals of the community are very little the subjects of each other's thoughts and conversation; the generality being too busy in thinking of themselves, to employ many of their thoughts elsewhere. Had one, by the help of magic, or by whatever means, the power of rendering himself invisible, and should he, in using the privilege of invisibility, go about from house to house, over his whole neighborhood and town, he would, probably, find himself spoken of by his neighbors and acquaintances more seldom than he had expected; and, in all probability too, he would hear the very same persons speak quite differently of him at different times.

In few words; universal and unqualified approbation it is folly to expect. And although we should, by no means, be regardless of what others think or say of us, yet the best way, or rather the only good way, is to be more solicitous to deserve esteem than to win it—more solicitous to do well, than to obtain the credit of doing well; and thus, to proceed on in the straight line, without angling for praise, or being too fearful of reproach. Whoso acteth in this manner, and upon pure, evangelical principles, enjoys a consciousness of feelings far more delightful, than any thing that can spring from the unmerited applause of ten thousand tongues.

NUMBER CI.

SUMMARY CHARACTERISTICS.

"Wisdom and folly meet, mix, and unite,
Virtue and vice blend their black and their white."

Inferior animals of the same kind have in general a sameness of physiognomy, and so trifling are the shades of difference between them in any respect, that the portraiture of one individual describes the whole species. But as human animals are moral and accountable, and subject to law, a marvellous provision is made in the divine economy, for the identification of every individual; in so far that each is distinguishable from each by the look, by the voice, by the gait, by the handwriting, and by several other modes of difference, hardly describable, though plainly perceivable. Were it otherwise, the judge might be mistaken for the thief; the innocent and the guilty would be blended together, without the possibility of making any legal discrimination betwixt them.

The differences are no fewer, but perhaps more multifarious, in the features of mind. So that, if the minds of mankind were as visible as their bodies, the individuality of each person might, perhaps, be as clearly determined from the former as from the latter.

Of the different features of minds, including qualities of heart as they appear in overt act, the following are samples; in sketching which I am constrained, for the sake of necessary brevity, to personify the twenty-six letters of the alphabet.

A— is *noble*-spirited but not charitable; in a public subscription his name figures well, but a Lazar might starve at his gate.

B— is quite candid enough in respect to *practice;* but if you thwart merely his *speculative opinions*, he raves like a bear.

C— is a woman, peevish and querulous about little things; her heavy calamities she bears with pious resignation, and with more than masculine fortitude.

D— enters with spirit into a laudable public undertaking, so the plan comes from *himself*, or *he* has the direction of it; else he will have nothing at all to do with the business, not he.

E— lives in the *practice* of vice; but would insult a man who should say any thing derogatory of the *principles* of virtue.

F— takes pride in railing against pride; he hates the pride of fashion, and is proud of being out of the fashion.

G— and his wife, abroad or in company, are all milk and honey; their ill-nature they save for domestic use.

H— is easy of temper, but very far from compassionate; his easiness of temper is nothing but apathy.

I— is good or ill-tempered by fits and starts; now, he is so pleasant, that nothing can anger him; then again, he is so techy, that nothing can please him.

J— is rough and impetuous, but of a feeling heart; his mind, as respects anger, is like wood that in a moment catches fire, which as quickly goes out.

K— is slow to anger, but much slower to be appeased; once affront him, and he is *coolly* your enemy for ever.

L— is not hard to be reconciled in a matter, in which the fault lies altogether on the other side; but when he has been in fault himself, the consciousness of it stirs his pride and stiffens his temper.

M— feels strongly whatever relates to himself; other people's misfortunes he bears with singular calmness and fortitude.

N—, though possessed of no extraordinary share of wisdom, is affronted if you decline to follow his advice, and is equally affronted if any one presumes to advise him.

O—'s cringing sycophancy to superiors might be thought humility, were he not brutally imperious and overbearing to inferiors and dependants.

P— loudly complains of the needy friends he abandons, to escape the reproach of abandoning them in their need.

Q— frequently changes her friends for a slight cause, or for no cause, and always likes the last best:—with her, friendship is like a nosegay, which pleases only while it is fresh.

R— would appear well enough, but for his affectation of appearing *extremely* well, which makes him appear below himself; the vanity of being thought important rendering him ridiculous.

S— tamely acquiesces in what is generally believed, because it is generally believed; he wants no other proof of the truth of a thing, than its having a plurality of numbers on its side.

T— runs into extravagant singularities, from the vanity of appearing possessed of superior understanding.

U— would not be suspected of dishonesty, but for his frequently boasting that he is honest; nor of want of veracity, but for his habit of propping his word and promise with asseverations.

V— passes for wise, because he is taciturn,—perhaps not so much from gravity as stupidity.

W— might please every body with the eloquence and good sense of his conversation, if he knew only when to have done.

X—, a lady of fashion, affects exquisite sensibility, by her look, her manner, and her tones of voice; such is her tenderness, that she weeps over high-life scenes of fictitious distress; and such is her obduracy, that she regards, with unfeeling indifference, those vulgar objects of real distress, that have claims upon her practical charity.

Y—, a philosopher of the school of cosmopolites, possesses a fund of speculative benevolence, which he often makes use of in word, but never in deed: like his prototype, the pagan philosopher, *Seneca*, who wrote an excellent book upon charity, but, though he was rich, gave nothing away.

Z— endeavors to commute for his neglects and trespasses in some things, by a grave and punctilious exactness in others. He will go miles to church on a stormy day; in his worldly dealings, he is not altogether a *hard* honest man, but *hardly* honest.

NUMBER CII.

OF THE NECESSITY OF SEASONABLE PRECAUTION.

That "an ounce of prevention is worth a pound of cure," is an old and true proverb, which is applicable alike to a multitude of cases: the ills we suffer in life being, in a large proportion, either of our own procuring, or such as might have been prevented by timely care and precaution.

It seems to have been a standing custom of the Asiatics, in their epistolary correspondence, to conclude a letter with this sage advice, *Take care of your health;* a precept which, were it generally put in practice, would save the lives of multitudes in every country. The grave is peopled with myriads, who might still have enjoyed the light of life, but for the intemperate manner of their living; and with other myriads, whose deaths were occasioned by unnecessarily exposing their health.

The lovely Belinda falls into a hectic, in the flower of her age. The life-spring within her fails; the art of medicine is unavailing; "the worm of death is in her bloom." Yet what a pound of cure cannot remove, an ounce of prudence might have prevented.

There was a time, and a very long time, when in the Christianized world, it was thought a merit to torment and waste the corporeal part of our nature; when the body was considered as at utter enmity with the soul; when it was voluntarily subjected to cold, and nakedness, and to unmerciful scourging, in order to curb and break its rebellious propensities. We live, however, in a more rational age.

Blessed be the day of Martin Luther's birth, and blessed the work achieved by him! He gave the death-blow to this mummery, and brought the body again into favor with its superior in the partnership. But whether it be a relic of the old popish superstition, or to whatever cause it may be attributable, there are said to be ladies at this day, even *protestant* ladies, who mortify, distress, and consume their own precious bodies, by keeping them in *irons!* But this by the by.

It is no uncommon thing to anticipate the stroke of time. Often, very often, the vigorous and robust squander their health, and hasten the blow that levels them; while the feeble, by temperance and assiduous care, spin out life to an advanced age.

Many of our misfortunes, as we call them, spring from imprudence or neglect. Through the neglect of a small leak a ship is sunk, and its crew, perhaps, lost. The neglect of a few feet of fence may destroy a crop, and so may a few days' negligence or sloth in seed time or harvest. Angry lawsuits, and heavy pecuniary losses, not unfrequently might have been prevented, by a seasonable attention that would have required very little of time or labor. Some plunge themselves into inextricable embarrassment, which might have been avoided, had a portion of their leisure been devoted to the devising of a reasonable plan of living; and others, again, are impoverished by artificial wants, of which they might easily have prevented the intrusion. Indeed, of instances there is no end.

But that which is of the most importance by many degrees, is yet behind. There are means preventional of *moral*, as wel as of natural evil. Most of the vices that infest society, and bring utter ruin upon individuals, are more easy of prevention than of cure: and it is to be hoped that the time is coming when civil governments, blending Christian morals with state policy, will employ their power and influence fully as much to prevent crime as to punish it. That would be an era more happy than language can describe. But passing over what is remote and contingent, I will mention, and *but* mention, the actual and practicable powers of two kinds of government—*Domestic* and *Personal.*

Inconsiderate parents are apt to think that time will cure the faults of their children. This is a sad and fatal mistake. Not but that time, perchance, may cure the minor follies and errors of the juvenile mind; such follies and errors as are peculiarly incidental to the inexperience, the imbecile judgment, and the eager vivacity, of childhood and immature youth; but *immoral* propensities are strengthened, rather than cured, by time, which matures them into fixed habits. The bias to lying, profaneness, defrauding, or whatever immorality else, is not so very hard to cure when it first appears in the child; but if it be neglected then, it grows into an inveterate habit in the man. It is of importance, however, to premise, that the inceptive immorality of childhood is to be cured chiefly by *moral* means,—by example; by exhibiting to the view its odious nature and direful consequences; by cogent and convincing appeals to the understanding, and affectionate appeals to the heart:—and not altogether, or chiefly, by the infliction of punishments.

One of the most important objects of domestic government, is so to train up children that they may have a due government of themselves. This is a point, on which the worth or worthlessness of character greatly depends; for discreet and well regulated self-government, is the surest prevention of the deplorable excesses of passion and appetite, since it keeps upon them a stronger and a more steady rein than any other human government does, or can keep. Neither is the science of self-government so hard to learn, nor the practice of it so very difficult, provided it be commenced as well in good season, as in good earnest. But the longer it is neglected, the greater is the difficulty; till, at last, it becomes next to impossible for one to rule his passions, or to restrain his appetites. Immoral habits, which might have been easily prevented by timely discipline, attain gigantic strength by long indulgence.

It is out of our power to alter the structure of our bodies: we must take them as they are, for better or for worse. We cannot change our complexions, or fashion our own features. We cannot add to our stature, or make even a single hair of our heads white or black. But it is not altogether so with the mind. We may, with the divine helps afforded us, improve and meliorate that. We may keep our passions and our appetites in subordination to our reason. And in this necessary and noble exercise, should every one be employed, day by day, who wishes to be wise, or hopes to be happy.

NUMBER CIII.

OF OUR PRONENESS TO GO FROM ONE EXTREME TO ANOTHER.

It often happens, that when we set ourselves to straighten a crook, instead of making it quite straight, we crook it the contrary way, or carry things from one extreme to the other.

A youth of an ingenuous, liberal temper, is apt to be not regardful enough of his own interest. He esteems money as trash, and scorns to employ his cares about it. As it comes to him easily, it goes from him freely. He gives, he spends, he squanders, till at length, experiencing embarrassment, he resolves to become frugal and provident. But such a youth seldom stops at the true point, but leaps, at once, far beyond it. Heartily sick of extravagance, he makes a covenant with avarice, and becomes unfeeling, illiberal, and miserly.

The extreme of confidence often runs into the extreme of jealousy. Of those who live to a considerable age, very few, perhaps, leave the world, with as good an opinion of mankind as they had when they began it. To the eye of the ingenuous but inexperienced youth, the world appears bright and charming. He looks to meet with justice, candor, and honor, in his intercourse with his fellow-beings. Fancy gilds the objects of his hopes, and whatever is promised him by hope, he regards as sure and certain. Presently, however, the illusion begins to vanish. He meets with disappointment; he encounters cold-blooded selfishness, deceit, fraud, and perfidy; his confidence in men turns to suspicion; the world, he concludes, is a cheat; he hastily says in his heart, that all men are rogues and liars; and he becomes sour and misanthropic. By how much his opinion of mankind was too favorable in his younger days, by so much is it too uncharitable in his advanced age.

Self-convicted credulity often runs into skepticism: and so, also, a zeal to free themselves from all shackles of superstition, is very apt to drive men upon the fatal rocks of infidelity and irreligion.

Gibbon, the historian, no less celebrated for talents and learning than notorious for infidelity, was, in his youth, an implicit believer in, and a zealot for, the nonsensical popish doctrine of transubstantiation. To the arguments and expostulations of his father, and other Protestant relatives and friends, he was utterly deaf. But happening, of himself, to find out an argument which convinced him of the monstrous absurdity of that doctrine, he rejected it, and, along with it, rejected the whole system of divine revelation; which he in the manner of Voltaire encountered with the weapons of sneer and contempt, rather than by fair and manly reasoning. Nor is it unlikely that the rank infidelity, so general, a few years ago, among the learned and the fashionable in Europe, sprung chiefly from the same root. Identifying the monstrous doctrines and superstitious rites of the corrupted church in whose bosom they had been educated, with the Gospel itself, and discerning clearly the ridiculous absurdities of the former, they hesitated not to explode the latter.

Some men of impetuous tempers, but of feeling hearts, are possessed by turns, of ferocity, and, on the other hand, of an undue measure of indulgent feelings. In their gusts of anger hard words, and sometimes hard blows, are dealt out for petty offences, or for none at all. But no sooner has the tempest subsided than they deeply relent; and, passing into the other extreme, they smother their little ones with caresses, and indulge them in every thing. A certain nobleman of former times is said to have been so remarkable in this respect, that his domestics threw themselves in his way whenever they saw him angry, in order to be beaten by him; well knowing that he would reward them bountifully with gifts, as soon as his passion was cooled.

Again, some fathers frame in their own minds a system of paternal government that is fine-spun in theory, but impracticable. They will govern by rule and plummet. They will begin in season, and effectually whip old Adam out of their children. So they do begin, and so they proceed; sternly marking every childish foible, till, finding their efforts baffled, they rather cast away, than remit the reins of government, and let their children do as they will.

Beware of extremes. Several of the minor virtues of our nature degenerate into folly or vice, when carried beyond the due measure. Sensibility is not more lovely in its proper degree, than contemptible in its extravagance. A sentimentalist, puling over an uprooted flower, or a maimed butterfly, excites disgust rather than sympathy. Good-humor, candor, and generosity may all be carried to an extreme. If our good-humor render our moral characters flexible, and our hearts too yielding; if our candor degenerate into a sort of indiscriminate approvance of truth and error, of right and wrong, of the good and the evil; if our generosity infringe upon the sacred laws of justice, by a hospitality exceeding our means, or by giving gifts in preference to paying honest debts;—in these, as in divers other cases, too much of a good thing turns it to a bad

NUMBER CIV.

OF DESPISING SMALL THINGS.

"He that despiseth small things shall fall by little and little."
ECCLESIASTICUS.

THIS text, though apocryphal, is consonant to the whole tenor of human experience.

Time, which is of such invaluable account to every human being, is made up as of little particles, that ever are flying away from us, and never to return: no, never.

———"Time that ensueth
Is but the death of time that went before.
Youth is the death of childhood; age of youth."

How inconceivably small are the passing moments! yet they are not to be contemned. For of these is the whole duration of life composed; and it is the assiduous and wise use of moments, that crowns life with honor. On the other hand, by undervaluing the moments and neglecting to employ them, whole days and years are lost.

We often complain of the shortness of the whole, and, at the same time, are daily making prodigal waste of the parts. We carelessly throw away thousands of the small fractions of time; else, in most cases, we should have time enough.

So it happens that, in the acquisition of knowledge, the race is not always to the swift. Many a *wonderful* boy, that confided altogether in the native force of his genius, has been left far behind his contemporaries of smaller talent, but of unwearied assiduity. And scarcely does history record the single instance of a man, truly great in point of knowledge, who did not diligently improve even the small fractions of his time. In short, with the exception of a few remarkable cases, much more is effected by the dint of application, than by the dint of genius. The fabled mouse, with unwearied diligence, ate in twain the cable which a giant could not have parted with all his strength. And besides, if it be of great value to know how to bear tedious moments with fortitude and patience, it is of still greater value to be able to prevent their being tedious; which can be accomplished only by turning them to good account, through assiduous diligence in proper and useful pursuits.

Nor is the apocryphal text that I am commenting upon, of less pertinent application to the interesting subjects of economy and morals.

It is the hand of the diligent that maketh rich. Most estates have been acquired by little and little; by regular and well-applied industry, and by a prudent care against waste in even the smallest matters. By these means, in a long series of years, estates have grown up to such magnitudes as the owners themselves would be puzzled to account for. They had met with nothing that could be called *great good luck*. The wheel of fortune never turned them out a prize, nor did they ever gather a single sheaf from the field of speculation; and they themselves can hardly see how their estates have so increased. The truth of it is, that small annual savings, so judiciously managed as to be made constantly productive, will, in the space of half a century, count up to the magnitude of considerable wealth. On the contrary, many of the estates that are spent, leak out chiefly in small streamlets. The heirs, or owners, are neither stained with gross vices, nor chargeable with wanton prodigality. But small things they have contemned, or at least neglected. And what from lack of industry, or the misapplication of it, and what from incessant little wastes, their all is gone at length, and they look about them deeply wondering how the catastrophe has happened.

Turn we now to the consideration of Morals:—and here also our text holds true. Seldom does a man commit a crime of the blackest grain, till he has ripened himself for it by degrees. It is by little and little, he plunges into the depths of turpitude. He begins with contemning small things; with disregarding the minor points in the code of morality; and, step by step, he advances, till at length he becomes capable of crimes, of which the bare thought would have struck him with horror at first.

Here, a youth of estimable qualities, associates with the idle and dissipated; not because he feels any desire for the intoxicating cup, but because he loves sport and jollity. Presently, however, his moral nature is deteriorated. By imperceptible degrees, he slides into intemperance, profanity, deep gaming; and turns out, at last, either a desperate villain, or a lumpish sot.

There, a youth of good talents, of considerable learning, and possessed of pleasing social qualities, is seen, nevertheless, from his very cradle, to trespass often in the small way against truth and integrity. He begins with petty falsehoods and petty frauds; mere childish or juvenile roguery, which the doting parent interprets as a mark of sprightly genius, rather than as the inceptive blossom of foul corruption. Unchecked in childhood, and perhaps flattered for his art and cunning; as he advances in age, his genius takes a wider range. By little and little he proceeds on, till at last he adventures upon great things, and is arraigned before the bar of justice as a perjurer, a swindler, a forger, or a thief.

In short, were all the tenants of our state prisons to publish a true and full account of themselves, it would be found that puerile immoralities, tolerated and encouraged, were the seeds which had ripened into so fearful a crop.

NUMBER CV.

OF CUTTING THE COAT TO THE CLOTH.

Cervantes, in his inimitable Don Quixote, finely ridicules the custom of larding conversation and writings with proverbs or old sayings, by his dealing them out, by dozens, from the simple lips of *Sancho.* So also, the polished Chesterfield is known to have warned his son against this species of vulgarity, as well as against all *unfashionable vice.* But notwithstanding these high authorities, there is a great deal of pith in some old sayings; for, in fewest words, they convey the lessons of sound experience. Of adages of this sort, few have a more extensive, or a more useful meaning, than the one which here follows :—" *Cut your coat to your cloth.*"

The literal sense nobody can mistake, and nobody's general practice is wide from it. But its metaphorical sense is daily contravened in the practice of no inconsiderable part of the sons and daughters of the giddy race of Adam, and more especially in the present age, and in this so highly favored country. Nor is any single frailty among us of more mischievous consequence, than the perverse effort to enlarge the coat beyond what the cloth will allow. Thousands are the hapless victims of this prevailing folly. Thousands, at this very moment, are pining in poverty and straits, who might have been at their ease, had they always cut their coat according to the measure of their cloth. And though what is past admits of no remedy, yet it may be made to have a salutary bearing upon things to come; since hardly any thing has a more direct tendency to make us prudent, than the imprudences of which we feel the smart.

Be it so! And then, many of those who are now grieving that their all of earthly substance is lost, will yet, by God's blessing, restore themselves to a competence, and smile in the sunshine of contentment.

It has been remarked by a writer of other times, that "he who is ignorant of the art of arithmetic is but half a man." Meaning that one who goes on with his affairs at random, or without calculation, must needs conduct them ill, whatever be his natural talents or capacity.

We are told of a noble *Venetian*, who ordered his steward to deal out to his extravagant son no more money than he should count when he received it; and that the prodigal youngster, having been used to nothing but the pursuit of his pleasures, was led, by the labor of counting his money, to reflect upon the labor it cost his father to get it; and thence was induced to retrench his expenses, and alter his manner of life.

In like manner, only a little attention to arithmetic, as respects the apportioning the size of the coat to the measure of the cloth, might save from ruin many a goodly young man, and many an estimable family, of the present generation.

"It is seldom seen," observes the great Locke, "that he who keeps an account of his income and expenses, and thereby has constantly under view the course of his domestic affairs, lets them run to ruin; and it is not to be doubted but many a man gets behindhand before he is aware, for want of this care, or the skill to do it."

The arithmetic that is here recommended, is by no means complex or puzzling, but is plain, and level to every common understanding. Therein the only question to be asked and solved is, *can I afford it?* No matter that the thing is cheap. No matter that *this* is comfortable, and *that* is fashionable; no matter that such a style of living is most respectable in the eye of the world. Before you purchase the one, or go into the other, ask yourself the simple question, whether you can afford it, and let the true answer be the regulator of your expenses; else your circumstances will soon be ruined past all hope.

With all those, in short, whose utmost means of living are small, resolute abstinence from all extraordinary expense, and rigid frugality, along with well-directed industry, so far from being marks of meanness, are noble virtues.

There are yet some other respects in which the sage advice, to cut the coat to the cloth, is to be carefully heeded: of these I will now mention only one, namely, the effort, more especially in early life, to build up the fabric of reputation too high and magnificent for its basis.

This is an error of no uncommon occurrence. The youth of ardent feeling is in haste to acquire fame, and neglects no opportunities of self-display. His own indiscretion in this respect is seconded by that of his friends, who by means of extravagant encomiums on his genius, puff him into notice. Thus he is made to enter upon the theatre of life with a reputation impossible for him to sustain. He is like a trader, who attracts and disappoints, by exhibiting to view the whole of his goods in the shop-window. His stores are all seen at once. They dazzle at first view, and expectation stands a tiptoe. To unfounded expectation, disappointment succeeds of course, and he sinks as far below his true level, perhaps, as these adventitious circumstances had raised him above it. Better, far better had it been for him, if his coat had been cut to his cloth.

One should beware of taking upon credit a greater amount, not only of money, but of *reputation*, than one will be able to make good. In the last respect, as well as in the other, it is a dangerous experiment for a young man to pass himself for more than he is worth.

On the contrary, there is no less truth than beauty in the following lines of the poet :—

> "I have learn'd to fear
> The blossom that is early, and its leaves
> Too soon exposéd to the chilling spring.
> But much I hope from the more modest bud,
> That hides its head and gathers secret strength,
> Scarce blown at mid-summer."

NUMBER CVI.

A SOLEMN MONITION.

> "Ill habits gather by unseen degrees;
> As brooks run rivers, rivers swell to seas."
>
> DRYDEN.

UPON the face of our country, in most other respects so free and happy, there are two *plague-spots*, of awful magnitude, and of mortal aspect: the one is the involuntary slavery of so large a portion of its population; and the other, the voluntary and chosen slavery of numberless multitudes, to the all-destroying power of strong drink. How wide is this deadly evil spread! How immensely numerous,—how deplorably wretched, are its victims!

Among this vast group of *miserables*, are to be found many of opulent parentage; many, who did once inherit wealth themselves; many, who once were respectable and respected; many who once were distinguished for industry, economy and thrift; many, who were once bright in intellect, and possessed of amiable qualities of heart; many, who once had a delicate sense of honor and a nobleness of sentiment; many, who once felt, and deeply felt the endearing ties of relationship; whose company gave daily delight to parents, brothers, sisters, wives, and children; many, who were the hope and pride of their kindred, the ornaments of society—till the cup of abomination poisoned them, soul and body.

Now, they are as lazy as poor; now, their once comely visages are changed to disgusting and hideous; now, their bodies are debilitated and corrupted; now, every fine and noble feeling is utterly extinguished, and all sense of honor and shame is gone and lost; now, brutal ferociousness succeeds to the former suavity of temper; now, natural affections themselves are extinct; now, the aged and woe-struck parent is wantonly insulted, or shamefully neglected and disregarded; now, the estimable, the once so dearly loved wife, is assailed with opprobrious language and wounding blows; now, both wife and children are forsaken—or, even worse—are made to endure, day and night, the brutality of a drunken husband and father, who, instead of supporting them, has become their fiend-like tormentor.

This picture, so far from being overcharged or aggravated, is but a faint copy of the ghastliness of the original.

Our country is invaded, and, in a considerable part, already conquered. The enemy has entered every town, almost every village, and is dragging away, year by year, fresh numbers of our citizens into slavery for life; a slavery worse than Algerine, worse than is any where endured by the wretched Africans. This innumerable multitude of doubly, and most deeply-fallen men—scattered about over the whole face of our country—are not merely a dead loss to, but a dead weight upon, the general society. And, moreover, they are drawing others into the same vortex of perdition; each being like a mildewed ear of corn, which blasts the ears contiguous to it. Assuredly then, it behooves all who have any regard for religion, morals, or country, to employ their united and assiduous endeavors to stay this plague, ere it infect and consume the general mass of the population.

Of the habitual and confirmed drunkards, there seems very little hope of a thorough cure. Somewhere it is related in substance, that a *monkey*, having been accustomed to the taste of strong drink, began to love it; that one day, watching his opportunity, he helped himself, and drank so freely that he became sick and dizzy, and fell into the fire and burnt his foot; and that never after, though repeatedly urged, could he be prevailed with to drink so much as a single drop.

Would that, in similar cases, the like prudence were found in *man!* *He*, on the contrary, the more he experiences the effects of the raging poison, is the more bewitched after it. Though it makes him dizzy and sick, loathsome and self-loathed, and occasions him much worse bodily ills than befell the monkey; yet all this but increases the greediness of his desire, and strengthens the chains of his bondage. One, of very many, masters the habit after it has become inveterate, and thereby entitles himself to no small degree of honor. With some others there is, all their days, a struggle between moral feeling and appetite. They sometimes *scotch* the snake, but never *kill* it. Their condition is like that of the fabled Sisyphus, condemned to the fruitless toil of rolling up a steep hill a heavy stone, which ere he gets to the top, ever comes tumbling back, and compels him to begin his labor anew.

But as to the general mass of drunkards, such a marvellous stupefaction befalls them, that they seem to lose all moral sense, and all regard to consequences :—they are of the hospital of *incurables.*

In no wise is it to be expected, that very many of those who have become real drunkards will ever reform ; yet, where the habit is not fixed and inveterate, to master it is comparatively easy.

If you are but just beginning to form this most pernicious of habits, pause,—for Heaven's sake, pause !

> ———— "The hour's now come ;
> This very minute bids thee ope thine ear,
> Obey, and be attentive."

See the pit lying before you. It is naked ; it hath no covering ; one step further, and you are ingulfed, and for ever lost. While it is yet in your power, dash from your lips the cup of intemperance.

> "For in the wreath that decks the flowing bowl,
> Fell adders hiss, and poisoned serpents roll."

What ! though *young*, do you need stimulants already ? I heartily pity the poverty of your spirits. Assuredly, the *young* should have enough of that commodity—enough of genuine, unsophisticated animal spirits, *of their own.* If a young man now needs stimulants to make him cheerful and lively, what a lifeless lump, what a mere inanimate clod, must he be, when his youth is departed. And besides ; he that requires daily doses of strong drink in the season of youth, is almost sure to be a drunkard at middle age. Perhaps you may think you are in very little danger yet, or in none at all. And so thought tens and hundreds of thousands before you, till they were inextricably involved in the awful snare.

It is one of long experience, who addresseth you. The hand now writing is withered with age, and must soon be mouldering in the dust.

THE END.

www.ingramcontent.com/pod-product-compliance
Lightning Source LLC
LaVergne TN
LVHW020938110826
845150LV00004B/897

* 9 7 8 1 4 2 5 5 5 1 7 1 1 *